TROUBLED WATER

TROUBLED WATER

A Journey Around the Black Sea

JENS MÜHLING

Translated from the German by Simon Pare

First published in English in 2021 by
The Armchair Traveller
4 Cinnamon Row
London SW11 3TW

This paperback edition published in 2022

Originally published under the title *Schwere See*
Copyright © 2020 by Rowohlt Verlag GmbH, Hamburg / Germany

Translation copyright © 2021 by Simon Pare
Map copyright © Jens Mühling
Extract from *Southern Adventure* by Konstantin Paustovsky translated by
Kyril Fritz-Lyon
Extract from 'The King' by Isaac Babel translated by Peter Constantine

A CIP catalogue record for this book is available from the British
Library

ISBN: 978-1-914982-01-9
eISBN: 978-1-909961-77-7

Typeset in Garamond by MacGuru Ltd

Printed in the UK

The translation of this work was supported by a grant from the Goethe-Institut

GOETHE
INSTITUT

www.hauspublishing.com
@HausPublishing

For Şeyma
Denizkızım benim

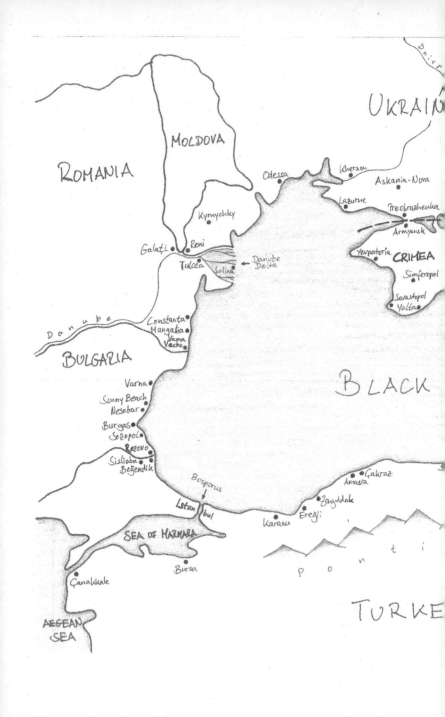

Contents

Foreword

They had just warmed up in prayer at the old Chabad synagogue in Odessa, upper bodies swaying, the amens ringing out rhythmically, when the sirens began to wail. Rabbi Avroom Wolf rolled his eyes behind his metal-rimmed spectacles. What was he meant to do? He should really have sent his congregation off to the bomb shelter, but these were the evening prayers before Passover night. Wolf and his closest advisers briefly put their long, bushy beards together before reacting the way most people in Odessa reacted to air-raid alarms at the time – they ignored them.

'Amen!' Wolf cried.

It was spring in the war-torn year of 2022, and the first horse chestnuts were flowering in Odessa. Two months earlier, Russia had invaded Ukraine. Violence had returned to the shores of the Black Sea – not that it had ever been absent for very long in the past millennia. Europe was in turmoil, and nightly maps of the frontline on TV news around the continent had seared the embattled sea's outline into people's minds.

Four years earlier I had made the journey around the Black Sea that is the subject of this book. As I reported on the Russian invasion, I revisited some familiar stretches of coastline. In the Romanian area of the Danube delta, during the first days of the war, I watched Ukrainian refugees scramble onto a passenger ferry to reach safety on the far bank of the border river. In Istanbul and Georgia I spoke to Russian anti-war protestors who, fearing reprisals, had fled their country. Lastly, I travelled from Moldova into Ukraine to report on the mass exodus of Jews from Odessa and to see Avroom Wolf, whom I had met during my Black Sea odyssey four years earlier.

Shortly before those evening prayers we had sat together in his office on the upper floor of the old synagogue. Wolf's impressive beard was whiter than I remembered it. The war had left its mark on him.

As a Jew he had his own perspective on the invasion Russia had launched with the flimsy pretext that Ukraine needed liberating from Nazis. He counted out names in the air on his fingers.

'Zelenskyy, the Ukrainian president, is Jewish. Groysman, the former prime minister, is Jewish. Ex-president Kuchma has a Jewish son-in-law …' This continued for some time before, eventually, his hands sank back into his lap. 'I know rabbis all over the world, and none of them has less trouble with Nazis than I do here in Odessa. There are more people killed by anti-Semites in Israel.'

And this was coming from someone from Israel. Avroom Wolf had been born fifty-two years previously not far from Tel Aviv and was the father of eight children, all born in Ukraine, where he and his Israeli wife Chaia had lived since 1992. His ancestors were from Nuremberg. Only some of his family survived the Holocaust after escaping from Germany while it was still possible. One of them was Wolf's grandfather, who was fourteen at the time. He was long since deceased, but his wife was still alive in Israel. Wolf had recently talked to his ninety-eight-year-old grandmother on the phone and asked that she whisper to her husband, on her next visit to the cemetery, that the Ukrainian Jews were now fleeing to Germany. 'He would never have believed it.'

Not that Avroom could believe what was happening in Odessa just then either. When the congregation – a few dozen Hasidic Jews in their timeless black-and-white robes – made their way to the Passover meal after evening prayers, they passed brightly lit barricades in the otherwise dark streets, as well as anti-tank barriers, sand-bag defences, and soldiers cradling assault rifles. Odessa was girding itself for an imminent advance by the Russian army, which had been trying for weeks to take Mykolaiv, the nearest major city to the east. Even closer, to the west, lay Transnistria, the separatist-held region of Moldova where another Russian troop contingent was stationed. There was also a threat to the port city from the Kremlin's Black Sea fleet patrolling out at sea.

From the very first days of the war, the city had been subjected to almighty explosions as the Russians bombarded military facilities on the outskirts. Tens of thousands of Odessans had panicked and flooded over the nearby Moldovan border or across the Danube into Romania. The synagogue had witnessed scenes that reminded Wolf of his grandfather's stories of the flight from Nuremberg. First, the Jewish community had evacuated the Chabad congregation's two orphanages and sent several busloads of children from Odessa to Germany. News of the rescue operation had spread, and Wolf's mobile had rung day and night as desperate Jewish parents asked if there was room on the coaches for their children. The rabbi had helped out wherever he could. Waving goodbye to the escaping children, he felt transported back in time. 'They were scenes from the 1930s.'

Back then the Germans had practically annihilated Jewish life on the shores of the Black Sea. Over one million

Ukrainian Jews were murdered during the Holocaust, roughly a tenth of them just in Odessa, where one in three inhabitants was Jewish before the war. Only New York and Warsaw had boasted larger Jewish populations at the time.

By Rabbi Wolf's estimations, approximately thirty-five thousand Jews had been living in Odessa before the Russian invasion. No one knew for sure, just as no one could tell how many had left the city since the outbreak of this war. The decimation of the community was evident from the Passover procession – it consisted almost entirely of men whose wives and children had fled abroad. Men of fighting age were not allowed to leave the country, or else the congregation would have been even sparser.

It was shortly before curfew when the Passover pilgrims reached the closed-off administrative district. Soldiers blocked the procession's path before stepping aside following a few words from Rabbi Wolf. The congregation had booked out the majestic, seafront Hotel London, Odessa's oldest and finest establishment, in order to be able to celebrate in spite of the curfew. It was owned by a local Jewish businessman.

The chandeliers were already burning brightly in the function room, and the bedside lamps in the hotel rooms wouldn't be turned off either that night. No light switch was to be touched that feast day because that was work, and work was a sin. It was taboo to use a phone, a camera, a cigarette lighter, or even a tap, and when someone accidentally set off the movement-sensitive soap dispenser in the men's toilets, he went a bit pale around the gills.

Rabbi Wolf, however, was quite lenient in how he interpreted these rules. When war broke out, quite a few members of the community had rung him to ask if they were permitted to flee on the Sabbath. 'Of course,' he answered. 'Run!'

As the unleavened matzo bread was passed around, the rabbi stood up at the head of the table and raised his wine glass. The gathering fell silent.

'We are celebrating the day of our liberation,' Wolf said, his striking head set off by the midnight-blue curtain along the back of the dais. 'The day the sea parted for us.'

The rabbi began to recount the story of the exodus from Egypt. The enslavement of the people of Israel. Moses appearing before the pharaoh to declare, 'Let my people go!' The people of Israel departing in such a rush that there was no time to leaven the bread, and their flight, pursued by the Egyptian army. The waves drawing miraculously aside, then engulfing the despot's army.

'It is customary,' Wolf concluded, 'that we do not sleep tonight and that we tell stories of that day until daybreak. So may each and every one of you pronounce "l'chaim" and speak his thoughts about freedom.'

As the meal ran its course, one guest after another raised his glass.

'L'chaim,' one exclaimed. 'What, I ask you, is a Jew? In the Soviet Union you were a Jew if it said "Jewish nationality" in your passport. Other people say that anyone with a Jewish mother is a Jew. But I say that a Jew is someone who rejects slavery and chooses freedom.'

And the listeners cried in unison, 'L'chaim!'

Another man stood up. 'They say many people chose to accept slavery back then because escape seemed too dangerous. We must always ask ourselves: Are we one of the few who desire to be free?'

'L'chaim, l'chaim!'

'When the pharaoh's army drove the Jews to the shores of the sea,' another man added, 'the fleers splintered into four groups. Some said: "We have to fight!" Others said: "No, pray!" A third group said: "Let us surrender!" And the final group said: "Let us drown ourselves in the sea!" But ultimately a different path opened up for them. May we always make the right decision!'

'L'chaim!'

'Slavery starts in the mind,' a man cried. 'Defeat your inner pharaoh!'

And so it continued. With every 'l'chaim' that evening, the relevance to the present became more and more explicit, the exodus from Egypt increasingly a template for the exodus from Odessa.

'We are talking about then,' I heard Rabbi Wolf say later at the table, 'but we mean now. That was always our strength as Jews. We have a long memory, and we use it to move forwards.'

Wolf spoke fluent Russian, having learned the language in the predominantly Russian-speaking south of Ukraine. If he forgot a word, he paraphrased it until the assembled faithful gave him a cue. He even told concentration-camp jokes in Russian, so dark that my hand paused as I jotted down his words. 'We cannot always only weep.'

He had every reason to weep, mind you. For three decades Wolf had strained every sinew to rebuild the Jewish tradition in Odessa. His efforts had resulted in the establishment of two orphanages, two Jewish schools, two kindergartens, an old people's home, a university, and three synagogues.

'It took just one day to destroy all that,' Wolf said. 'Never again will things be as they were before.' He knew that far from everyone who had fled would return, even if the war were to finish tomorrow. 'Emigration,' he said, 'is in our Jewish blood.'

As I listened to him, my mind turned to all the emigrants and immigrants, all the outbound and the returnees I had met during my journey around the Black Sea four years earlier. It seemed as if, in those war-torn days, Odessa was witnessing a repeat of the eternal drama that afflicted this body of water whose coastal residents had been in constant and mostly involuntary motion for thousands of years. Along its shores I had come across people who had lost their homes as a result of war, displacement, ethnic cleansing, and other man-made disasters. Some of them had been forced to flee from one stretch of the coast to another many times over the generations. The hardest hit were the countless minorities of the Black Sea area, the peoples and tribes who were unfortunate enough to fall through the cracks between nation states and lose their toeholds on the Black Sea coast every time the borders shifted again.

Rabbi Wolf was all too familiar with this old Black Sea drama, not only because he was a Jew but from family experience. He had seven siblings, five brothers, and two sisters. Three of his brothers were rabbis – one in Israel, the other two, like Wolf, in Ukraine. The youngest Wolf brother, forty-year-old Benjamin, led a synagogue in the Crimean city of Sevastopol. Fifty-year-old Josef Itzhak was a rabbi in Kherson, which was located between Odessa and Crimea. Until the peninsula's annexation the Wolf brothers had travelled regularly back and forth between the three Ukrainian Black Sea ports. When Russia annexed Crimea in 2014, however, a controversial border had suddenly been erected between Benjamin and his brothers. Now that the Russians had invaded and occupied Kherson, the frontline had cut Avroom off from the other two.

Avroom had last seen his brother from Kherson a month

before the outbreak of war in Kharkiv in eastern Ukraine, where the local rabbi was getting married. The Crimean-based brother had also been invited, but he was unable to enter Ukraine from the occupied peninsula. Avroom had last met him at a Jewish conference in New York six months earlier.

Of course, the three brothers continued to see one another on a regular basis – through their phones. What did they talk about? 'Solely about our mother,' Avroom joked. This was the only subject on which the rabbi evaded my questions. His brother in the occupied city of Kherson in particular was in a politically precarious and militarily perilous situation.

When I visited Rabbi Wolf at his office in the synagogue again on the Sunday after Passover, he phoned his brother in Kherson. The news from the occupied city was bad. The Russian army had deposed the Ukrainian mayor, introduced the rouble as the official currency, and rerouted the internet through Russian providers. They were apparently preparing a sham referendum in which Kherson's inhabitants would vote to break away from Ukraine – even though the toppled mayor estimated that nearly half the population had fled the city.

I listened quietly as the Wolf brothers talked in Hebrew. Josef Itzhak sounded exhausted. Until, that is, the two brothers burst into childish giggles – they hadn't lost the Wolf family's sense of humour. When Avroom mentioned that he had a journalist with him, Josef Itzhak switched to Russian.

'I'm sorry,' he said, 'I can't talk to you.'

How was he feeling? There was silence for a few seconds. 'My soul is heavy,' he replied.

When Avroom hung up, he told me that he had been on the phone to his brother long into the night the previous day. Josef Itzhak faced a dilemma. If he stayed, he would put his life in danger; if he left, he would be abandoning his community.

Leaving entailed a second dilemma: if he emigrated to Russia via Crimea, the Ukrainians would forever hold it against him, but fleeing across the frontline to Ukraine would alienate the Russians.

Even as Wolf uttered these words, his eyes were already glinting with the next one-liner.

'What is a dilemma?' he asked. 'A greengrocer on Odessa market accidentally giving you back too much change. Because then you have a decision to make – do you tell your wife or not?'

Wolf was still chuckling as his phone rang again.

'You won't believe this,' he said after glancing at the display. 'It's our mother.'

The seventy-five-year-old lady was calling from Israel. Her voice also sounded as if her soul was heavy, but the rabbi was soon chortling along with her too.

'Mothers!' he said after hanging up. 'She told me to hurry up and convince my brother to get the heck out of Kherson.'

Wolf's giggling was still ringing in my ears as I gazed out over the Black Sea from the barricades on the promenade that afternoon. The water was a metallic grey, the air full of screeching gulls. Everything seemed peaceful, but just the previous day Russian rockets had fallen on Odessa, and memories of the explosions still made my knees go weak. One of the missiles had struck a residential building; the dead included a mother and her three-month-old baby. The number of civilian casualties in Ukraine already ran into the thousands. The tens of thousands, some even said. There were more and more horrific accounts of executions, torture, pillaging, and rape in the Russian-occupied areas. Around seven million Ukrainians had fled abroad; another seven million had abandoned embattled regions for safer parts of the country. Europe had

not seen a flood of refugees on this scale since the Second
World War.

In the harbour, nothing moved. The war had brought trade
to a standstill. The Gulf of Odessa was strewn with mines to
keep the Russian navy away from the coast. Shortly before my
arrival, the *Moskva*, one of the Kremlin's largest cruisers and
the pride of the Black Sea fleet, had been sunk not far from
here. I stared at the grey surface of the water on the horizon
and tried to picture the steel behemoth listing and sliding
slowly, bow first, into the deep as inquisitive dolphins circled
its sides and air escaped from its doors and portholes and
bubbled swiftly to the surface. I imagined the water pouring
into engine rooms and cabins, into the lungs of drowning
sailors, and the ship sinking down and down until it reached
the dead lower layer of the Black Sea, where a lack of oxygen
means that there are neither animals nor plants. The *Moskva*
glided through lifeless, empty water before finally settling on
the bottom among the conserved, spectral wrecks of Ottoman
gunboats, Bulgarian pirate ships, Venetian sail frigates, and
ancient Greek galleys whose wooden hulls could not rot in
the depths of the Black Sea because they sustained no organisms capable of decomposing timber. The *Moskva* lay there on
the sea floor now – one more exhibit in the great underwater
museum of Black Sea wars.

A green double-decker coach was waiting outside Odessa's
main railway station the next morning. It had been provided
by an Israeli aid organisation, and two buses were still carrying Jewish refugees across the border into Moldova every
week. Families heaved battered wheeled suitcases into the
hold. The women boarded the buses with their children
while all the men stayed behind, apart from a few pensioners who were allowed to depart despite mobilisation. Dogs

barked in animal carriers, and a grey tomcat slunk from seat to seat.

Like most people on the coach, Viktoria Malis wanted to go to Israel, swapping the Black Sea for the Mediterranean. The day before, in Odessa, she had said goodbye to her Jewish grandfather Ilya Israelevich Malis, who was born in 1941 in Azerbaijan to parents who had fled there from the Nazis. After the war, his family had returned to Odessa, where Viktoria was born during the final years of the Soviet era. This slender, blonde woman with bluish-green eyes was now thirty-three and had, until the war, worked as a logistician in a bread factory. Her husband Dmitri, a car mechanic, had dreamed of emigrating even before the war, repeatedly urging Viktoria to make the most of her Jewish origins to offer their two children a brighter future. She had only agreed when Russian rockets demolished a military base not far from their dacha.

Mobilisation meant that Dmitri was staying behind in Odessa for now, while Viktoria sat upstairs on the bus, third row on the left, with seven-year-old Eva and babe-in-arms Artur. They were heading for the Israeli consulate in Moldova. I was sitting behind the three of them – this bus was my lift out of Ukraine. Together, through the windows, we watched Odessa slip away: first the classical architecture of the centre, then the prefabricated apartment blocks of the suburbs, and then the wide Ukrainian steppe.

'Mama,' I heard Eva ask, 'are there apples in Israel?'

Berlin, July 2022

The Flood

Prologue

It seemed to him that the Black Sea
had risen to the skies, to come
pouring down on the earth
for forty days and forty nights.

Konstantin Paustovsky, 'The Colchis', 1934

We saw them coming towards us as we travelled the last few miles to Mount Ararat, in eastern Anatolia, where Turkey borders Armenia and Iran amid endless slopes of scree. They were walking along the sides of the road in small groups – men, most of them young with dark beards and nothing in their hands, except for a few carrying small plastic bags. It was March, and snow still lay on the winding pass roads. I wondered how fast you would have to walk in these men's thin jackets if you didn't want to freeze.

Mustafa, whose taxi I'd got into in Agri because the next bus to Dogubayazit left only the following day, motioned with his chin to the walkers beyond the windscreen.

'Pasaport yok, para yok.'

No passport, no money.

I looked at him quizzically. 'Syrians?'

He shook his head. 'Afganlar.'

They must have come to Turkey via Iran, I thought.

Mustafa nodded as if he could read my mind. 'Afghanistan – Iran – Istanbul.' He was silent for a moment before a grin splayed his moustache. 'Istanbul – Almanya!' he said, suggesting that the Afghans' intended destination was my home country.

The moustache hardened into a line when I tried to persuade Mustafa to stop the car. I wanted to talk to the refugees and ask them what they needed, even if I'd almost certainly be unable to provide it. *Forget it*, said Mustafa's frozen moustache. *Not for all the lira in the world.*

We drove on towards Mount Ararat, which has an ancient and enigmatic bond with the Black Sea. Again and again, men

3

would come around a bend in the road, in twos, five at once, then none for a long time, then suddenly a dozen followed by another dozen – and for a moment I was convinced that the road beyond the next bend would be black with people. But then no one else appeared for ages.

Every time a bunch of men approached us out of the distance, Mustafa would briefly take his hands off the steering wheel, turn his palms to the sky, and shake his head in silent bemusement, as if he were asking himself, or me, or maybe God, what on earth was to be done with all these people who could not stay where they were.

* * *

I've seen the Black Sea from all sides, and from none of them was it black.

It was silvery as I drove along the deserted beaches of the Russian Caucasus coast in the spring, as silvery as the skin of the dolphins hugging the shore as they pursued shoals of fish northwards.

It turned blue in May as I reached Georgia, the ancient Colchis of Greek legend, where the beaches are black but not the water.

In Turkey it seemed to take on the green of the tea plantations and hazelnut groves along its shores, and it was still green when I reached the Bosporus in late summer.

The first storms of autumn coloured it brown as the birds headed south and the tourists headed home over the Bulgarian coast.

In Romania's Danube delta the sky seemed to hang so low over the sea that its lead-grey colour rubbed off on the water.

When I reached Ukraine, the waves scraped dirt-grey ice along the beaches.

Only in Crimea did the winter sun brighten the sea again, and here it assumed the hue it will forever have in my memory – a cloudy, milky green, like a soup of algae and sun cream.

* * *

Journeys seldom start where we remember their starting. This one may well have begun under my blind grandmother's dining table.

Occasionally, as the grown-ups traded their grown-up stories, my sister and I would crawl between their legs to the end of the table, where Grandma sat. We would creep up quietly behind her chair. The back was wickerwork, the holes big enough for us to poke our fingertips through. We would prod Grandma in her bony back and, although she had heard rather than seen us coming, she never failed to greet our recurring prank with an indulgent, horrified shriek.

'Oh, are those mice I can feel?'

Squeaking, we would pull our mousy fingers out of the back of the chair and scuttle back under the table.

In Neunkirchen, the small town in the Siegerland area of western Germany where my grandmother lived until her death, stands a memorial:

JOH. HEINRICH VON KINSBERGEN
LIEUT.-ADMIRAL
BENEFACTOR OF THE POOR
* 1.5.1735 † 22.5.1819

The admiral's name – or, rather, not his name but his title

– cropped up from time to time in the grown-up conversations on which my sister and I eavesdropped from under the table. 'The Admiral' stuck in my childhood memory like some kind of semi-mythical character. From what I could grasp, he was a distant relative of ours, a great-great-great-great-great-grandfather who had pitched up in Holland back in the mists of time and acquired considerable fame and wealth there as a seafarer. He had left part of his vast fortune as a fund that, on request, offered grants to impoverished family members back home in the Siegerland. In my imagination, 'The Admiral's money' that the adults occasionally mentioned in Neunkirchen took on the proportions of a pirate's treasure trove, a glittering stash of gold coins just waiting to be discovered by me, The Admiral's legitimate heir.

I was to find out from my aunt Gertraude and her Neunkirchen friends Elfriede and Ingeborg at a family Christmas many years later that I wasn't the only one with his eye on The Admiral's money. In my grandmother's hometown there is, besides the memorial to the seafarer, a street called the Van Kinsbergen Ring. Local people call it the 'potato bug ring' in view of the amazing number of needy Neunkircheners who came crawling out of the woodwork after van Kinsbergen's death, claiming to be related to the generous admiral. His alleged descendants had multiplied like potato bugs.

That Christmas, Gertraude, Elfriede, and Ingeborg also told me that the legacy payments from Holland had dried up long ago – my treasure trove had apparently been confiscated as reparations after the Second World War.

To digest my disappointment, I began to compare my childhood memories of The Admiral with his real-life biography. I learned that it was not van Kinsbergen himself but his father who had emigrated from the impoverished Siegerland in the early eighteenth century to sign up as a soldier in Holland. He had swapped his German surname, Ginsberg, for the more common local variant Kinsbergen when he married a Dutch woman, with whom he had a son named Jan Hendrik. (In an interesting inversion of his father's self-renaming, Jan Hendrik was identified as Johann Heinrich on his memorial in the Siegerland, due to the contemporary practice of translating foreign names into their German variants.)

The immigrant's scion joined the navy at fifteen. I realised with some perplexity that the man who would later become an admiral had gone to sea not only for the Dutch crown but for the Russians too. In his mid-thirties, van Kinsbergen had accepted Catherine the Great's offer of joining the tsarina's war against the Turks and commanding part of her fleet, which had recently made its first sorties into the Black Sea. In 1773, van Kinsbergen engaged a considerably larger Turkish force off the Crimean coast with two gunboats and, after a battle lasting several hours, put them to flight. This skirmish at Balaclava was Russia's first naval battle on the Black Sea and, thanks to my alleged great-great-great-great-great-grandfather, it resulted in a great victory.

I wasn't sure if this was any cause for pride. Catherine's campaign against the Turks, which van Kinsbergen continued to support in the following years, ended in 1774 with the defeat of the Ottoman Empire. Russia did what the world's largest country had always loved doing – it grew. Catherine incorporated into her empire large swathes of the northern Black Sea coast that had previously been controlled by the Crimean Tatars, allies of the Turks. A few years later, after van Kinsbergen had returned to Holland bedecked with Russian medals, the tsarina went one step further. She subjugated the Tatars and annexed their Crimean homeland. The peninsula,

Catherine declared in 1783, would be Russian 'from now on and for all time'.

In order to conceal the fact that Crimea had ever been anything but Russian, Catherine erased almost all traces of the Tatars. Mosques and madrasahs, caravanserais and khans' palaces were razed, and the first of several waves of Tatar refugees set out for Ottoman shores.

This wasn't the first time – and it wouldn't be the last – that roads around the Black Sea turned black with huddled masses as autocrats transplanted whole peoples and extinguished all sign of them from history. Dozens of Black Sea minorities moved up and down the coast, sometimes repeatedly and always against their will, because they stood in the way of imperial expansion or national destiny, the communist future, the Thousand Year Reich, Pan-Turkism, a vision of Greater Romania or the Bulgarian National Revival ... in short, because wood shavings fell where sovereigns planed, or because, as Stalin reportedly said, you can't make an omelette without breaking eggs. Over a century and a half after Catherine, it was Stalin, the arch-carpenter and master omelette-maker, who had the remaining Crimean Tatars herded onto cattle trucks and deported to Central Asia. And they were by no means the biggest egg in Stalin's Black Sea omelette.

Back then, under my grandmother's dining table, I knew nothing of displacement, ethnic cleansing, refugees, or people who cannot stay where they are. The story of The Admiral's emigration from the Siegerland to Holland already exceeded the bounds of my imagination. As far as I could tell, van Kinsbergen was the only one of our family who hadn't lived where the rest of us lived. I attributed this to his seafaring life. His home was his ship – that was the only explanation I could come up with.

The outside of my grandmother's home was clad with black slate, like many old Siegerland houses. Recalling those pitch-black streets today, resting there in the valleys beneath the weight of their slate, I am overcome by an archaic, childlike sense of astonishment and disbelief that anyone on this earth could ever leave their homeland behind.

* * *

My journey may have been a circular one, but the Black Sea not only isn't black, it isn't round either.

The geographers of the ancient world compared the shape of its coastline, which is upwards of 4,000 km long, with that of a Scythian horseman's bow. The taut bowstring runs the length of the southern shore in what is now Turkey, whose course appeared straighter and more bowstring-like to the ancient Greek settlers there than it really is. West and east of Turkey, the two limbs of the bow describe steep north-ward arcs – past the beaches of Bulgaria and Romania in the west; along the Georgian and Russian coasts in the east – before curving around more gently towards their point of convergence. They meet in Ukraine, from whose southern shore Crimea hangs down like an archer's clenched fist. The imaginary arrow this bow would send hurtling north points almost exactly at Moscow, although no ancient Greek could yet have guessed as much. By the time the Muscovites made their appearance on the world stage, the Scythians had long since exited.

Yet whenever I trace the sea's outline with my finger on a map, it is not a bow I see but a horse's head. The horse's muzzle is nosing Georgia to the right, and its ears prick up into Ukraine and Russia on either side of the Crimean peninsula. The north-eastern ear is the Sea of Azov, one of two bodies of water connected to the Black Sea. It was along the river Don and through the Sea of Azov that the Russian tsars advanced to the Black Sea coast in the eighteenth century. To the south-west lies the more famous entrance, being the neck on which the horse's head is poised: the Bosporus, the narrow straits leading to the Sea of Marmara, the Aegean Sea, and the Mediterranean realms of antiquity. This is the route Jason and the Argonauts are reputed to have followed on their quest for the Golden Fleece, which took them along the southern coast to modern-day Georgia and then on a long detour home to Greece via the Danube.

The voyage of the *Argo* is a legend, but it is based on the actual discovery of the Black Sea by ancient Greek seafarers, who may have sailed their ships through the Dardanelles and the Bosporus as early as the second millennium BC and had definitely achieved this feat by the beginning of the first millennium BC. Generations of Greek poets and philosophers later depicted what those sailors encountered there as the edge of the known world, fraught with danger and inhabited by all kinds of weird and wonderful peoples and creatures including cannibals, hellhounds, man-slaughtering Amazons, dwarves mounted on flying cranes, Cyclopes, lice-eaters, and werewolves.

The real peoples living along the coasts of the Black Sea in ancient times received equally short shrift in Greek literature. The languages of horse-borne tribes such as the Scythians were meaningless gibberish to Greek ears, and their purported tendency to say 'bar bar bar' soon earned them the epithet of 'barbarians'. This collective noun for nomads entered the Greek psyche and took root there. To judge by Hellenic literature, they embodied all that was alien to the Greeks, a threat to their very civilisation and everything they abhorred, feared, and scorned. It is difficult in retrospect to establish who was to blame for this animosity and whether it was mutual, because we only have one side of the story – the barbarians didn't write down what they thought of the Greeks.

When the shards of the ancient world were later pieced together to forge the identity of an entire continent, the Europeans internalised the story of the barbarians along with the rest of Greece's cultural legacy, and this myth, long since cut loose from its historical moorings in the Black Sea, acts to this day as a means of differentiating ourselves from others. We need barbarian neighbours to make us feel civilised. For centuries, the French considered the Germans barbarians, the Germans the Slavs, the Poles the Russians, and the Russians were spoilt for choice among the Mongols, the Tatars, the Turks, the Caucasians, and the Chinese.

On the whole, Europeans tended to draw the line between civilisation and barbarism where it best served their interests. You could wage war or embark on colonial campaigns with fewer scruples if you pre-emptively declared your adversary to be an enemy of the civilised world, if you could appeal to an instinctive revulsion ingrained in the continent's psyche since ancient times. Here are the civilised, there the barbarians. Here is our kind, and there are the others: the foreigners; the backward; the unwashed; eaters of strange foods, and men who let their children and wives run wild; cruel, bloodthirsty monsters; cannibals; unbelievers; our inferiors; natural-born slaves; sub-humans.

Tellingly, this image of the barbarian did not originate among the Greek seafarers who founded the first trading outposts on the Black Sea coast in the eighth century BC and lived in close symbiosis with the nomadic peoples of the hinterland

– this being the inception of the distinctive ethnically mixed communities that would shape the Black Sea for thousands of years. It was in fact Athenian intellectuals who dismissed barbarians as enemies of civilisation, even though they knew the Black Sea only from hearsay and rarely stepped outside the colonnades of their academies (which perhaps explains why they were so quick to pass judgement on people of no fixed abode).

This was by no means the first historical contact between sedentary peoples like the Greeks and nomads like the Scythians. What was novel in this case, though, was that their encounters were recorded in literature, and that this literature forged the self-image of a continent. As Neal Ascherson puts it in his sublime study of Black Sea history, 'In this particular encounter began the idea of "Europe" with all its arrogance, all its implications of superiority, all its assumptions of priority and antiquity, all its pretensions to a natural right to dominate.'

Once you have tried to discern the menacing Scythian bow the Greeks saw in the shape of the Black Sea, it is very hard to shake it from your mind again.

* * *

I have a very clear memory of the moment the Black Sea suddenly moved from the margins to the forefront of European perception.

I was on a pleasure cruise around Sevastopol's harbour in March 2014. Less than a fortnight earlier, Russian soldiers had appeared in Crimea and surrounded Ukrainian barracks. Although their uniforms bore no insignia or rank, no one had any doubts about where they came from. Parliament had been dissolved and replaced with puppets under the Kremlin's orders, a hastily arranged referendum on Crimea's integration into the Russian Federation had been announced for the next day, and Ukrainian and Russian warships were facing off in the harbour – and yet tour boats continued to ply their trade between the destroyers as if everything were completely normal.

I had travelled to Sevastopol as a journalist to report on the act of political piracy that was taking place. I had no idea at the time that in 1773, not far from that same harbour, on the south-western coast of Crimea, Jan Hendrik van Kinsbergen had laid the groundwork for Catherine the Great's annexation of the peninsula. All I knew was that I was witnessing Russia's second annexation of Crimea.

The tour boat passed close to the warships' towering grey hulls. The Ukrainian and Russian Black Sea fleets still shared the port in that tense time before the Crimean referendum, and I had hoped that out on the water I might gain a better understanding of their muddled positions. The boat was full of Russians from Sevastopol, high on alcohol and patriotism, who made no secret of the fact that they wished a plague on the Ukrainians.

'Fascists!' they roared at the ships flying blue-and-yellow flags. For weeks now, Russian propaganda had constantly dubbed all Ukrainians fascists. *The same old story*, I thought. *A country on the warpath in search of some barbarians to fight.*

One man stood slightly apart from the others by the railing, staring silently out to sea. He was the only person apart from me who didn't join in with the shouting. As we disembarked at the end of our tour, I approached him to enquire why he was there.

'To say goodbye to the sea,' he said tersely.

He was a Tatar. He had been born in Uzbekistan after his

parents were deported under Stalin, and only when the Soviet Union collapsed, and Crimea and the rest of Ukraine gained its independence, had he been at liberty to return to the land of his ancestors.

'Now the Russians are taking over again,' he said gloomily. 'I'm not going to wait for them to expel us a second time. My wife has family in Ankara. The day after tomorrow, we're going to put the kids in the car and leave.' His lips twisted into a bitter smile. 'It won't be the first time we've had to start from scratch.'

I watched him for a long time as he walked away along the promenade and into an unknown future. A woodchip had fallen. An egg had been broken.

* * *

The Black Sea is bounded by six states. Clockwise, in the order I visited them, they are Russia, Georgia, Turkey, Bulgaria, Romania, and Ukraine.

Six and a half, if you count Abkhazia, a renegade part of Georgia that is kept on life support by Russia to prevent Georgia from joining any Western alliances.

Seven, if you count Moldova, formerly known as Bessarabia, which lost its coastline in the Second World War when Stalin moved the border inland.

Seven and a half, if you count Transnistria, a renegade part of Moldova, which is kept on life support by Russia to prevent Moldova from joining any Western alliances.

Eight, if you count Poland – the old Poland at its point of maximum expansion when *szlachta* noblemen persuaded themselves that their country's ruling class was descended from the Sarmatians, an ancient barbarian tribe.

Eight and a half, if you count the Donetsk People's Republic, a renegade part of Ukraine, which… you can fill in the rest.

Eight and a half, if Crimea belongs to Ukraine. Eight and a half, if Crimea belongs to Russia. Nine, if you'd prefer to let Crimea stand alone.

Nine and a half, if you count the ruined empire of ancient Greece, whose vestiges I encountered on every shore in the form of weathered stones; in place names mangled by foreign tongues; in family stories of scattered Black Sea Greeks; on the menus of countless Aphrodite Restaurants, Poseidon Cafés, Olympus Hotels and Amazon Bars, written in Cyrillic, Latin, and Georgian letters; and in the deep-seated Black Sea tradition of always expecting the worst from your neighbours.

* * *

Where should I start? After my finger helplessly circled the sea several times on the map, I eventually settled on a spot that is a long way from the coast but has a great deal to say about the origins of the Black Sea – which is why I found myself driving over a pass on a snowy March day with groups of penniless, passportless people walking towards me.

Arriving in Dogubayazit, I saw women in full-length robes that trailed in the Anatolian dust. The looks Kurdish men gave them as they walked past reminded me of starving wolves. I saw fly-covered cow's heads in butcher's shop windows, I saw prayer beads clicking in tea-drinkers' hands, and everywhere I looked, at the end of every street and over every roof, I saw Mount Ararat. The mountain floated above the town as if some trick of perspective were at work. If this had been a movie set, you would have had to shrink it to make it more credible.

I checked into the Hotel Nuh, named after the famous

seafarer who allegedly ran aground here a long time ago in his boat: Noah, the admiral of the Ark. The hotel's owner was a white-haired Kurd called Jakub who had named not only his guesthouse Nuh but also one of his sons. In the Qur'an, Nuh's ship had been stranded not on Mount Ararat but on Mount Judi, which lies near Turkey's borders with Syria and Iraq. However, the Christian pilgrims to the Ark – who were funding Jakub's twilight years and his son's studies in Istanbul – came here, to Mount Ararat.

Had come, anyway. Up until two years ago, before the event that a man called Cervat told me about the next morning as he drove me to the foot of Mount Ararat.

'Bang!'

He held an invisible rifle against his cheek and fired it at the cloud-veiled summit.

'Bang! PKK! Bang!'

Due to the purported threat of terrorist attacks, the army had closed off all access to Ararat for the past two years

The mountain is over 300 km from the nearest coast, the shore of the Black Sea. In my mind's eye, I tried to submerge Mount Ararat in the rising waters of the Flood. It wasn't easy. And yet there is a kernel of truth in the legend of the Flood that connects the mountain to the Black Sea – a sea that not only isn't black, but in fact hasn't always been a sea.

In the early stages of its development, long before humans appeared along its shores to argue over the exact internal borderline of that Siamese-twin continent of Eurasia, this body of water wandered in parallel to the grating dance steps of the two tectonic plates. Over the course of a tango lasting millions of years, it was sometimes linked to the Caspian Sea, sometimes to the Mediterranean, and at others it became a landlocked lake cut off from its neighbouring seas.

The bottom of the sea tells us about the circumstances in which it drifted out of the last ice age into the more recent past. About 150 m below the current surface, there are the visible contours of an earlier lake, much smaller and shallower than the sea is today. Discovering this substrate in the late twentieth century, scientists came across the remains of freshwater organisms, whereas in the upper strata they found only deposits of typical sea creatures. So far, so unsurprising: over the millennia, a smaller lake had been transformed into a larger sea. It was only when the researchers noticed that there was no real transition between the two sedimentary zones that they began to scratch their heads. It looked as if the lake had filled up comparatively suddenly with huge quantities of salt water, radically altering its ecosystem within a very short space of time.

When did this happen, and why? The researchers dated the traces of life found along the line of the former lake shore. They established that the upheaval must have occurred within the last 8,000 years, in the sixth millennium BC, when the sunken lake's water level had been considerably lower than that of the nearby Mediterranean. The two bodies of water were separated then as now by a narrow land bridge – the passage between the Balkan Peninsula and Asia Minor. A dramatic film began to play inside the researchers' heads. As the ice age waned and meltwater topped up the oceans, the level of the Mediterranean rose to such an extent that the sheer mass of water eventually spilled out of its bowl, flooded the Balkan land bridge, and streamed into the next valley to the north. The whole process sped up when the pressure of the water, thrusting earth and rock aside, tore a breach in the isthmus – creating the present-day Bosporus. From this moment on, the waters of the Mediterranean must have poured into the Black Sea basin with such force that the level of the lake rose by up to 15 cm per day. Transposed to the horizontal, this equates to the shoreline eating its way inland in flatter areas at a rate of more than 1 km per day.

For the people living on the lake shores in those dark days, the drowning of their world must have been an incomprehensible and unimaginable disaster. What could have inspired their gods to such wrath? As they and their livestock fled desperately to higher ground, they must have come up at first with some tentative explanations, which developed over the ensuing years and decades into recriminations, pledges of atonement, self-flagellation, and religious legends. Even centuries later, when they had long since built a new life for themselves far from their ancestral homes, people must have still spoken in whispers of the great flood that had wiped away the past and marked the beginning of a new future.

When these campfire stories were set down in writing thousands of years later, a deluge of Flood literature rolled out from the shores of the Black Sea. In the Old Testament, the exodus of humans and animals ends on Mount Ararat, whereas in the Qur'an it is on Mount Judi. Both of these versions resemble the Sumerians' *Epic of Gilgamesh* and their earlier *Atrahasis* story in which the ship of salvation lands on Mount Nisir, a mountain in what is now the Kurdish part of Iraq. The ancient Greeks were also familiar with the legend of the Flood, which they explicitly associated with the Black Sea, albeit in the opposite direction. In the first century BC, the historian Diodorus of Sicily heard from the inhabitants of the Aegean island of Samothrace that back in the mists of time, the Black Sea had burst its banks and poured through the Bosporus, engulfing their island. In addition, Strabo reports in his *Geographica* that the rivers flowing into the Black Sea had once caused it to overflow.

Is it possible that the origin of all these stories was an authentic natural disaster that gave the Black Sea its present form? The 'deluge hypothesis' is, as its name suggests, a theory, and among geographers and oceanographers it has its proponents and its critics. If there is one sea, however, whose genesis lends itself to legends of the Flood, then it is the Black Sea.

* * *

We left the foot of Mount Ararat behind and drove south. Cervat wanted to show me a place in the mountains where, several decades ago, one of the many Christian Ark-seekers thought they had stumbled upon a promising lead. A few miles from the Iranian border, we turned off the main road onto a track that wound its way uphill between reddish crags. After a quarter of an hour's drive, Cervat stopped the car. We got out and saw before us a long and deserted valley. The dusty ground was strewn with scree and looked totally parched, as if it hadn't seen a drop of rain since the Flood.

Cervat pointed to the slope opposite. There was an indentation visible in the rock: a long, dark blotch on the stone.

'Nuh'un gemisi,' Cervat announced solemnly. Noah's Ark.

The indent was perhaps 100 m long and a third as wide. It was pointed at both ends and, with a great deal of imagination, reminiscent of a ship's hull. With slightly less imagination, it was reminiscent of a Turkish *pide* bread.

We stood there in silence, staring into the distance. Suddenly, out of nowhere, two barefooted boys appeared, their inquisitive eyes darting back and forth between me, Cervat, and the impression in the rocks. I wondered where they had come from, where they lived, and what they were doing here, but we had no common language.

'Nuh'un gemisi?' I asked, gesturing towards the imprint.

The two boys nodded silently, as though they did not entertain the slightest doubt that long ago a ship had run aground here in the middle of this arid mountain landscape.

I contemplated the imprint and tried to rewind the film in my mind. Dust coalesced into weathered wood; beams took shape and curved up into ribs, a spine, a ship. Figures came scuttling out of the mountains, half-starved, their eyes crazed, humans and beasts virtually indistinguishable from one another. Water crept up from the valley, lifted the laden ship off the rocks and propelled it northwards, on and on, across a never-ending sea heaving with flotsam and corpses. Then the water level fell; the sea shrank, retreated, and seeped away until it was no bigger than a valley. The Ark came to a rest, and out climbed Noah. He drove the animals onto the land, dismantled the ship into its component parts, took a deep breath and settled on the lakeshore as a herdsman.

Russia

Chornoye more / *Чёрное море*

That sea, the blessed sea of a blessed childhood,
is now nowhere to be found—except within myself.
It is gone, probably gone to the same
place where time also goes.

Pavel Florensky, *To My Children*, 1919

The beginnings of a bridge

'Hang on, I've got something for you.'

Oleg's huge head dived into the freezer. We listened to him rummaging around inside it for a while before he pulled a long rigid frozen fish out into the spring air.

'Here you go!'

'Oleg—'

'It's for you.'

'But—'

'A present.'

He walked towards me with a broad grin on his face, clutching the fish's tail like the hilt of a Jedi lightsabre.

'Oleg, I'm staying at a hotel. How am I supposed to cook that thing?'

'Which one?'

'What?'

'Which hotel?'

'The Fortuna.'

'Tell Sasha to fry the fish for you. The guy at reception. He's a friend of mine. We beat each other up once.'

'Why did you beat each other up?'

Oleg shrugged his shoulders. 'It's what we do to seal friendship around here.'

'Can't you seal friendship without beating each other up?'

He thought about this for a second before shaking his head vigorously. 'You don't know the other person properly if you don't.'

I nodded as if I could see the wisdom in this.

The freezer was steaming in the April sunshine. Oleg had

forgotten to shut it, which was hardly surprising given all the brandy. His mate Elvis, the soberest of us three, clicked the lid back into place, while Oleg disappeared into the common room to find a bag for my present.

This freezer stood on the western tip of the Taman Peninsula on the banks of the Kerch Strait, the narrow channel separating Russia from Crimea – and Asia from Europe, if you believe one of the many definitions used to draw this indefinable continental boundary over the centuries. The freezer stood in Asia.

We were sitting in the courtyard of a fishing cooperative that had seen better days. Rust and salt were gnawing away at the corrugated-iron roofs of the sheds, piles of nets drying between them. A few peeling upturned rowing boats lay on the beach, covered in seaweed and half buried in the sand, like the shells of dead tortoises.

I had arrived in the nearby town of Taman the previous day, after a flight from Moscow to Krasnodar and a long bus journey across the southern Russian steppe. That morning, I had borrowed a bike to cycle to the very end of the peninsula. Oleg and Elvis both worked for the fishing cooperative, and they had caught me trying to squeeze my bike through a hole in the fence; I wanted to get to the shore, and the fence was in my way. Then, instead of chucking me out, they tied me to a chair and forced me to drink homemade brandy.

They didn't really tie me to a chair, of course. They merely welcomed me with the sort of Russian hospitality you cannot easily refuse.

The fishing cooperative was a typically Soviet set-up whose post-Soviet decline had affected its employees to varying degrees. Elvis, a small wiry Crimean Tatar with the facial features of a Mongolian steppe warrior, seemed to have come to terms with the new situation. His wallet was bursting with photos of kids, his smile relaxed, and his alcohol consumption moderate – at least by local standards. Oleg, on the other hand, oozed dissatisfaction from every pore of his bear-like physique. He set a hellish drinking pace, withdrawing after the first few glasses into blank-eyed gloom, from which he would occasionally stir to resume his long jeremiad about the continual slights Russia had to endure.

'The world only likes us as long as we're weak…' I watched the accordion-like wrinkles on his brow play a heroic march in a minor key. 'But the moment we get up off our knees, everyone tries to beat us down.'

His glazed eyes were riveted to the horizon. Over there in the distance, Russia was getting up off its knees. The sounds of a building site drifted over to us on the gusty wind. Pneumatic drills, rollers, crane winches. Just over a mile from the fishing cooperative's beach, the outline of a brand-new bridge jutted out into the Kerch Strait, bending slightly to the right at first before curving back in the opposite direction. It looked like a gigantic question mark. We screwed up our eyes, shelled Black Sea shrimps, and observed the world's largest country in the act of growing. The bridge, whose inauguration was scheduled for the next few weeks, spanned the gap between the south-westernmost tip of the Russian mainland and annexed Crimea.

That April day was slightly more than four years after Moscow's occupation of the peninsula. In March 2014, Vlad the Expander had announced Crimea's return to Russia's embrace with similar pathos to that employed by Catherine the Great in her day. In contrast to that first annexation, however, the blot on this second forcible acquisition was that the Crimea of 2014 could only be reached from Russia by air and by sea, as the narrow spits connecting it to the northern mainland led to Ukraine. Hence the bridge. It had been built over the Kerch Strait at great speed in the past four years, drawing a 19 km, €3.5 billion line under the annexation and binding together what, from Oleg's perspective, belonged together.

'Crimea was always Russian … always … we merely took it back … how can you blame us for that?'

Listening to his lament with a vague foreboding that his self-pity might suddenly veer into belligerence, I couldn't get out of my head two lines of verse Alexander Blok wrote shortly after the October Revolution as a declaration of his simultaneous love and hatred for the ignorant West, which so persistently misunderstands Russia's clumsy embrace:

Is it our fault if your skeleton cracks
In our heavy, tender paws?

This uncompleted bridge was the missing link in my otherwise uninterrupted pathway around the Black Sea. Other than the mouths of rivers, the only two major breaks in the coastline were the straits at Kerch and Istanbul. Both had been referred to as 'Bosporus' since ancient times, and both were commonly designated as the continental dividing line between Asia and Europe. The Bosporus in Istanbul had been bridged long ago, unlike the Cimmerian Bosporus, named by the Greeks after the nomadic Cimmerian people who had once lived here.

I gazed into the distance in the hope of making out on the other shore the port city of Kerch, the final destination of my journey around the Black Sea. But the furthest end of the bridge was lost in the haze, and Crimea was out of sight. The first cars would soon start to cross. The road to Crimea would then be open, but there would still be a gaping hole in the straits, albeit one not apparent to the naked eye. The Ukrainian government still regarded the annexed peninsula as Ukrainian territory, despite Kiev having lost control of Crimea. The Ukrainians considered the construction of the bridge an illegal act, and they had declared that they would prosecute anyone crossing it for violating their country's borders. It was an empty threat, for in actual fact no one in Kiev was now in a position to monitor the traffic in the Kerch Strait. And still, a suggestion of excommunication hung over these waters. You couldn't cross the Cimmerian Bosporus without arousing Ukraine's wrath.

It wasn't political qualms that kept me away from the bridge, though; it was a kind of hare-and-tortoise ambition. While the Russians drew their line under history westwards towards the Crimean shore, I wanted to travel in the opposite direction, clockwise around the entire sea with the ultimate goal of standing on the other side of the bridge – without having crossed it.

The afternoon passed slowly. At some point, Elvis's wife turned up with their two small daughters, the staccato rhythm of the drinking toasts slowed somewhat, and Oleg's mood levelled out. We grilled shashliks and looked out to sea. Wooden stakes, with the cooperative's nets slung between them, poked up out of the water just off the beach. Beside them, two dolphins suddenly surged through the waves, big and grey and gleaming – the first of many I would see on my journey around the Black Sea. I stared at them like a child, mouth open and eyes wide, whereas Elvis's daughters barely glanced up from their father's phone.

Elvis had family on the other side of the strait. When the annexation of Crimea and the building of the bridge were announced four years earlier, he and his wife were delighted because it would make it easier to visit their relatives. Their relatives, on the other hand, as Crimean Tatars, were anything but delighted by the takeover. As in so many Russian-Ukrainian families, the political events had driven a wedge between Tatars on either side of the Kerch Strait. There were arguments, Elvis told me ruefully. Instead of bringing the family together, the bridge had split them apart.

I asked Elvis whether there was a mosque for the Tatars in Taman.

'Not one in the whole Krasnodar district.'

'Cossack soil!' The subject had shaken Oleg out of his brooding. 'Ancient Russian land! The government doesn't want any mosques here. Only church bells shall ring out here!'

I wanted to object that the land here had been Tatar soil before Catherine the Great made it Cossack soil, and that the Cossacks had only ended up here because Catherine had expelled them from their Ukrainian homeland, but I held my tongue.

We discussed fishing techniques instead. Oleg and Elvis told me about the tower method. Two wooden perches are mounted, equidistant from the shore, on long poles about 3 m above the surface of the water. Behind them, a box-shaped net is stretched with a fish trap along its seaward side. Two men take up position on the towers and stare patiently down at the water. At the sight of a shoal of mullet, they guide it into the middle of the box using movable nets, close the front, and wait for all the fish to be caught in the trap.

Oleg and Elvis assured me that the tower method was practised only here on the Taman peninsula. Extremely local, like most fishing techniques. A few miles down the coast, you'd find people fishing very differently. This particular method was originally Turkish, and local fishermen still referred to the core components – the towers, the watchmen, the nets – by their Turkish names. I wrote down the terms phonetically: *karava, cherbukhan, giz*.

Not six months later, as I reached the Bosporus on the opposite shore of the Black Sea, I saw two wooden towers looming up out of the water on the Anatolian side and, perched on top of them, two men; it was the spitting image of the sketch Oleg and Elvis had drawn on my pad. But when I read out their Russian counterparts' technical terms to the fishermen on the Bosporus, their faces were blank. Something had got lost on the towers' long journey around the Black Sea.

Night was falling as I hung the fish from my handlebars and cycled back to Taman.

Hotel Fortuna

Arriving at my hotel in the dark, I discovered that Oleg's present had vanished. The plastic bag was still hanging from the handlebars, but there was now a gaping hole in it and the fish was gone. It was probably lying on the verge somewhere, staring up at the moon.

Taman, a dusty dump in the steppe, lies on the northern shore of the eponymous peninsula on the Asian side of the Cimmerian Bosporus, a few miles from the end of the Crimean bridge, and is flanked by rippling water on one side and rippling grass in every other direction. This flat and practically treeless grassland stretches in a more or less uninterrupted swathe from here to Mongolia; well before Slavs settled on the Black Sea coast, an ever-changing cast of nomadic mounted peoples advanced to the edge of Europe along this corridor of Asian steppe. The list of these barbarians is long. The Cimmerians were followed by Scythians, the Scythians by Sarmatians, then Goths, Huns, Alans, Avars, Khazars, Magyars, Pechenegs, Mongols, and Tatars.

Dikoye Polye ('the Wild Fields'): that is what the Russians called these grasslands, which long formed the disputed south-western frontier of the Russian Empire until Catherine the Great conquered the peoples of the steppe and extended her tsardom to the coast. The day before, I had travelled for five hours across this steppe in a long-distance bus from Krasnodar, the district capital, to Taman. The air over the sea of grass on either side of the road flickered in the heat, millions of songbirds skimmed inches above the ground catching insects, and the scent of wild herbs through the bus's open window was so intense that the eyes of the elderly Russian man sitting next to me had grown moist.

'You could season shashliks with this air!' he cried. 'You only need to hold the skewers out of the window.'

My hotel in Taman was called Fortuna because it belonged to an Armenian who had made a killing on the Russian lottery a few years earlier. A local TV reporter had asked him at the time whether he was planning to hightail it back to his native country with his winnings. The Armenian had interpreted this as a veiled threat and had therefore stressed on camera that he would invest the money in Russia. And that was how he had gone from being a guest worker to a guesthouse owner.

The Fortuna hadn't brought its proprietor much luck, to be honest. 'For sale', said a tattered poster that seemed to have been attached to the front of the hotel for quite a while already. My footsteps echoed in empty corridors: I was clearly the only guest. I heard the story about the lottery win from two of the owner's relatives, who ran the business in his absence – an elderly Armenian brother and sister with near-identical sombre features. Neither of them knew the owner's precise whereabouts. The only thing they did know was that his business wasn't doing well – and that things rarely turned out well for Armenians. Their faces became even more sombre when I told them that I'd recently seen Mount Ararat.

'Our mountain!' the man cried in a plaintive voice.

The woman sighed. 'The Turks stole it from us.'

Both of them asked me where I was heading. I started to list the countries bordering the Black Sea, but I only made it as far as Turkey.

'Our coast!' the man cried in a plaintive voice.

The woman sighed. 'The Turks stole it from us.'

Neither spoke for a long time after that.

Paradoxically, the two Hotel Fortuna employees were the most miserable people I came across in Taman. Everyone else in the small town was in high spirits; I met barely anyone during my three-day stay who did not rejoice in the bridge-building. Those who had found work on the huge building site, or who were hoping to make a living from tourists from every corner of Russia who would soon pass through their town on their way to Crimea, rejoiced. Those who had relatives on the peninsula rejoiced that they would no longer have to take the sluggish, chronically overloaded ferry to visit them in the summer. The director of the local history museum rejoiced because her display cases were now full to bursting with archaeological artefacts – Cimmerian horse harnesses, Roman drinking vessels, Genoan coins – found while the bridge's groundworks were laid. Last but not least, the joy of Taman's residents was shared by the 2,500 entrants into a nationwide poetry competition that the office responsible for the bridge's construction had recently launched to encourage patriotic eulogies of their feat. The victor had not yet been chosen when I was there, but here is a sample of what I read:

Crimea and Russia
Forever inseparable
Wedded by a bridge
That looks like a temple

The bridge was indeed something of an unexpected windfall for Taman. The town, with a population of 10,000, had hitherto wallowed in such oblivion, even by Russian standards, that its old name of Turkish origin, Tmutarakan, had become a national byword for any godforsaken provincial backwater – a kind of Russian Hicksville. Soon though, thanks to the bridge, Taman would no longer be a dead end on the tip of a promontory but Russia's last stop before Crimea.

There was as yet little sign of this earth-shaking change. The bridge was a building site, the holiday season had not yet begun, and Taman seemed to be only just stirring from hibernation. The local museum was open but deserted, the model Cossack village on the edge of town still closed. A Soviet tank on blocks in the market square stood as a memorial to the Great Patriotic War, and its aerial counterpart, a fighter plane, greeted you on the road into town. Both of them were mounted on concrete pedestals with the constantly cited – and constantly wrong – dates carved into them: 1941–1945. As everywhere else in the former Soviet Union, the hushed-up war years of 1939 and 1940 – when Stalin was still making common cause with Hitler to carve up Central Europe – were missing.

Some of my Russian friends had nodded knowingly when I told them that my journey would take me to Taman. They knew the place from a short story by Mikhail Lermontov, who spent a few nights here in the 1830s when he was a young cavalry officer. The old fisherman's hut that served as his quarters at the time, and as the setting for his later story about smugglers, was still there. It had been turned into a small Lermontov museum containing a few items from the author's estate including, much to my astonishment, a dog-eared and obviously well-thumbed copy of a book called *L'Imitation de Jésus-Christ*. It was a French translation of *The Imitation of Christ* by Thomas à Kempis, the medieval mystic from the town near the lower Rhine where I went to school. I'd never read the book, even though – or perhaps because – I'd received a copy after my high school exams, like every leaver from our Thomaeum High School, named after Thomas. I had trouble coming to terms with the fact that a book that in my teenage years seemed to epitomise all the boredom and remoteness of my provincial hometown should suddenly cross my path here on the Black Sea coast, a source of inspiration that a writer close to my heart had kept close to his heart as he rode through southern Russia.

On my second day in Taman, I was followed by a small brown stray dog with a greedy eye on my rucksack. It tailed me down to the beach. When I put my bag down in the sand, the dog sniffed at it, only to turn away in disappointment. Then it trotted down to the edge of the water and did something unexpected: it dipped its nose and began to lap at the water. I stared in amazement. Never before had I seen a dog drink seawater. I stuck a finger in the water and licked it. Because the shallow Sea of Azov is predominantly freshwater, it hardly tasted of salt.

After this incident with the dog, I got into the habit of trying the water whenever I reached a new stretch of coast. In

Taman it was barely saltier than the yoghurt-based drink the Turks call *ayran*. South of the Cimmerian Bosporus, where the Sea of Azov ends and the Black Sea begins, the taste was noticeably more intense, but it was only when I got to the Bosporus at Istanbul and the Sea of Marmara that I experienced the familiar gagging reflex I knew so well from the Mediterranean holidays of my childhood.

Pasha the Turk

He was wearing a sky-blue skullcap when we first met, and a cream-coloured one when we parted ways. Pasha appeared to change his *taqiyah* daily, but he kept his head continuously covered from morning to evening, even when it wasn't time to pray. He never removed his crocheted head covering, not at the wheel of his car nor when he took his breaks outside the grocery shop on Taman's main street waiting for clients, a short, slim man standing beside an old white Lada.

When he revealed to me on our first taxi journey that he was a *Turok* – that is to say, a Turk – I studied his face somewhat quizzically from the side. The skullcap; the pointy, hawklike face; the salt-and-pepper moustache; the gold teeth.

'A Turk?' I asked. 'You mean, a Tatar?'

'A Turk.'

'Really? Türkçe konuşuyor musunuz?'

His answer in Turkish was fluent, unlike my stammered question about his language skills. Having taken a Turkish course in Berlin a few years earlier, I'd been capable of ordering a kebab quite fluently ever since. Pasha, on the other hand, had grown up in the language.

It took me a few taxi journeys to understand that he and his parents were Meskhetian Turks. That is, Georgian Turks

– or Turkish Georgians, depending on your point of view. The Meskhetian Turks had lived on the southern margins of Georgia, close to Turkey, since the sixteenth century. Where they originally hailed from remained an unresolved matter that only attracted their neighbours' interest when the Turks and Georgians along the border discovered nationalism. In Turkey, they were henceforth regarded as Turks who had emigrated and assimilated to Georgia, whereas to the Georgians they were Georgians who had adopted Islam and the Turkish language under Ottoman influence. And so, both the Georgians and the Turks claimed the Meskhetians as their own while also viewing them as a bastardised, second-class people of mixed heritage. In this sense, Pasha's ancestors shared a fate with countless ethnic minorities in the regions bordering the Black Sea. They fell through the cracks in the mosaic of emerging nation-states, and it was not they themselves but rulers in distant capitals, irked by this melee of peoples on the margins of their supposedly pure nations, who decided to which state they should belong.

One aggravating factor for the Meskhetian Turks was that Ioseb Jughashvili – aka Joseph Stalin – though no fan of nation-states, was a partisan of good old Russian-style imperialism. Scenting an opportunity to annex border areas of Turkey during the Second World War, the Soviet dictator pre-emptively expelled the Meskhetian Turks from their homeland. In light of his plans, they suddenly struck him more like Turks who might just, who knows, feel more loyal to the enemy than to the Soviet motherland. Stalin was an advocate of simple solutions. Justifiably or not, the Meskhetian Turks were a headache. No more Meskhetians, no more headaches. They had to go.

Pasha's parents were newlywed at the time. His father was

twenty and his mother eighteen when, out of the blue, one winter's day in 1944, soldiers came pounding on their door in the southern Georgian village of Zarzma. Along with over 100,000 other Meskhetian Turks, they were herded into cattle wagons that rolled eastwards from Georgia and only came to a halt several thousand miles later. Roughly a third of them died during their deportation or shortly afterwards from hunger, thirst, hypothermia, disease, or a broken heart. Ultimately, Stalin's planned expansion into Turkey came to nothing, but the 'leader of peoples' had managed to purge his mind entirely of one.

The Meskhetian Turks were dumped out of those cattle wagons into the steppes and deserts of Central Asia to find themselves under military supervision. Pasha's parents ended up in a temporary settlement near the Uzbek capital, Tashkent, where the fourth of their six children, Pashali Shazimovich Ritvanov, was born in 1958.

Although Pasha had never seen his parents' native land, he grew up in Uzbekistan in the knowledge that he was either a Georgian Turk or a Turkish Georgian, depending. His parents told him that there had been mountains in Zarzma as well as forests and lakes, seasons, real summers and real winters, not just cotton fields and dust, as there were in Uzbekistan. At home, with his family, Pasha spoke Turkish. Beyond their four walls, he spoke Uzbek with the Uzbeks and Russian with all the other Soviet minorities whom Stalin had exiled to Central Asia to ease his troubled mind: Crimean Tatars, Volga Germans, Pontic Greeks, Kalmyks, Chechens, the Ingush, Karachays, and Balkars.

Pasha showed a gift for languages in this Tower of Babel and became a Russian teacher. He worked his way up to deputy head of a high school and might well have become headmaster, had Moscow's loss of control of the republics in the dying days of the Soviet Union not led to a surge in long-repressed nationalist sentiment among the Uzbeks. Some of them suddenly began to question why they should put up with Stalin's transformation of their homeland into one big multicultural omelette. Pogroms erupted in the ethnically piebald Fergana Valley in 1989, and several hundred Meskhetian Turks were killed. The survivors took to their heels.

'And then?' I asked Pasha as he was telling me this story in his taxi. 'Then you finally went back to Georgia?'

I realised I was longing for a happy ending.

Pasha gave a short, dry chuckle.

'As if! The Georgians wouldn't let us in.'

The Georgians, having rediscovered their feelings of nationhood after the long Soviet-imposed hiatus in similar fashion to the Uzbeks, were suspicious of how Georgian the Meskhetians really were after they had lived elsewhere for the best part of half a century. They made it clear to the wannabe returnees that it would be preferable if they returned somewhere else – a place better suited to them, even if the Meskhetian Turks didn't come from Turkey and had indeed never been there.

Pasha, who had four children by then, initially ended up, like many other Meskhetian Turks, in Azerbaijan, Georgia's neighbouring Turkic-speaking republic, where he continued working as a teacher. It was only when teachers' salaries nosedived amid the general post-Soviet chaos and, to compound his misery, illness struck his twin sons that he took a doctor's advice and moved. Pasha's sons needed sea air, the doctor said. Pasha's wife suggested they join her mother who had fled, along with other Meskhetian Turks, to the Russian Black Sea coast. So Pasha found himself in Taman. That was twenty-three years ago.

He had only been to Turkey once – for his daughter's wedding. After moving to Taman, Pasha had been unable to find a teaching post and had taken on a succession of odd jobs to make ends meet. During one assignment on a building site, he made friends with a Turkish man from the Isparta area who had been posted to Russia by the construction firm he worked for. This man was Pasha's age, and when he mentioned that he had an unmarried son back home in Turkey, Pasha offered him his daughter's hand. Arranged marriages were not unusual among Meskhetian Turks – Pasha himself had married a wife of his parents' choosing.

'My daughter wouldn't agree when I first told her, but I'd given my word and I couldn't take it back.'

He flew to Istanbul with his weeping daughter. They travelled south by bus for eight hours until they reached the village where the wedding was held. The next day, Pasha returned to Taman because he needed to work. He saw very little of Turkey, but what he did see gave him the impression that his daughter's tears would quickly dry.

'She's happy now.'

I hoped he was right.

'The Turks in Turkey,' Pasha continued, 'didn't know there were Turks in Russia. They asked me if we kept the faith. Of course, I said – we fast during Ramadan, we slaughter sheep for the Feast of the Sacrifice, and we don't touch vodka or bacon. They were amazed.'

I was amazed too. It was the first of many convoluted stories of immigration and emigration, leaving and returning, that I was to hear on my way around the Black Sea, and in retrospect it wasn't even the most convoluted one, but it did set a tone that would become increasingly familiar in the months that followed.

On the day I left Taman, I walked to the main street to say goodbye to Pasha.

'I never imagined I would meet someone who spoke Turkish here.'

'We aren't the only ones. There are Greeks around here who speak Turkish too.'

'Greeks who speak Turkish? In Russia?'

'In Vityazevo. A little further down the coast.'

'Could you drive me there?'

Greek wine

The steppe spooled past the Lada's windows. Over the millennia that had passed since the nomads of antiquity galloped across the oceans of grass to Europe, the majority of the Wild Fields of southern Russia had been parcelled up, ploughed, and planted – but every so often, between the fields, a small accidental nature reserve would appear, where it seemed as if nothing had changed since barbarian times. Wormwood bushes and quivering thistles towered above the scrubby grass, whose colour was just shading from wintery yellow into spring green. When the gusty wind flattened the blades, it looked like waves rolling across the steppe.

We passed through the occasional village comprising a handful of low-slung wooden houses with fruit trees in their gardens, their blossom-laden boughs hanging low over the road. The turbulence we created tore the flowers from the twigs and left white confetti clouds swirling in our wake.

'Back then, when your parents chose a wife for you … did you like her straight away?'

The pulsating spring air outside the windscreen made it easier to ask intimate questions.

'Of course. She was a good girl.'

For a while we said nothing, but then a twitch of sudden memory wrinkled Pasha's face.

'There was this Russian girl. In Uzbekistan. We met at university before I married.' This was followed by a long pause, Pasha's silence telling a story for which he couldn't find the right words. 'But my father was against it.'

'Why?'

He glanced at me, as if to say, *Isn't that obvious?*

'Why, oh, why ... because she wasn't Turkish, that's why.'

I looked at him out of the corner of my eye. It was hard to read his fixed expression. 'Would you have rather married the other woman?'

'Oh, rubbish. She wasn't Turkish, so how could I have married her?'

'Was it hard to forget her?'

He shook his head. 'After the wedding, I never thought of her again.'

Something in his voice told me this wasn't true. As we drove on in silence, I wondered if Pasha really had given away his daughter as breezily as he claimed.

When the road curved back towards the sea after a good hour's driving, the landscape was different from the countryside on the Cimmerian Bosporus, where the grassland had reached almost to the water's edge before the slightly raised coastline fell away steeply to a narrow strip of sandy beach. In the small seaside resort of Vityazevo that we were passing through, the shore was flat, the beach was as wide as a football pitch, and inland, blocking my view, were dunes – the only ones I saw along the entire Black Sea coast.

Pasha stopped outside a car repair workshop. A young

woman was standing in the doorway, her left hand in the pocket of her blue overalls, a cigarette in her right. Pasha got out.

'Does that old Greek still work here? The one who speaks Turkish?'

The woman smiled as she studied him. 'There are more than enough Greeks around here, Pops, but we all speak Greek.'

It took us some time to explain to the woman and her fellow mechanics who it was we were looking for. It turned out that the old man who had once repaired Pasha's Lada no longer lived in Vityazevo, but one of his colleagues promised to call in a substitute Greek.

A few minutes later, a black SUV pulled up outside the workshop. The driver got out and shook my hand. He was about thirty, with dark hair, pale, chubby cheeks, and sad puppy eyes.

'I'm Misha.'

I started to introduce myself slightly awkwardly, but Misha cut me off after the second sentence. 'Get in. You can spend the night with us. Mum will tell you everything.'

I waved to Pasha through the car window, and he tapped two fingertips on his cream-coloured skullcap.

Where most automatic gearsticks have a knob, the one in Misha's SUV sported a grinning skull. Misha loved this skull. He couldn't take his hand off it and stroked its forehead absentmindedly throughout the whole drive.

He and his mother ran a small guesthouse in Vityazevo. The tourist season hadn't yet begun, the guesthouse was empty, and, after parking the car in the courtyard, Misha pressed a master key into my hand.

'Pick a room. Mum will make you something to eat.'

We ate cheesecake with sugary tea under the walnut tree in the courtyard. Larisa, Misha's mother, had her son's pale complexion, but instead of his sad puppy eyes she had narrow, slanted cat's eyes that lent her face a permanent air of amusement. Smiling, she explained that there were two kinds of Greeks in Vityazevo, and I had chosen the wrong kind.

'You have to speak to the Pontic Greeks. Vityazevo belongs to them. We Tsalkans are only here because my son has ants in his pants.'

The Pontic Greeks owed their name to the old Greek word their ancestors had used to describe the Black Sea in ancient times: 'Pontos Axeinos', meaning 'the inhospitable sea', the sea of barbarians. Later, when Greek seafarers had grown more accustomed to the Black Sea coast and the coast had become more Greek, they had altered the name to its similar-sounding opposite: 'Pontos Euxeinos', 'the hospitable sea'. The abbreviated form 'Pontos' had survived and been incorporated into most of the languages spoken along the coast as a loan word for the Black Sea, as well as clinging to the descendants of those who had coined the original term – the Pontic Greeks.

I had heard a great deal about the Pontic Greeks but nothing about the Tsalkans. They too were originally Black Sea Greeks, Larisa explained, but their ancestors had bowed to power relations in the Ottoman Empire and learned Turkish, though they hadn't converted to Islam as other Pontic groups had done. Later, in the nineteenth century, when the Russian–Ottoman struggle for control of the Black Sea triggered transfers of Christian and Muslim communities between the two empires, the Tsalkans' Anatolian ancestors had emigrated to the Georgian part of the tsar's realm. Most of them settled west of Tbilisi, not far from the Meskhetian villages in the Tsalka region from which they derived their name.

That, however, was just the prologue to a long history of migration which, in Larisa's case, had begun not south of the Caucasus but to the north. Long before her birth, her grandparents had fled through the mountains to Russia. Larisa didn't know why they had left Georgia, but counting backwards brought me to the time of the Russian Civil War, which had uprooted large sections of the Soviet population in the aftermath of Lenin's October Revolution.

Larisa had given birth to Misha in 1988 in the mountain spa town of Yessentuki. His father disappeared from their life at an early stage. Larisa spoke Russian to her son while his grandmother taught him the Turkish of the Tsalkan Greeks. Misha grew up amid the chaos of the post-Soviet transition, a time of economic hardship during which the Caucasus emptied in eerie fashion. Anyone who could leave did so. The Russian Jewish community emigrated to Israel or Germany, which was also where the Russian Germans headed. In the same period, many Greeks also 'returned to their historic homeland', as it was described at the time, although the words 'homeland' and 'return' sounded even more abstract in their case than they did for the Jews and Germans. It had been millennia rather than mere centuries since their ancestors' ships had rowed through the Bosporus into the Black Sea. Such had been the divergence in history, customs, and even language between the Pontic and Hellenic Greeks that understanding one another was problematic in many regards.

This did not deter the Pontic Greeks, though. Of the 500,000 estimated to have been living in the Soviet Union's republics as it collapsed, at least half emigrated to Greece during the 1990s. They included Larisa and Misha, who found a new home in Cyprus.

That might have been the end of their story, but then

something happened which even now Larisa and Misha were unable to explain fully.

'Tell him.'

'What?'

'How you got ants in your pants.'

'What is there to tell?'

'If you don't tell him, I will.'

'Go ahead.'

One day when Misha was seventeen, a relative who had happened to move from the Caucasus to Vityazevo invited Larisa and her son to come on holiday to the Black Sea. They travelled on the Russian passports they both still held, spent two weeks with the Pontic Greeks of Vityazevo, then flew back to Cyprus.

When the next school holidays came around, Misha longed to go back to Vityazevo. He spent the following two holidays on the Black Sea too, but this time without Larisa. This went on for several years until Misha, who by now had left school, didn't return home. Over the phone he said, 'I'm going to stay for a little longer.' He said this once, twice, five times, then the sixth time he said, 'Mum, I'm staying here.'

Larisa had painstakingly built up a new life for herself in Cyprus and found it hard to imagine returning to a country she had been so relieved to quit a decade earlier. However, she found it even harder to imagine life without her son. Eventually, she smiled her feline smile, packed her suitcases, and followed Misha.

'Explain to him.'

'What?'

'What kept you here. You can't explain it to me, but maybe to him.'

Misha glanced uncertainly at me. 'Life's just more interesting here … for a man. Does that make sense?'

'You mean there was a woman involved?'

He shook his head. 'Only later.'

Larisa laughed. 'And then twice in quick succession!'

Misha seemed glad to change the subject. 'Mum said, "Marry anyone you want, as long as she's not a Muslim." But they really turn my head, those Chechens, those Ingush women, those Turkish girls! Twice I've married Christians, but I promise you, Mum, the next one will be a Turk!'

We tried a few more times that afternoon to coax Misha into saying which fateful wind had blown him to Vityazevo. Had he felt like a Pontic outsider in Cyprus, a member of a minority for whose exceptionalism he didn't fancy paying the price? Hadn't he been able to round off his childhood to his satisfaction? Was it a sense of unfinished business with Russia? Had he grown bored of EU-regulated life in Cyprus? Had Russia seemed more interesting, with more possibilities for a young man whose background meant he would never really belong?

Misha seemed incapable of explaining to himself what it was. He squirmed and evaded our questions. Maybe, I finally thought, he had suffered a bout of genetic nostalgia for the Black Sea that had skipped a few generations after his ancestors left the Ottoman Empire.

In the early evening, Misha shifted his skull from P to D and drove me to the winery. Larisa wanted me to meet some 'real' people, some Pontian Pontic Greeks, which meant just about every Greek in Vityazevo except for the two Tsalkans.

The winery was at the other end of town. On our way there, we drove along the seafront past an almost unbroken line of concrete hotels and cafés at various stages of completion. From all sides came the sound of hammering and drilling – the whole place was getting ready for the tourist season, the period between June and September when half of Russia comes to roast its pale flesh beside the Black Sea, the only practicable bathing waters on the entire chilly half-continent. Annexing Crimea may have more than doubled the length of the Russian part of the Black Sea coast, but it was still only a sliver in relation to the enormity of the country.

The Pontic Greeks' influence on Vityazevo only became apparent to me when I saw the columns, statues, and temple friezes on the fronts of the buildings along the beach. Atlas lookalikes panted under balconies. Goddesses bared their marble-white breasts. A furious Zeus hurled aluminium lightning bolts. I noted the names of the hotels and cafés with disbelief: Avrora, Jason, Argo, Pontos, Odisseya, Illiada, Nika, Poseidon, Attika, Kolisey, Parfenon ... neon Cyrillic signs spelled out these mythical words to the Slavs in a strange blend of alphabets: Russian characters with a Greek slant.

This Hellenic symphony reached a crescendo at the Old Greek winery.

'You can't bottle wine in a cube-like warehouse,' Valeriy Stavrovich Aslanov said. 'Wine is sacred. Wine requires a temple – a Parthenon!'

And that is precisely what the bottling plant Aslanov had built in the middle of his factory site looked like: a concrete copy of the Parthenon. It had slightly fewer columns than the original but made up for this by boasting two golden griffins on its roof that the Athenian version lacked. And a cellarful of wine in oak barrels. And a tasting room with plush chairs. And a black grand piano. And a glass floor looking down into an artificial excavation site furnished with fragments of Greek amphorae. And ...

'And my next plan is to have an apartment added to the

roof,' Aslanov said. 'With a lift to take me straight down to the barrels. That'll be the life, my friends! Drinking, sleeping, drinking, sleeping, drinking …'

His listeners laughed dutifully. Aslanov raised his glass, and the Riesling shimmered, moon-coloured, in the evening sun.

'To friendship between peoples!'

'To friendship between peoples!'

'An excellent toast, Valeriy Stavrovich!'

'Hurray to friendship between peoples!

Aslanov was a former judo instructor who had managed to take over the local kolkhoz during the wave of privatisations. The collective farm had been built on the ruins of a Greek Orthodox church that the Bolsheviks had torn down because it stood in the path of a socialist future. As it became increasingly clear this socialist future would be paused for a while, Aslanov built his wine palace on the ruins of the kolkhoz. Now here he was, sitting on his office terrace with a view of the Parthenon, a short and broad-shouldered nouveau-riche sixty-five-year-old man, surrounded by his entourage of obliging drinking pals. He wore a tracksuit top with a hammer-and-sickle badge on the front, and silver *kombolói* – Greek worry beads – slid through his fingers. The worry beads and the Soviet symbol struck me as a contradiction, but this was only one of many contradictions that weren't contradictions to Aslanov.

'My German friend, you know the good thing about the Soviet Union?' He swirled his glass and stared pensively at the revolving Riesling, as his audience waited in feigned anticipation for the answer. 'The nations didn't mix as they do today.'

'Well said, Valeriy Stavrovich!'

'That's quite right.'

'There's a lot of truth in that.'

There was no truth in it whatsoever. Aslanov was born in 1953, the year Stalin died. He hadn't lived through the forced resettlements of so many communities in the pre- and post-war years, including the Soviet Pontic Greeks. In the 1930s, Stalin sent about 150,000 of them to labour camps because the Greeks weren't nearly eager enough in their backing for his plans to collectivise Soviet agriculture. In other words, they didn't want to starve. In 1949, four years after the war, Stalin had approximately the same number deported from the Black Sea coast to Central Asia in a cloak-and-dagger operation. To this day, no one knows why. Maybe because the government in Athens had handed out passports to the Greek diaspora between the wars as part of its 'Megali Idea' for one grand Greek state encompassing the former Byzantine possessions around the Black Sea. This idea came back to bite the Pontic Greeks, as it made Stalin suspect their loyalties.

Only some of the Soviet Greeks returned from Central Asia after Stalin's death, and many had to look for new homes, as other people had occupied their ancestral houses and villages in their absence. In Vityazevo, however, pre-war Greek life resumed pretty much as before – or so it may have seemed to a young man growing up here in the 1950s and 1960s. Aslanov said that the place was '99.9 per cent Greek' in his youth.

'Other than us, there was only one Russian and one Moldovan family. And an Armenian one later on.'

I wasn't sure how much of this calculation could be attributed to the Riesling. Or maybe Aslanov's memories were tinged with family sentiment. His great-great-grandfather, a Greek Orthodox priest from the Turkish port of Trabzon, had turned his back on the Ottoman Empire in 1837 and emigrated with his congregation to the Russian Black Sea coast, where the Pontic Greeks later founded Vityazevo. To this great-great-grandfather the town also owed the church that was later demolished by the Bolsheviks. The Greeks grew cotton, tobacco, and wine along the shore and sold their produce to nearby Cossack settlements. Cotton and tobacco production had been transferred to other parts of the Soviet Union during the planned economy era, but wine remained.

Later, as Aslanov was showing me around his Parthenon, he proudly pointed out three oil paintings he had commissioned specially for the wine cellar. They were portraits of three Pontic heroes: David Megas Komnenos, the last ruler of the lost empire of Trebizond; Alexander Ypsilantis, the Pontic Greek general who had fought in Russian employ to free Greece from the Ottoman Empire; and Ioannis Kapodistrias, the first head of state of independent Greece.

I liked Aslanov. He was a puffed-up small-town oligarch, and I preferred to remain ignorant about his path to success, but deep down he seemed to be as amused by his wine temple's eccentric décor as I was. He showed off all his useless, expensive tack with great pride, but also with a broad grin, as if it were not himself, Valeriy Stavrovich Aslanov, who had amassed it but someone else – maybe the man whose name was printed in his Greek second passport: Valerios Aslanidas tou Stavrou.

As we said goodbye – and the Riesling may have been to blame – I felt a sudden surge of awe and disbelief inside me that I was facing a man who was, by many twists and turns of fate, an heir to Greek antiquity, and yet to this man Russia was home. Aslanov had never considered emigrating to Greece. He was a Pontic Greek, and his homeland was here on the Black Sea.

Horseless Cossacks

The next morning, I bade farewell to Larisa and Misha and walked to the bus station. On the way there, I happened to notice a parked car whose number plate sported a tricolour sticker in black, blue, and red with the letters DPR across it. I stopped in surprise. The abbreviation stood for the Donetsk People's Republic, one of the separatist regions of eastern Ukraine that had been fought over for years.

Two men in shorts were standing by the car, so I approached them. They were from Donetsk and had driven across the Russian border to Vityazevo.

'For a seaside holiday?'

They laughed, but they didn't sound particularly amused. One of them raised his right hand and rubbed his thumb and forefinger together.

'That's why we're here. There's no work back home.'

They were driving up and down the coast from one construction site to the next, in the hope that someone somewhere would need a hand.

I asked them about Donetsk. What was life like there now? I remembered the depressing atmosphere while I was reporting on the war there a few years earlier.

'Normal,' one of them said. 'There's still gunfire, but we've got used to it.'

The other man laughed, and this time he did sound amused. 'My wife used to tell our kid, "Come inside, it's starting to rain!" Nowadays she shouts, "The shooting's started. Come inside!" And our kid says exactly the same as before: "It's only a little bit, Mum. I'll come in if it gets any heavier!"'

I took a *marshrutka*, a Russian shared taxi. On our way south, I saw the fluorescent Cyrillic shopfronts gradually lose their pseudo-Greek allure as the names of the hotels and cafés became more and more Russian: Admiral, Laguna, Kapitan, Kontinent, Sputnik, Planeta ...

Shortly after Vityazevo, the road curved inland. Half an hour later, hills sprouted from the steppe on either side of the carriageway and increased in size until the grass cover was rent in places, exposing bare rocks. The first foothills of the Caucasus.

When the road rejoined the coast in Novorossiysk, I got out. Warships of the Russian Black Sea fleet were lying at anchor in the roadstead – armour-clad giants, grey, hulking, and motionless, like crocodiles digesting the banquet they had devoured in Crimea.

On the promenade stood a large and clearly not very old monument. An officer in the uniform of the tsarist army was pulling his horse along behind him. The man's bronze body was slanting towards the shore while the anxious horse dug its hooves into the ground. It looked as if destiny were tugging the two figures in opposite directions.

'That's exactly what it was like back in the civil war,' said the honey-seller I struck up a conversation with at a market near the port.

The civil war had ended here in Novorossiysk for the White Army troops loyal to the tsar. British navy ships evacuated them from here to Crimea in 1920 with the Red Army hot on their heels. Over 35,000 soldiers watched the Russian coast fade into the distance forever.

'There was no room on board for the horses,' the honey-seller said. 'The Cossacks had to leave them behind. Some shot them, so they wouldn't fall into the hands of the Reds, but others couldn't bring themselves to do it.'

When Lenin's revolutionary troops marched into

Novorossiysk shortly after the evacuation, thousands of riderless horses were roaming the Pontic steppe. It must have looked like a performance of an ancient Black Sea drama, but one with an incomprehensible twist. Were the barbarians played by the Whites or the Reds, by the exploiters of the working class or the butchers of the bourgeoisie? Who were the nomads and who the settlers? And why, in hell's name, was no one riding the horses?

The honey-seller was wearing a *papakha*, a Caucasian fur hat.

'Cossack?'

His moustache quivered with indignation. 'Everyone in Novorossiysk is a Cossack, young man.' With a more conciliatory gesture, he pointed towards the harbour. 'Ask Sveta, the woman selling gingerbread. She knows all about Cossacks. A few stalls further down.'

Sveta-the-woman-selling-gingerbread was about fifty and had the physique of a woman who does not spurn what she sells to others. She advertised her gingerbread to passers-by in a voice as sweet as honey. 'Try the one with tender plums that melt in the mouth … you'll get hooked on the maize ones. Have a taste …'

She told me about her great-grandmother who had galloped over the battlefields with the Whites until she lost a hand in a skirmish.

'Chop! Hacked off with a sabre. We Cossacks are fighting women. Want to see my medal? The mayor awarded it to me for giving two Tajiks a good thrashing here at the market. They were going after a Russian guy. You have to show those black-arses who's boss.'

She told me about her son, who was a well-known local biker and a Cossack.

'He's a big fan of your German culture.'

I was amazed. A Goethe buff in leathers?

'I bought him a German ring at a flea market. If I send you a photo, could you tell me if it's genuine? It's from the war, with a skull on it. From those, oh, what are they called?'

'SS?'

'That's right! He just loves your culture.'

Right at the end, just before we said goodbye, Sveta told me about a Cossack friend of hers who taught youngsters to fight. 'So they can defend themselves when black-arses get funny with them. There's a tournament tomorrow morning. Why don't you take a look?'

That evening, I went out to join the hundreds of anglers dotting the harbour's long breakwater. Peering out into the darkness, they seemed to register movements I couldn't detect. A few young men, more ambitious than the rest, ran up and down the breakwater, barking coordinates to one another – '11 o'clock', 'ahead on the left' – pointing excitedly at the water, suddenly flicking their lines out into the void, far out into the blackness, and, even though their manoeuvres appeared to be more show than strategy, they reeled one big fish after another onto the shore.

The tournament was being held in a Soviet sports hall south of the city centre. Stepping over the threshold was like passing into a different element: I was engulfed by a cloud of dense, moist air saturated with teenage sweat.

On the mats laid out in the middle of the gymnasium, two boys in white battledress and blue padded helmets, maybe thirteen or fourteen years old, were pounding away at each other. This technique was known as 'army hand-to-hand combat', although to my unpractised eye it looked as if each were trying to kill the other with a combination of the most painful punches, kicks, and throws they could muster. When one of them crumpled to the floor and couldn't get up again, the other kicked him again and again, screaming 'hee-yaa, hee-yaa' each time. Only when the kicks got too close to the fallen boy's head did the referee signal the end of the fight.

Certificates were handed out at the end. The director of the local cadet school gave a speech, punctuated by roars of approval from the assembled Cossacks.

'Russia needs men who are ready to fight!'

'Lyubo!'

'More than ever before!'

'Lyubo!'

'You are Cossacks! The future belongs to you!'

'Lyuboooooo!'

On the way out, I spoke to the director, a man with the wariness of a Soviet bureaucrat in his eyes.

'From where? Germany?' His eyes widened with panic. 'I can't talk to you! Not without the district council's permission. Ask in Krasnodar.'

'I only wanted to know about the Coss—'

He brushed me off like an annoying insect.

Vassiliy was more approachable. He caught my eye outside the gymnasium because he was wearing the biggest *papakha* of all – or at least that was what it looked like, until I realised that I'd mistaken his black locks for a fur hat. Vassiliy's torso was swathed in a bright red knee-length Cossack tunic gathered at the waist by a military belt. Spilling over this belt was a belly of such enormous dimensions that I wondered how he stayed upright.

He had six medals pinned to the chest of his tunic, three

on the right and three on the left. Vassiliy explained each one to me in order.

'For services to the Cossack people. For maintaining law and order in the Kuban region. For promoting the education of adolescent Cossacks. For winning back Crimea. For—'

'What was that about Crimea?'

He raised his eyes from his chest. They were pale blue, like the sky, and shining with pride. 'We won it back!'

Vassiliy and a hundred other Cossacks had chartered a boat to Crimea in February 2014 – on the same route the White escapees from the civil war had taken almost a century earlier. They had set out to make the world's biggest country a little bigger. For the first few weeks, they had been posted along the northern border of Crimea to block access from the Ukrainian mainland. Shortly afterwards, during the referendum on the peninsula's incorporation into Russia, Vassiliy kept watch over the parliament building in Simferopol. I almost gasped out loud at his story. I still had very precise memories of the Cossacks I'd seen standing outside the parliament in those chaotic March days: men with their legs wide apart, simultaneously menacing and ridiculous, dressed in cobbled-together camouflage kit, some with Cossack whips hanging from their belts, with *papakhas* of every shape, size, and texture on their heads. So one of those fur hats had been resting on Vassiliy's curly mane.

As I listened to the customary monologue about the 'Ukrainian fascists' from whom they had saved their Russian brothers and sisters in Crimea, I wondered how Vassiliy could be so blind to the historical irony of his words. His ancestors, the Cossacks of the Russian Black Sea coast, had been driven out of Ukraine. Catherine the Great had resettled them here in the eighteenth century after crushing the centre of the

Ukrainian Cossack state – the island of Khortytsia in the river Dnieper.

This expulsion was the decisive turning point in Cossack history. From the fifteenth century, they had lived as bandits on the steppes, in the disputed frontier region between the settled civilisations to the north and the nomadic peoples to the south. They gathered in the Wild Fields, a felt-bearded bunch of escaped serfs, runaway prisoners, army deserters, destitute farmers, and other outlaws who chose to lead a life as free barbarians rather than bow to the laws of their native civilisations. They picked up their riding skills from their nomad neighbours, but they were no less proficient as sailors. On land and water, they plundered what they needed to get by. Their most spectacular rampages took them east across the Urals to the Pacific coast of Siberia and south across the Black Sea into the Ottoman Empire, where their pirate ships even raided Istanbul on occasion.

In the Ukrainian borderlands between Russia, Poland, and the Crimean Tatar empire, they established their most powerful host, the Hetmanate of the Zaporozhian Cossacks, whose members dug in on a water-bound fortress downstream from the Dnieper Rapids. At the height of their power, the Cossacks ruled over an anarchic steppe state from here and were a constant thorn in the side of their enemies, who included not only the tsars in Moscow but also the kings in Warsaw and the khans on the Crimean peninsula. Catherine the Great's predecessors had tried to defeat the Ukrainian Cossacks or forge alliances with them, with no lasting success. It was only when the tsarina advanced on the Black Sea coast that the Zaporozhian Hetmanate was finally vanquished, along with the other peoples of the steppe.

The Cossacks never recovered their former glory. Once

Catherine had destroyed their fortress on the Dnieper and driven the Zaporozhians out of Ukraine, she increasingly harnessed their battle skills to her imperial ambitions. The Cossacks were employed as frontier guards protecting the southern borders of the tsarist empire against the remaining nomadic tribes and the mountain peoples of the Caucasus. They soon became a common sight in Russia's cities too, patrolling the streets on horseback in their flamboyant uniforms. They were especially feared by Jews, Armenians, and other non-Russian city-dwellers for whom the Cossacks traditionally had no time. One of their most notorious roles was to crush popular uprisings by whipping protestors and riding roughshod over them – something they did more and more frequently in the latter days of the empire. Many workers dragged themselves home from an early-twentieth-century protest with horseshoe-shaped bruises on their bodies.

During the revolution, the Cossacks were divided into two parties: White and Red, monarchists and communists – the former loyal to the tsar's murdered family beyond death itself, the others willing to defend the new regime in the Kremlin henceforth. After the civil war, the White Cossacks disappeared into Stalin's camps, with the exception of those who had escaped abroad with the remnants of the counter-revolutionary troops. That was the end of their Cossack careers; from that day on, they no longer rode horses but drove omnibuses in Berlin or taxis in Paris instead.

The Red Cossacks had no further role in Stalin's new state either. After they had done their bit on the front line in the civil war, they suffered the same fate as the rest of the Soviet population. Their identity was no longer to be defined by their individual past but by a collective future, and if someone didn't like that future, then they had none. In one final desperate act of rebellion, some Soviet Cossack groups threw in their lot with the Nazis during the Second World War, which merely accelerated their demise.

The Second World War was the last conflict ever waged with horses and, when it was over, an era of life on the steppes passed into history. It was the end of an age of barbarians, nomads, and horse-riding tribes. It was the end of a life of freedom in the Wild Fields. It was the end of an age when the steppe was so wide and so empty that a warrior's shadow stretched to the horizon at sunset. The Bolsheviks preferred a different kind of steed, which drew a line under the cavalry and the wild grasslands: the tractor. The steppes were brought under the plough. The Cossack villages became collective farms. A region where hooves had beaten the ground for millennia now echoed to the roar of combine harvesters. Erstwhile cavalrymen retrained as tractor drivers, mechanics, and machine operators. Only occasionally were they allowed to dust off their *papakhas* and sing the old Cossack songs – long since reworked into anthems to the freedom of the working man and woman – during cultural performances at the *kolkhozes*. They were degraded to caricatures of themselves, sad folklore warriors, dressed up but unarmed.

I was not surprised when Vassiliy told me that he was a car mechanic in real life. His monologue about heroically winning back Crimea was hard to stomach, but I was aware that I simply romanticised the Cossacks in a different historical state than he did. I was focusing on their freedom-loving Ukrainian iteration, whereas he preferred the Russian imperialist kind. What was common to both was that they no longer existed. The present-day Cossack revival bore little relation to either. It was a new invention, an amalgam of warmed-up resentment, chauvinistic posturing, hollow machismo, bushy moustaches, furry *papakhas*, gleaming medals, and brutal combat sport.

'You're from Germany?' Vassiliy asked. 'I have some friends there. In Heidelberg. Russians from here who emigrated to Germany. I mean, we used to be friends. I'm afraid we aren't friends any more.'

I looked at him quizzically.

'We fell out. I went to visit them in Heidelberg. When I told them I'd been in Crimea, they called me a criminal. No wonder – the poor guys had been fed all kinds of terrible myths about Russia in Germany.'

One of Vassiliy's mates joined our conversation.

'It's good that Russian emigrants keep tabs on things in your country.'

'Keep tabs?'

'If not, you'd never cope with those refugees. They said on TV that the Germans don't dare to put the black-arses in their place and that now the Russians are doing it for you.'

Vassiliy nodded vigorously.

'Ever since half the Caucasus invaded Novorossiysk, no one dares to do anything here either. Not even the police rap those crooks over the knuckles. We Cossacks have to see to it ourselves.'

'By the time the police book them, they're already off groping the next Russian woman. We take care of things faster. Snip, snap – can't grope anyone with broken fingers.'

After we said goodbye, the two of them got into a not particularly new-looking black BMW. Vassiliy had trouble squashing his belly behind the steering wheel. And off they went – two Cossacks with no horses but lots of horsepower.

A few minutes later, I sat down on a park bench near the gymnasium to take down from memory what the Cossacks had told me. Hardly had I begun to write when a man came staggering towards me. He looked in a bad way. His overalls were torn, his teeth at war with one another, his breath fetid.

'Write this!' he slurred. 'Write down what … what I say! And then you can tell it to your … that … your Trump!'

'I don't think so.'

He stopped short when he heard my accent. 'French?'

I shook my head.

'German?!'

I nodded.

'Haaaaa!'

Jerkily, he pulled up one sleeve of his overalls. He had a pale blue tattoo emblazoned on his bicep. A cross surrounded by four Cyrillic letters: ГСБГ. It hit me as he slurred his next sentence that this was the acronym of the Soviet occupying forces in East Germany.

'We …' His voice almost cracked with indignation. 'We Russians … withdrew. But those bloody Yankees … stayed!'

A BLACK SEA LEXICON

Entry no. 1: *Rapana venosa*

In 1963, in Novorossiysk bay, which I saw through the windows of my bus as I continued my journey in a south-westerly direction, a marine biologist called E. I. Drapkin first noticed the presence of a particular aquatic creature in the Black Sea. It was a snail, a specimen the size of a child's fist with a thick, pointy shell that was grey-green on the outside with a bright orange interior. When Drapkin tempted the animal out of its spiral home and inspected its proboscis, he realised he was looking at a predatory snail.

Drapkin initially considered his find to be an exemplar of

Rapana bezoar. It took later researchers to identify what it really was: *Rapana venosa*, the veined rapa whelk, a carnivorous snail native to the Sea of Japan. No one knew exactly how it had ended up in the Black Sea. It had probably stowed away in a freighter's ballast tank. Maybe it had clung alongside other molluscs to the barnacled hull of a ship. It cannot be ruled out that it was accidentally introduced when Japanese oysters were seeded in the Black Sea.

Soon after Drapkin's discovery it became clear that the rapa whelk hadn't come in peace. The snail had no natural foes in its new environment, apart from a few species of starfish too small to threaten a fully grown *Rapana venosa*. However, it did find a huge quantity of food. The rapa whelk eats mussels, oysters, and other molluscs, boring through their shells with its radula. It excretes a biotoxin before sinking its proboscis into the flesh of its paralysed prey. It can suck a shell dry in under an hour.

The snail crept, drilled, and slurped its way into the ecosystem of the Black Sea throughout the 1970s and 1980s. Wherever it appeared, it decimated the mollusc stocks. Turkish mussel divers reported how previously abundant areas of the seabed were transformed into deserts before their eyes. The population of Black Sea oysters was brought to the brink of extinction.

Nothing could halt the *Rapana venosa*'s advance, not even the divers who partially switched from harvesting mussels to snails in the eighties. The whelks are edible. Turkish fishing companies have specialised in extracting the firm greyish flesh from the shells and exporting it, frozen, to Japan and Korea – countries bordering the waters from which the snail originally emigrated to Europe.

Veined rapa whelks are now on the menus of waterside

restaurants on the Black Sea as well. I had them cooked with garlic, onion, and white wine in Bulgaria and as a cold mayonnaise salad in Crimea. They have a similar texture to octopus, with a tangy aftertaste that reminded me of liver. Tourist shops sell the snail's characteristic shells as souvenirs. It isn't hard to find them yourself either, as there are heaps of them on many shorelines. I recall a beach in northern Bulgaria so deep in washed-up snail shells that you could hardly see the sand beneath them. The crunch they made under my feet almost drowned out the roar of the surf.

'There are lots of Turks in Germany, right?'

Andrey Zatsepin was a little over sixty, a man with friendly eyes and a white ruff-like neck beard of the kind worn by ship's captains in old paintings.

'Here in Russia, the immigrants come from Central Asia and the Caucasus. They've been coming here to seek their fortunes since the end of the Soviet era. The same is true in the sea: immigrants find a niche for themselves, and they sometimes adapt better than the species that were there before them.'

Zatsepin was a marine biologist. He worked for Moscow's influential Institute of Oceanology, which maintained a small branch office on the Black Sea coast – its 'Southern Department', on the north-western fringe of a seaside resort called Gelendzhik.

In the kitchen of the institute's hostel, Zatsepin poured me a glass of red wine called Fanagoria, made from a local grape variety grown on the Crimean peninsula, which was surprisingly dry for Russians' usual taste. Zatsepin told me over the course of several hours about his forty years of research on the Black Sea. It was one of the most interesting bodies of water in Russia, he said. Changes could often be observed earlier and more easily here than elsewhere because this isolated sea, cut off from the oceans, reacted very sensitively to outside interventions. For instance, the veined rapa whelk hadn't been able to inflict the same damage in the Mediterranean because it had more natural enemies there.

Our conversation soon turned to Crimea, which Zatsepin visited regularly. He was in close contact with the scientists at the Oceanological Institute in Sevastopol. He also exchanged data with researchers in the other countries around the coast. Only with Ukraine had all contacts been severed. The Odessa Maritime University had halted cooperation with Russian scientists shortly after the annexation of Crimea – in response to political pressure from above, Zatsepin presumed. He hadn't been to Ukraine since the rift, not least because he feared being arrested. His trips to annexed Crimea were well documented, and that made him guilty in Kiev's eyes – even though the annexation had done him nothing but harm, Zatsepin said with a smile.

'When Crimea was still part of Ukraine, I was paid an international flat rate for my business trips – 2,500 roubles per day. Now they pay me only the national rate: 100 roubles.'

There was something forced about his smile. It was obvious that Zatsepin was anything but overjoyed by the falling-out between Russia and Ukraine.

'It wasn't easy to get the Black Sea neighbours around a table together beforehand, but this has made it completely impossible. I can't see any way out of this Crimean stalemate.' He sighed. 'My colleagues in Crimea are happy about joining Russia. I can't condemn something that makes my friends happy, but the way it happened …'

Zatsepin left his sentence incomplete, just shaking his head in silent disagreement before assuring me that he had never voted for the man responsible for the annexation.

Later, as Zatsepin described the species that had been accidentally introduced into the Black Sea's ecosystem over the past decades, I thought back to the ashamed expression that had come over his face as he talked about Russia's might-is-right policy. Roughly speaking, biologists divide creatures into three groups: native, non-native, and invasive species. Aggressive newcomers like the predatory snail *Rapana venosa* fall into the third category, because they do not take their place in alien ecosystems peacefully but fight for it against other species. This classification raises many questions that biologists generally view as being beyond their remit. Which generation of immigrants no longer count as immigrants? Aren't today's natives simply yesterday's invaders? And if those invaders are superseded by new invaders, should we pity them?

The classification becomes even trickier if you apply it to humans – something that biologists, for good reason, avoid doing. Nevertheless, Zatsepin, a hydrophysicist, saw as clearly as I did that his compatriots had played the inglorious role of invaders in the history of the Black Sea. They hadn't exactly enriched the human ecosystem in the two and a half centuries since they first conquered the coast.

Perhaps that is why the Russians are so pathologically afraid of new invaders, I thought the next day. This idea occurred to me at the Gelendzhik bus station as I took my place in the queue at a ticket counter. I obviously wasn't moving forwards fast enough, because a woman suddenly elbowed her way into the space between me and the customer in front.

'Excuse me, I—'

Hearing my accent, the woman turned to look at me, full of curiosity. 'Not from here?'

'No, but I—'

'From where?'

'Germany, but could you—?'

'Full of Muslims over there, isn't it?'

'Er …?'

A gloating grin split her face. 'I saw on TV how they're overrunning you. Pissing on your churches, screwing your women. It's shit, eh?'

By now I had lost count of the times people had mentioned 'the refugees', 'the Muslims', or 'the black-arses' supposedly competing for my living space. Since the row over Crimea, the Kremlin propaganda machine had taken to painting everyday life in the West in the grimmest of lights. The way it was portrayed on Russian TV, Europe had fallen to the barbarians.

In the bus from Gelendzhik to Novomikhaylovsky, I saw an icon stuck to the dashboard, a triptych of the Mother of God, the Saviour, and Saint Nicholas. The plastic-framed image was so tightly wedged in between the instruments that it looked a bit like one itself – a speedometer of the soul. Not for the first time, I was amazed by how the strange coexistence of incompatible things had become so routine in post-Soviet Russia. Icons in buses, busts of Lenin at bus stations.

I asked the driver to drop me off when a concrete monument bearing the inscription 'Orlyonok' appeared on the right-hand side of the coast road. Orlyonok ('little eagle') was the name of a huge holiday camp stretching for a good two miles along the shore. It had opened in 1960 and for decades was one of the largest pioneer camps in the Soviet Union.

Hundreds of thousands of children from every corner of the USSR had spent their holidays here, where the irradiation of the southern sun and the ideology of Lenin had turned their bodies and minds red.

The ideology was gone, but Orlyonok was still there. What, I wondered, remains of a pioneer camp when the pioneer neckerchiefs, the pioneer songs, the pioneer badges, and the pioneer spirit are gone – along with the pioneers themselves?

'Childhood,' Olga said. 'What remains is childhood.'

She was deputy director of the camp school, a short, chubby woman with something mask-like and inscrutable about her kohl-ringed eyes.

The school's Black Sea classroom was packed with display cases full of objects found on the beach. On the wall, there was a large map showing the sea and its surrounding states. I noticed that Crimea was still part of Ukraine on this map.

'Tell our guest what you've learned about the Black Sea.'

Twenty pairs of eyes were trained on us. A boy of thirteen or fourteen broke into a wide grin. 'That it's black!'

General merriment.

'And why is it black?' Olga asked sharply.

A girl put up her hand. 'The sea bottom is whipped up in storms, turning the water black.'

'Any other explanations?'

'It seemed darker to the Greeks than the Mediterranean because the water here isn't as translucent.'

'And because there are more clouds hanging over this sea than there are further south!'

'Anyone else?'

'In some old language or other, the word for "black" is like the word for "north". People in the south called the sea black because for them it lay to the north.'

'That's correct,' said Olga, 'although it's not just "some old language" – it was Persian.'

I threw in a few questions of my own, but before the conversation could really get going, the afternoon bell went, and the kids charged out of the room. It was the last day of the children's three-week stay on the Black Sea. The next morning, they would travel back to Smolensk, to Voronesh, to Kostroma, to Moscow, or Perm, and be replaced by the next cohort of pupils who would be succeeded by others, again and again until the end of the summer.

After showing me the rest of the school, Olga took me on a tour of the huge campsite in her small car, past Soviet residential blocks that, half a century after they were built, resembled concrete memorials to communist failure. They still signalled faith in a future that had long since slipped into the past without ever having materialised in the present.

'They'll all be crying tomorrow.' Olga smiled. 'We call the car park over there the Square of Tears. It's where holiday romances end as the lovers climb onto their buses. You can't imagine the sobbing.'

It was dark by the time we got to the beach, where a farewell disco was in full swing. A few hundred teenagers – the youngest of them eleven, the eldest sixteen – were dancing to Russian technopop on the sand. Olga and I stood on the sidelines and watched. I seemed to recognise characters from my own youth. Shy loiterers clinging to bottles of lemonade. Precocious alpha males casting condescending looks. Girls dancing extravagantly. Bashful wallflowers.

Off to one side, beyond the reach of the bright spotlights, a silent couple stood side by side on the promenade, gazing out over the dark sea. The boy's hand was caressing the girl's back with tiny tentative motions, ready to draw back at any second, as if it were all a bit of an accident. The girl had her arms crossed over her chest, not responding to his touch. Only Olga and I could see that she was smiling, not the boy from whom she was hiding her face behind a curtain of blonde hair.

Olga followed my gaze. 'Teachers used to ban things like that, but what can you do? It's the age when love starts.'

She was no longer young, but Orlyonok had already ceased to be a pioneer camp by the time she started working there.

'What else has changed since Soviet times?'

She thought for a moment before shrugging indifferently. 'There used to be ideology.'

'And now?'

'Now there's none.'

With that she seemed to consider the subject closed. On our tour of the holiday site, she had described in detail the camp's sport and educational programme, which sounded ambitious but interchangeable with what was on offer at any international summer school.

Without ideology, but with love. If that summed up how times had changed, then the change was massive. I stared at the young faces and wondered if this generation would finally manage to drag Russia out of the swamp of grievance, self-pity, and aggression in which their parents and grandparents were bogged down.

'Olga,' I said. 'What do these kids believe in? What do they think about?'

She turned her mask-like eyes towards me and studied me in silence. It was impossible to read her expression. I sensed that she had an answer on the tip of her tongue, but then she just nodded towards the romantic couple.

'You can see for yourself what they think about.'

That was all I got out of her.

When I headed further south the next day, my rucksack was clinking with two items found on the beach and pressed into my hand by Olga in that Black Sea classroom. They now lie side by side on my desk in Berlin. A snail shell and an oyster shell, *Rapana venosa* and *Ostrea edulis* – the invasive predatory mollusc and its most tragic victim. This oyster species has survived only in a few protected areas of the Black Sea, as rare a sight in its waters as Greeks are on its shores. Only their shimmering oil-coloured empty shells still wash up on the beaches, where they lie in the sand like bits of Greek temples, fragments of abandoned ruins, the last testament to a vanishing Black Sea civilisation.

A Caucasian without a moustache

Beyond Novomikhaylovsky, the road wound its way up the increasingly steep mountain slopes. The passengers on my bus swayed their upper bodies to the rhythm of the left-hand and right-hand hairpin bends. For the first time, I noticed that the mountain peoples of the Caucasus were gradually mixing with the Slavic population of the plains. A few rows in front of me sat a young man with the kind of aquiline beauty seen in Georgia, Chechnya, or Armenia. I looked around and spotted other passengers with dark hair, curved noses, thick eyebrows, long lashes, and those drooping eyelids that make some faces look sleepy and others arrogant. This physiognomy generally suited men more than women, which was the exact opposite of Slavic looks.

In Tuapse, I changed onto a train to Sochi. This was the only stretch of railway on the entire Black Sea that did not connect the coast to the hinterland but ran along the seafront instead. To the left of the tracks, I saw the mountains rearing higher and higher into the sky, while the vegetation at their base seemed to change as I watched. Cypresses appeared, palms, ferns, cacti, mandarin, orange and lemon trees, wild grape vines, lush climbing plants, and brightly coloured flowers. Simultaneously, the Slavic place names vanished from the signs in the railway stations and were replaced by Caucasian and Turkic words: Gizel-Dere – Dederkoy – Shepsi – Magri – Makopse – Ashe – Chemitokvadzhe – Shakhe – Loo – Uch-Dere – Dagomys – Sochi.

Sochi! I got off the train and inhaled the sweet fragrance of the south. On my way into the city centre, I passed the old summer houses aristocratic families had built on the Russian riviera in imperial times, little suspecting that construction workers would move into them after the revolution. Lenin transferred ownership of the villas to the working people and had them converted into sanatoria for the Soviet Union's industrial workforce. In one princely residence, miners nursed their lung ailments; in another, steel smelters rested their battered backs. The proletariat recovered from the class struggle under the palm trees, little suspecting that after the next revolution Sochi would be transformed into a yacht club for Russia's oligarchs. Now the city positively reeked of new and dirty money.

It would be easy to believe that Sochi's only constant was the exotic flora that defined the beguiling image of the Black Sea riviera through all those revolutions. This impression was deceptive, however. Until the nineteenth century, I now discovered, only the climate had been subtropical in Sochi, not the vegetation.

'Forget the palm trees, the mandarins, and the lemons ...'

A mutual acquaintance had put me in touch with a botanist who now proceeded to slash down the seafront greenery before my very eyes. With every click of his fingers, he erased some more exotic plants, like a magician making rabbits vanish.

'… the juniper, the eucalyptus trees, the cacti …'

Everything that was thought of as typical and characteristic of the Russian riviera had only been introduced in the nineteenth century. It was possible, the botanist told me, that subtropical plants had been native to the Black Sea coast once before, a few thousand years ago, but the last ice age had pushed them southwards, and they weren't able to make it back across the arid regions of Turkey by themselves. It was the landscapers of the late Russian Empire who had given them a helping hand by planting the subtropical coastal stretch between Batumi and Sochi with imported Mediterranean bushes and trees.

My botanist had grown up in Sochi and spoke very affectionately about the introduced plants in whose shade he had spent his childhood. It only occurred to me later that despite the fact that the subject matter of his monologue was similar to what the marine biologist Andrey Zatsepin had told me about the invasive species in the Black Sea a few days earlier, the tone couldn't have been more different. According to the botanist, human beings were enlightened gardeners who plugged the gaps in God's plan by deliberately planting species where they would flourish. In the oceanographer's version, human beings destroyed their livelihoods by allowing species to spread to places where they didn't belong and did nothing but harm.

I couldn't shake off the impression that you could also tell these two migration stories the other way around. With the veined rapa whelk, humans had tapped into a new source of food from the Black Sea; the imported Mediterranean plants had displaced the existing vegetation along the coast. Whichever way you sliced it, it seemed to me that people, whether scientists or laypersons, judged the movements of trees and snails first and foremost according to the benefits they brought them.

As for the movements of their fellow human beings, that was another story that had been told over the centuries with changing portents. It was imperialist policy purposefully to mix peoples together; it was nationalist policy forcibly to separate them. Each in its time had seemed to people to be as sensible and natural as it later struck them as being wrong and unnatural – and both had had a drastic impact on the demographic structure along the shores of the Black Sea. Numerous peoples had been unlucky enough to be resettled a first time under imperial auspices and a second time, later, for nationalist reasons. Some, such as the Pontic Greeks, had the triple misfortune of falling victim to Stalin's landscaping of the Soviet Union, which involved transplanting people to fit his own unique criteria. Some peoples had transgenerational bad luck. They emigrated after the end of the Soviet era to the countries from which their ancestors had fled or been driven long, long ago, only to be perceived as alien because of a shift in migrating and non-migrating people's perceptions of one another.

At Sochi's city museum, I came across an old propaganda poster hailing Stalin's impact on the class composition of the Soviet Union. It said that between 1913 and 1937 the proportion of workers and collective farmers (i.e. desirable elements) had risen from 16.7 to 90.2 per cent of the population, while the proportion of bourgeoisie and private farmers (i.e. class enemies) had fallen from 15.9 to 0.0 per cent. Literally zero point zero. Stalin's green fingers had eradicated every weed in the Soviet garden.

I headed to the ticket office in Sochi harbour. Eight of the nine windows were shuttered. At the ninth counter sat an old attendant, who told me that she didn't sell tickets because there were no passenger vessels to sell tickets for. All the Black Sea lines had been axed in the post-Soviet era, apart from a speedboat to Batumi on the Georgian coast that ran only in summer.

'Now that we have capitalism,' the saleswoman said, 'it's no longer worth it.'

I'd heard those same words two weeks earlier in Novorossiysk harbour. These didn't appear to be the salad days of maritime traffic on the Black Sea.

Ruminating on this, I left the port. The fact that the speedboat to Batumi was not yet operating was a problem. To the south of Sochi lay the separatist region of Abkhazia, one of the trickier parts of the coastline, politically speaking. The Abkhazians had broken away from Georgia in 1992 and had since considered their small Black Sea republic an independent state. Officially, so did the Russians, who had unofficially pretty much annexed the area. To the Georgians, on the other hand, Abkhazia was still part of Georgia. Which was why I couldn't enter the separatist region from the north – the Georgians regarded border crossings from the Russian side as illegal and would refuse to let me out again at the territory's southern end. I would first have to travel around Abkhazia, head into it from the Georgian side and leave again by the same route.

Since the boat wasn't running, I booked a flight to the Georgian capital, Tbilisi. Sochi airport lay to the south of the city, not far from the Russian–Abkhazian border, so I made time for a little detour on the day of my departure.

The border fence cut an isolated pebble beach in half. The

shore was empty apart from a family having a picnic on the Russian side. There was a concrete platform jutting out into the sea, and the fence came to an abrupt end in the waves. As I approached the border installations, I saw a head appear briefly in the window of a watchtower, and the Russian soldier cast me an indifferent glance before withdrawing from sight again. On the Abkhazian side, the beach came up against a cliff plunging into the sea.

For a long time, I stared at the invisible extension of the fence that divided the water; no border had ever seemed more pointless to me. Maybe because the fish could swim back and forth without a care. Maybe because the border between land and water seemed so much more existential than the one between land and land. Or maybe because my journey had taught me that all borders drawn between peoples are fluid at best.

The taxi driver who took me from that beach to the airport was an old Armenian. He was wearing aviator sunglasses and had a magnificent walrus moustache as white as snow, as thick as a mole's pelt, and as wiry as a hedgehog's prickles.

He asked me where I was from. I only needed to say 'Berlin' and he was off.

'Germany! I served there! Back in the day, when the bloody Soviet army was stationed in East Germany. I was with this Sabine. Heck, what a woman she was! We wanted to get married, but the bloody commissars said, "No chance. No fraternising with Germans." They transferred me to another base 200 km away. I was sick of the miserable Soviet Union and its damned army after that. I went on strike. They sent ten different doctors to declare me mad, but not one dared do it. They put me in military detention instead. When I came out, the captain said, "Now shave off that bloody moustache!" I said, "Never! This moustache is my pride and honour. A

Caucasian without a moustache is like a Caucasian without underpants!" I copped another ten days in detention for that. When I got out, the captain said, "All right, if you won't shave it off, then from now on you have to shave the rest of the unit, starting with me. Cut my hair!" I took out the scissors and trimmed every last damn hair off his head. I shaved him as bald as a rat's arse, that pederast! That was his reward for taking Sabine away from me! That got me ten more days' detention. I didn't see my Sabine for forty years. But then I wrote her a letter – it was last year. I hadn't forgotten her address, and she still lived there. She's had two kids since. Her husband died in an accident. She visited me this year. She liked the Caucasus, and next year—'

'WATCH OUT!'

My cry came too late. We were hurtling towards a barrier blocking the entrance to the airport. I threw my hands up in front of my face and heard a loud crack as the car smashed the boom aside. The Armenian hadn't spotted it. Maybe his sunglasses were to blame, maybe Sabine was.

The car screeched to a halt.

'Damn!'

The Armenian got out to inspect the bonnet, which was miraculously unscathed. There was no damage except for a tiny scratch on the windscreen. The barrier slanted up into the April sky, as the impact had knocked it off its hinges. Next to it was the pay and display machine we ought to have stopped at. A whirring CCTV camera was straining its neck to make out the cause of the accident. We tried in vain to mend the barrier. After several attempts, the Armenian burst out laughing and kicked out at the boom before turning towards the camera and shaking his fist at it.

'That'll teach you to stand in the way of a Caucasian!'

Georgia

Shavi zghva / შავი ზღვა

Would that the sea, stranger, had dashed thee to pieces,
ere thou camest to the Colchian land!

Apollonius of Rhodes, *The Argonautica*, 3rd century BC

The thieves of Poti

Russia and the sea disappeared behind dense cloud. The plane flew in a south-easterly direction for just under an hour, sticking close to the ridge of the Caucasus mountains whose snowy peaks I saw from above, peeking through the otherwise unbroken cottony white blanket – mountains higher than the sky.

Next morning, after a short night in Tbilisi, I got on the train that would take me back to the coast. The six-hour journey went straight through the heart of that breathtaking mountain landscape whose inhabitants like to say that God originally created it as a refuge for himself, but when he had handed out every other part of the Earth to other peoples, the Georgians suddenly turned up, having slept through the distribution ceremony in a drunken stupor. God therefore had no option but to give the most beautiful country of all to the most bibulous people of all.

I heard this story from one of my neighbours on the train, an old Georgian farmer with a broad, virtually toothless grin. I had to listen closely to pick up the mumbled Russian in which he laid out the long and glorious history of his people. Did I know that it was the Georgians who had invented wine-making? Or that their curious alphabet was one of the oldest in the world? Had I heard that they had adopted Christianity as their state religion before any other nation? Was it clear to me that the Russians were still living in caves long after the Georgians had built cathedrals, composed hymns, and written epics?

Later, I often thought back to this farmer's crooked smile when I tried to reconcile the country's statistical hardships with its apparent splendour. I knew that over one million Georgians had emigrated to Russia or Western Europe in search of work since the collapse of the Soviet Union, and that the remaining four million were some of the poorest people in Eastern Europe. However, it was just as hard this time as on previous visits to recognise the Georgians' abstract poverty in the reality beyond the train windows. The railway tracks swung this way and that between steep rocky outcrops and through valleys of such surreal verdancy that I felt as if farmers here needed only to let the seed trickle from their pockets before sitting back in anticipation of the most abundant of harvests. Crystal-clear mountain rivers ran alongside the tracks, and plump cows, sheep, goats, pigs, and geese grazed beside their banks. Shepherds lay in the grass and watched the train pass, as if unable to grasp the haste with which some people raced through their idyllic land.

It caused the Georgians no little pain that with the loss of Abkhazia they had forfeited one of the most sublime parts of their country. In the dying days of the Soviet Union, long-repressed animosities between the Abkhazians and the Georgians in the subtropical coastal region had escalated into all-out civil war. Russia had provided clandestine backing to the separatists, who had proclaimed an independent republic of Abkhazia in July 1992. By the time the defeated Georgian army withdrew, both sides were mourning several thousand dead. Some 250,000 people, roughly half of Abkhazia's population then, had been forced to flee, most of them Georgians. Only a handful of countries around the globe had recognised Abkhazia's independence, and yet Russia still found it worthwhile to keep the small Black Sea republic alive.

That war had ended almost three decades earlier, but Georgians still gnashed their teeth when talking about the loss of

Abkhazia. The previous evening in Tbilisi, I had met a Georgian who had grown up in Sukhum, the Abkhazian capital. In the final phase of the war, shortly after his nineteenth birthday, the Georgian army had put him in command of a battalion tasked with protecting fleeing civilians from attacks.

He shook his head grimly. 'You don't want to hear the kinds of things I saw.'

This statement was so emphatic that I believed him. He'd never been back to Abkhazia. What he knew of how the region had evolved since the Georgian withdrawal he had learned purely from hearsay, but when I mentioned that I was going there, he painted the bleakest picture possible for me – and for himself. It was as if he were trying to convince himself that his former homeland had fallen into the hands of barbarians to make it easier to cope with its loss.

'Half the population are criminals, and the other half are drug addicts. Watch out for yourself there.'

Further west, the railway tracks descended towards the flatter Black Sea foreshore. When the train pulled into Poti on the Georgian coast, I changed onto a bus heading north and soon found myself facing yet another pointless-looking sea border, but this time on the southern perimeter of the separatist republic. A low barbed-wire fence attached to poles that had tilted in the wind ran the width of the beach and into the water. On the far side was a watchtower. A Georgian border officer was leaning against the bottom of the ladder. I waved to him, and he ambled slowly over to me. We shook hands across the barbed wire.

The police officer was young and bored. He had a great deal of time to reflect on the peculiar border he was guarding and was obviously glad to be able to share his thoughts with someone. With his thumb, he indicated a second watchtower I could make out a couple of hundred metres away.

'Those are the Russians over there. They've occupied our country. Why? Mongol blood. For three centuries they were ruled over by the Mongols until they themselves became Mongols and now they can't stop invading other countries.'

He spat contemptuously in the sand.

When I asked him for how much longer a fence would divide this beach, he shrugged.

'God knows, but not forever. Look at the course of history. The Mongol Empire: crashed. The Roman Empire: disappeared. Your Nazi Reich: gone. These empires don't last forever. That one over there will disappear too.'

He raised his eyebrows when he heard I was planning to go to Abkhazia.

'Just be careful. There are a whole lot of criminals around. And the others are—'

'Drug addicts?'

'Right.'

My more immediate concern was getting hold of the entry permit I needed for the separatist region. The 'Ministry of Foreign Affairs of the Republic of Abkhazia' had been sending me cryptic e-mails for several days, requesting that I make some amendments to my visa application. It was becoming apparent that the procedure would take longer than planned, and so I decided to stay on the Georgian coast for the time being.

I travelled back to the port town of Poti, known as Phasis in ancient times and depicted as the end of the world in the legend of the Argonauts. Jason had once ventured this far into the Colchian empire to bring home the Golden Fleece.

Above the town towered the red-and-white-striped profile of a lighthouse, built in 1862 by a London-based engineering company called Easton Amos & Sons, equipped with a lighting system designed by the Parisian precision mechanic Augustin Michel Henry-Lepaute and later electrified by a nameless Soviet combine from Sevastopol. The lighthouse keeper, a man of barely thirty by the name of Jekati, was the only taciturn Georgian I ever met. Together we climbed the iron spiral staircase and looked down on the mouth of the Rioni river. A dozen dolphins were hunting fish along the indistinct line where fresh water and salt water met. I tried to imagine how, a few thousand years earlier, the *Argo* might have entered the river from the sea and arrived, unnoticed, in central Colchis. Reefed sails, silently dipped oars, whispered commands, nervous glances. Jekati nodded as I described my thoughts but made no comment. If you wanted to keep your mouth shut in this country, I thought, you would need to retreat to a lighthouse.

The town was laid out in a grid of long, dead-straight streets that ended at the sea to the south-west and ran towards the mountains in the north-east. They were lined with two-storey stone houses with square floor plans and tent-like metal roofs – a familiar sight along the Georgian coast. Against the backdrop of snow-capped summits, I kept seeing men walking along the streets, clutching life-size porcelain figures of sheepdogs, leopards, and mermaids to their chests. They would offer them to passers-by but didn't seem to have much success, as I saw them criss-crossing Poti with the selfsame figures until the day I left town. I wondered if they might be trying to get rid of a shipment left stranded in customs, until someone explained to me that the porcelain figures were made in Gori, Stalin's birthplace, and sold by hawkers nationwide.

In my mind's eye I pictured a Georgia traversed by sheepdogs, leopards, and mermaids.

On the day I arrived, an old woman addressed me in Russian as I was walking through a residential neighbourhood.

'Did you come by ship?'

That was obviously the way foreigners usually got here. The woman was sitting on a wooden swing in her front garden. I shook my head and asked her what life was like in Poti.

She hunched her shoulders. 'There's no work here. No one has any money. Everyone wants to leave.'

The swing rocked forwards and backwards, squeaking with every movement. The garden was covered with a pergola of wild grape, filtering the sunlight into a dappled golden pattern. The old woman was wearing a flowery headscarf. Laughter lines played at the corners of her mouth and eyes; her face looked as if it had been smiling for decades. It was yet another of these Georgian moments when I couldn't match what I heard with what I saw.

From an adjacent garden, a man's voice called out a few sentences to us in Georgian. The old woman pointed to the hedge from which these words appeared to be coming.

'They're inviting you to drink.'

I hesitated for a second.

'Go ahead, I know them. Good people.'

This was, as it turned out, simultaneously true and untrue. The four men behind the hedge were a hospitable bunch of thieves.

Their leader was a man of about sixty whom the others referred to as Uncle Bachugi. His bald head was as eloquent as an actor's in a silent film. At rest, Bachugi came across as cheerful, but he could silence his companions at a stroke whenever the smallest cloud veiled his features.

The four of them made no effort to conceal on which side of the law they stood, though they kept the details to themselves. As the toasts began, we raised our glasses more than once to former gang members who had apparently departed this life following work-related accidents.

'To my brother! He was a great thief!"

The youngest man present, a handsome youth with black curls by the name of Sandro, hadn't learnt Russian at school like the others. He insisted on describing events in English instead.

'Uncle Bachugi wants to drink with you.'

I nodded.

'A lot.'

I nodded somewhat more warily.

'Can you drink very much?'

I wobbled my head noncommittally.

Bachugi quickly took a liking to me for reasons I couldn't fathom.

'I can see that you are a good man,' he kept repeating.

It seemed to me that he was dying to relieve himself of some pearls of bandit wisdom by confiding them to a writer. His affection might also have had something to do with the homemade *chacha* that the four of them were drawing from a fifty-litre barrel in the garage. This Georgian brandy tastes like grappa, but the thieves were knocking it back like vodka – in one. Every new shot was introduced by an epic toast fuelled by an excess of heartfelt emotion, sometimes lasting for minutes but always liable to be brought to a premature end when Bachugi raised an impatient eyebrow.

The *chacha* erased from my memory almost everything the

thieves told me that afternoon. The next day, I had only the vaguest of recollections that Bachugi had talked about the war between Georgia and Russia, from which he and his gang had steadfastly kept their distance.

'Everyone knows Bachugi can fight, but I'm not getting involved in any wars.'

Sooner or later, I began to pour the *chacha* away under the table before raising the glass to my lips – a technique that had frequently saved my life in Russia. The third time I did it, I suddenly started to worry that cheating like this among thieves might carry the death penalty. I was relieved when, after a few more shots, Bachugi rose unsteadily to his feet and declared the boozing over. He drew my head towards him and planted a long kiss of friendship on my cheek before staggering into the house. Within seconds, I heard ear-splitting snores through the window.

A BLACK SEA LEXICON

Entry no. 2: *Engraulis encrasicolus*

The fishing trawlers in Poti's harbour were heavy, thick-hulled Soviet-era boats, built during the Cold War in such a way that the net winding machines could be easily dismounted, if necessary, and replaced with machine guns. Only two Turkish-built boats were smaller and lighter than the others – the *Argo* and the *Kolkhi*, which belonged to the same proprietor, obviously a lover of Greek myths.

On the last afternoon in April, I sat on the deck of the *Kolkhi* with four Georgian fishermen and a black-and-white ship's cat called Potsva. The ship was moored in the harbour. The windows were dulled by saltwater and cigarette smoke, but I still had to screw up my eyes when looking out at the sea, which was sparkling in the sun beneath a cloudless sky. Potsva the cat was dozing on a tattered woollen blanket. The fishermen, whose faces betrayed their direct contact with the elements, were sitting in a circle smoking: old Kia astride the wheel chair, Alik, Torma, and Avto on the bench with the cat. The air was filled with the pinging slap of halyards. There was no wind to speak of, only a gentle rocking that caused the horizon to move up and down the window. The *Kolkhi* creaked languidly on its moorings.

'It's the worst ship in the harbour,' joked Alik, the captain.

The four men would have loved to have bought a new boat long ago, a bigger one of their own, but the bank wouldn't grant them a loan. There was no money to be made in fishing, not in Georgia at any rate. Alik and the others handed over 60 per cent of the day's turnover to the ship's owner and divvied up the rest between themselves. After deducting petrol, they were often left with only 10 lari each – barely $3.

'Young people won't work for wages like that,' Alik said. 'Only idiots like us who love their work.'

Alik had picked me up at the harbour entrance as I was casting inquisitive looks at the fishing trawlers. It wasn't every day that foreigners interested in boats turned up in Poti, because the few foreigners who did turn up here tended to turn up in their own boats. The fishermen had borrowed a colleague's ID to smuggle me past the harbour guards and show me the *Kolkhi*.

The fishing season had just finished. May was the start of close season: the fish were spawning and there was no licensed catch for two months. The fishermen used this time to fix the holes in their nets, in their clothes, in their houses, in their cars, and in the hearts of their families. Business would only resume in July, slowly, with bass, mackerel, and goatfish, before at last November would spell the appearance off the Georgian coast of the fish everyone here was waiting for.

Engraulis encrasicolus.

Kapshia in Georgian, *hamsi* in Turkish, *khamsa* in Russian. Black Sea anchovies.

They are tiny fish, 10–12 cm long, and yet the gigantic, dense shoals in which they move around can weigh several thousand tonnes. They spawn in June in the shallow coastal waters off Odessa, from where they set out on their long journey around the coast, always following the same route. They swim with the sea's surface currents in an anti-clockwise direction, past the Romanian and Bulgarian beaches, past the Bosporus, and along the north coast of Turkey. They can cover up to 20 km per day, all the while filtering plankton out of the water and growing fat. It is winter by the time the grown fish reach the bulge in the south-east of the sea where Turkish, Georgian, Russian, and Ukrainian fishermen haul them out of the water in their billions from November through to the following spring. The shoal survivors who slip the nets continue past Russia and Crimea until, after a little under a year, the anchovies make it back to their starting point in the Gulf of Odessa. After spawning, their circle dance begins again. In good years, an unimaginable million-tonne mass of *Engraulis encrasicolus* performs its circumnavigation of the coast.

It was these anchovies, more than anything else, that triggered the ancient Greeks' colonisation of the Black Sea. When Jason chases after the fleece of a golden-wooled ram in the Argonaut myth, he is engaging in a literary re-creation of the fishing expeditions that brought his compatriots to the world's barbarian fringes. Workers at the Greek trading posts around the Black Sea dried and salted mountains of anchovies and filled them into amphorae. Merchant ships then transported these fish to the Aegean along with metals from the Caucasus, timber from the forested mountains along the southern coast, and grain grown in the Black Sea colonies' hinterlands.

Anchovies have left their mark on Pontic history. Evliya Çelebi, who combed every corner of the Ottoman Empire in the seventeenth century, devotes a whole chapter to them in his legendary *Book of Travels*. His fellow countrymen's love of *hamsi*, he wrote, knew no bounds. When the fishermen in Trabzon harbour, for instance, sounded the trumpet to signal that anchovies were on sale, every man would cut short his prayers, a steam bath, or even lovemaking to rush to the fish in whatever he was wearing at the time – even if that was nothing.

Even the imams and muezzins break the ritual worship. 'Prayer is forever,' they say, 'but hamsi is not forever.' … Its benefit is such that if a man eats it for seven days he will go to his wife and have his own 'fish' eaten seven times every night. It is very invigorating, easy to digest, has no fishy smell at all, and does not produce heat when you eat it. It is a cure for typhoid fever. If someone has snakes and scorpions in his house, he burns fish heads and fumigates the house with them, and the smell of it kills off all the vermin. This fish has hundreds of benefits and curative properties.

To this day, the whole country jokes about the anchovy lust of the Turks along the Black Sea. However, they are also a beloved delicacy on the sea's other shores. I saw a memorial to the anchovy in Novorossiysk harbour – a depiction in silvery metal of a teeming shoal of fish. 'Dedicated to the anchovies of the Black Sea by the grateful people of Novorossiysk,' it said on the plinth. 'During the hungry war years, the *khamsa* catch helped us survive.'

It didn't take long for the conversation on the deck of the *Kolkhi* to turn to anchovies. Alik and the other fishermen had a bone to pick with their Turkish colleagues. Or, rather, they had a bone to pick with the Georgian authorities for selling the best fishing permits to Turkish fishermen, who could afford to pay more than their Georgian counterparts. The Turks showed up off the Georgian coast in winter with their huge trawlers and ransacked the waters. The *Kolkhi*'s permit only allowed it to go six nautical miles (11 km) out to sea, and sometimes Alik and his crew were forced to watch the Turks hauling aboard fantastic catches while they returned to Poti with their nets half full.

Potsva the cat was still dozing on the bench on deck as we left the *Kolkhi*. On the way into town, we bought two bottles of cognac and dropped in on an old seaman who lived on his own in a room near the harbour. Padri was tall, broad-shouldered, and shy. He had huge bucket hands, yet, even after seventy years of life, he still hadn't figured out what to do with them when he wasn't working. They hung stiffly by his sides like discarded tools.

Padri, who didn't have any family, had retired a few years back, but his Georgian fisherman's pension didn't stretch very far. The plaster was crumbling on the ceiling of his room and red metal rods poked through the holes. The fishermen drank and sang Georgian songs. The more they drank, the louder they sang, and the louder they sang, the more anxiously I studied the crumbling ceiling.

Later, I talked to old Kia. He told me that he had once been an athlete before he started working as a fisherman.

'I was the fourth-fastest sprinter in the Soviet Union.'

He had come fourth in the 100 m at a championship in 1987. Had it not been for an accident, he might have got even better. One of his friends, a pole-vaulter, had come last in one competition. Kia wanted to cheer him up. 'Man,' he shouted, 'even I can do better than that!' Grabbing his friend's pole, he started his run-up despite never having vaulted before in his life. He rammed the pole into the ground just in front of the mat. It bent, Kia's feet left the ground, and the pole straightened, sending Kia flying – but unfortunately in the wrong direction. Instead of landing on the mat, he came crashing down on the track. All around, people cracked up laughing as he was carried away. Kia related this story with a grin on his face too, as if it was the funniest thing that had ever happened to him, even though it had cut short his running career.

Before turning his hand to fishing, he had worked for a while as a long-distance lorry driver, and he and his truck had travelled all over Siberia towards the end of the Soviet era.

'In some places you don't see a light in the darkness for days on end. Not one! No one lives there! The Russians have more land than they can occupy and yet they still have to take some away from us Georgians!'

When the drinking party broke up, Alik, the captain, took me home with him. He lived to the north of the harbour in a small two-storey house he and his twin brother, Bacho, had built themselves. The top floor wasn't finished yet – a few windows were still missing and the outside walls were unrendered – as the brothers had run out of money halfway through its construction. They were hoping that the next anchovy season would be profitable enough to allow them to continue.

Alik's brother had a fourteen-year-old son, who was fanatical about Real Madrid. He was enemies with Alik's sixteen-year-old son, who was fanatical about Barcelona. The house was also home to the twin brothers' wives and parents.

The grandfather was sitting in front of the computer with headphones on, smoking rollies he inserted into a long cigarette-holder. He too had been a fisherman once, on the *Argo* I had seen in the harbour. Since his retirement, he spent his days watching amateur videos of deep-sea fishermen on the internet.

His wife told me about the old days in Poti. 'Under the Soviets, every other man here went to sea.'

That was clearly a long time ago. Neither of her two grandsons was interested in fish. They took turns trying to lure their grandfather away from the computer so they could watch football highlights, but he was tenacious.

We ate smoked anchovies. Alik showed me how to gut them. You snap off the head and use the fish's sharp jaws like a knife, slitting open its belly with its own mouth to remove its innards. You eat the rest, complete with tail and fins. It tasted divine.

A quiet thirteen-year-old girl had dinner with us, a neighbour's daughter. She was being brought up by her grandmother because her mother was working as a nanny for an Italian family in Bologna. Many Georgians had gone to Italy in recent years to look after children, care for old people, and work as housekeepers. Alik had an interesting theory about the bonds between the Italians and the Georgians.

'They like us because we cook well, talk a lot, like to sing, and because we are warm-hearted. The Italians say the Georgians are how they used to be when they were still poor.'

Later that evening, Alik showed me the upstairs room where he had made up a bed for me. On a shelf at the far end of the room lay a fragment of a large amphora. All that was left of it were the russet-coloured pointed base and bits of the two handles.

Alik didn't know how old the amphora was. He'd pulled it out of a heap of anchovies on the *Kolkhi*'s deck one day. It was a fairly regular occurrence to find relics from the bottom of the Black Sea snagged in the drag nets. Virtually every fisherman in Poti had some old pottery shards at home, Alik said.

Swimming trees

An old taxi driver called Jeka took me from Poti to Anaklia, 30 km to the north. I had read about a new deepwater port that was being built close to the Abkhaz border at China's initiative.

Most Georgians talk loudly, but Jeka beat the lot of them. He roared his every thought into my earhole from the depths of his body. I assumed that it was the onset of deafness that drove him to yell, so as to make up for what he perceived to be his voice's diminished volume.

Before driving a taxi, Jeka had run a canteen and worked on building sites, but deep down, like all Georgians, basically, he was a historian. We had met in Poti at the foot of the equestrian statue of the Georgian prince Tsotne Dadiani, where local taxi drivers touted for business. Jeka had effortlessly drowned out all rival bids by shouting the prince's life story into my ear.

His specialist historical subject was the Mingrelians, the inhabitants of the Black Sea region around Poti. Just about every important Georgian, Jeka explained as he drove, was actually a Mingrelian – Prince Tsotne, of course, but also Lavrentiy Beria – Stalin's secret police chief – and the Red Army soldier who had raised the Soviet flag on the Reichstag during the Battle of Berlin in 1945. And, naturally, Jeka himself.

The route to Anaklia led not along the coast but through the interior. All of a sudden, Jeka turned off the main road into a village.

'I've got something to show you. You've never seen anything like it in your whole life!'

He stopped the car in the middle of the village. On the right-hand side of the street, I saw a few men in work clothes gathered in front of a tree, a large sycamore.

'Gamar joba!' Jeka pumped up the volume of his vocal chords even more than normal.

'Gamar joba!' the workers replied in unison.

While Jeka had a word with the men in Mingrelian, I took a closer look at the tree. It was twice as tall as the nearby houses. The earth had been excavated in a wide circle on all sides, and the workers had spared only an island roughly the size of the canopy around the trunk and edged it with planks that were holding the soil and the roots together. It looked as if the tree were standing in a big wooden flowerpot.

I heard Jeka's booming voice behind me. 'They're digging up the tree. Have you heard of Ivanishvili?'

I nodded. The oligarch Bidzina Ivanishvili owned half the country.

'The son of a bitch collects trees. A Japanese fortune teller convinced him to. For his sons' sake. They're albinos, and that Japanese guy said they needed old trees around them. Ivanishvili is making a park for them in Shekvetili, a little further down the coast. He's ransacked the whole of Mingrelia, seeking out the oldest trees and then having them dug up. He spends a fortune on it, but who cares when you're a billionaire!'

I stared at the tree. It was at least 30 m tall.

'It's 150 years old,' one of the workers said, guessing my

unspoken question. 'We lift it far enough to get the low-loader underneath it. It'll transport the tree to the coast, and from there it'll be taken by ship to Shekvetili.'

As we drove on, I couldn't get the image of the swimming tree out of my mind.

'That son of a bitch!' Jeka didn't think much of Ivanish-vili. 'We don't know how we're going to pay for firewood in winter, and that guy shells out millions to move trees!'

We soon reached Anaklia. Not much of the new deepwater port was in evidence yet. A few excavators were levelling a piece of waste ground by the coast – the construction work had only just begun.

We spotted something else, though. A low-loader was parked on the shore by the future harbour site. On its load bed stood a gigantic tree, its roots encased in a flowerpot of wooden planks. As we got closer, I saw that it was a eucalyptus. The bark was almost white, and the small elongated leaves were quivering in the onshore breeze. The tree was a good bit taller than the sycamore we had seen earlier, and beside it the lorry looked like a toy truck.

Jeka threw back his head, shaded his eyes with his hand and stared up at the topmost branches. 'Son of a bitch …'

The lorry driver was nowhere to be seen. A worker on the harbour construction site told us that another tree had stood on the shore up until a few days ago – a flowering magnolia, which had since been shipped. We exchanged phone numbers and asked the man to ring us as soon as the eucalyptus was taken away.

We spent the next two days hunting trees. We began in Jeka's own village, where a 200-year-old lime tree was in the process of being dug up. A few blocks away, Jeka had built a new house shortly before his retirement so that he and his wife could spend their twilight years there. However, his wife had died before it was finished. The house stood empty now, and Jeka was living at his sister's flat in Poti instead. There would have been no one to talk to in the village, and not talking would have been the death of Jeka.

We asked our way from one village to the next. In the area around Poti, we came across a good dozen oaks, magnolias, sycamores, eucalyptuses, lime trees, plane trees, and camphor trees being readied for transferral to the coast. Villagers quoted the most incredible sums of money that Ivanishvili was supposedly paying the landowners for their trees. Even the more conservative estimates were in the tens of thousands of dollars per unit. As a result, the oligarch's scouts were pampered and feted when they turned up, as they allegedly combed and remapped every corner of Mingrelia in their search for old trees. At the approach of the low-loaders, power lines were cut, roofs removed, and fences and walls shifted so that the old trees could be steered through the narrow village streets. A workforce of hundreds must have been involved in tending Ivanishvili's private park on the Black Sea coast.

Opinions differed about the reasons for such extravagance. Some people repeated the same story as Jeka about Ivanishvili's sickly children, for whom the trees were supposedly the ticket to a longer life. Other people believed that the oligarch had a botanical interest in collecting trees. Others thought he was plain mad.

In the village of Didi Nedzi, a new road had been specially built to allow old Valerian Jramaya's oak to be ferried away. There was a deep crater around its trunk. The oak was three times as old as he was, said Jramaya, who had recently celebrated his eighty-third birthday. It was a fairy-tale tree with a gnarled trunk and a magnificent sweeping crown that lent shade to his whole garden. Jramaya's great-great-great-grandparents had planted it, but he didn't seem too bothered about divesting himself of the family oak.

'I can go and see it if I miss it.'

There was something oak-like about Jramaya himself, who had been headmaster of Didi Nedzi's village school for four decades. He pushed me into the house with his muscular arms, forced me down onto the kitchen bench and placed shot glasses on the table.

'Thanks, but—'

'I'm not going to let you leave without tasting my home-made *chacha*.'

'It's really a bit early—'

'It's never too early to celebrate the start of a new friendship.'

'We still have a long way to drive.'

'Another good reason for a pick-me-up.'

'OK, just one, though …'

'Of course.'

Five shots later, I was still reeling from how Jramaya's silver tongue was breaking my resistance. He anticipated my every objection and deflected it with disarming elegance. His powers of persuasion, honed to perfection by a lifetime of playing the host, reminded me of the well-practised persis-tence with which some Italian men flirt with women.

Because he was driving, Jeka had escaped with no more than a polite sip. He chuckled at my tipsy philosophising on the subject of Georgian hospitality.

'You haven't seen anything yet! If I invite you to my home and the neighbours see I have a foreign guest, it'll be three days before they let you go!'

By the following afternoon, we had developed such a keen eye for old trees that we spotted one specimen after another that met the oligarch's predatory standards on the side of the road.

'Over there! That lime tree!'

In a village somewhere between Anaklia and Zugdidi, Jeka pulled up alongside a garden fence. The fragrance of lime blossom wafted in through the open car windows. Jeka waved to an old man sitting on a bench in front of the fence.

'What a splendid tree, my friend! That would be a good one for Ivanishvili.'

The old man nodded sadly. 'Brother, he was already here.'

This man's name was Merabi, and his voice sounded as if it was coming from inside a wine barrel – woody and creaky, with a dry aftertaste. He told us that the oligarch had come in person to inspect the lime tree.

'He was wide-eyed with wonder. "Amazing," he said. "Fantastic!" He named his price, offered me his hand, and I shook it. A done deal! Then the technicians came. "Brother," they said, "there isn't enough room here. The lorry won't fit into your garden." I said, "If my house is in the way, for God's sake, tear it down. To hell with it – I'll build myself three new ones with that amount of money!" I'd even worked on my neighbour, so he was willing to demolish his house too. But the technicians stood firm. "No chance," they said, "there isn't enough room." Damn, I could already feel the money on my palm! I thought my worries were over.'

On the morning of the third day, Jeka rang my hotel room in Poti. The worker from the harbour construction site had been in touch: the eucalyptus tree had disappeared from its parking place.

I walked down to the coast from my hotel. I didn't need to look for long. Far out at sea, the tree was sailing along the horizon almost directly opposite Poti. I blinked a few times to be sure that this weird sight wasn't a mirage. A tug was towing the upright tree behind it on a floating platform. It looked like a cartoon desert island – a tiny patch of land under a giant palm tree.

Jeka picked me up in his taxi. The drive to Shekvetili took us along the coast. For the best part of a half-hour, we were shadowed by the tree floating parallel to the road, but then the sea was obscured by some woods. We turned off onto a track that ran for a few hundred metres down to the shore. A dozen workmen were standing on a concrete landing stage alongside heavy construction vehicles, waiting for the tree to dock. We parked the car and joined them.

For a good hour, we watched as the tree drifted towards the shore from the horizon. Its branches were outlined black against the sky in the bright sunlight. Not a single workman moved; all eyes were riveted on the water. I had the distinct impression that I was seeing something for the first and only time. It seemed as if natural law had been weirdly inverted: the tree was moving, and the humans were rooted to the ground.

The swimming platform bumped into the concrete jetty with a grating thud. As the tree came to a quivering halt, the workers began to pump water into the platform to lower it, millimetre by millimetre, to the height of the jetty. I realised that it would take hours to level out the tree's path.

'That son of a bitch.' Jeka pointed to a villa a few hundred metres along the shore. 'That's where he lives.'

I wondered if the proprietor stood by his mansion's reflective glass facade to observe his ships arriving – an admiral of trees.

The private park stretched landwards from the shore, sepa-rated from the outside world by a tall fence dotted with clearly visible video cameras. The guards at the front gate were good-natured Georgians, but they merely shook their heads silently when I asked if I might not, just for a minute, just a few steps ...?

I walked around the entire perimeter fence, but the view of the newly planted trees inside was blocked by a ubiquitous screen of tall pines. Along the shore, the fence abutted the beach, which was not the colour of normal sand but dark, virtually black. I'd heard gossip that it derived its hue from magnetic particles, to which the Georgians attributed miraculous healing powers. As I was groping for the right word for this colour, I very nearly tripped over the corpse of a stranded dolphin. Its teeth were exposed, and there were glimpses of bright orange flesh through the rotting skin.

Maybe it was the dolphin that sowed sinister thoughts in my mind. As I watched a truck hauling the tree from the platform in the gathering darkness, I had a sudden sensation that I was witnessing an ancient and ill-fated Black Sea ritual. Something about this body of water seemed to incite people to folly, seemed to suggest to them that the abundance along its shores, both plants and humans, required an ordering hand to control it. Yet again, someone had decided to rearrange a coastal population and resettle it according to his own criteria, erecting fences, establishing a ghetto, and enclosing a community – this time, a nation of giant Mingrelian trees.

The eucalyptus rolled ashore at a snail's pace. A blurred almost-full moon had risen over the sea, and tattered black clouds scudded across its face. Against the light, I could see the eucalyptus leaves trembling, and I fancied, impossible though it was, that I could hear their dry rustling over the engine noise. The low-loader manoeuvred the tree slowly through the gates.

'What a sick son of a bitch …'

Jeka had suddenly popped up beside me. Together, we watched the tree recede into the distance until it had vanished into the estate.

Abkhazia

Amshyn Eikwa / Амшьын Еиқәа

But meanwhile, rumours of a little paradise said
to exist on the Caucasian coast, with a fantastic
abundance of food and other goods and a fabulous
climate, spread all over the Black Sea area and the
neighbouring regions. Everyone was striving to get
into that paradise, but it remained firmly sealed off.

Konstantin Paustovsky, *Southern Adventure*, 1960

A long story

'Are you a tourist?'

'A traveller, yes.'

'Why do you want to go to Abkhazia?

'I've heard it's very beautiful.'

'Is this your first time here?'

'In Abkhazia, yes, but I've been to Russia many times and to Georgia a few—'

'Russia? Where?'

'Many places.'

'Moscow?'

'Of course.'

'Petersburg?'

'Also.'

'Siberia?'

'Yes.'

'Where did you learn Russian?'

'On the road. Travelling.'

'Why are you so interested in Russia?'

'Oh, that's a long story.'

The young customs official clicked his biro a few times, in and out, before laying it down deliberately slowly and exactly parallel to the edge of the desk I was sitting at. He leaned his upper body towards me, placed his elbows on the plywood tabletop, and, smiling, cupped his chin in his hands.

'I've got time.'

When the entry permit from the Abkhazian foreign ministry finally arrived, Jeka had driven me to the foot of the Enguri

TROUBLED WATER

Bridge, the only crossing that still linked Georgia with the breakaway republic. I had walked over the bridge with a group of Mingrelian widows, who were braving the midday heat in black dresses, carrying black parasols. They lived in the south of the separatist region and were on their way back from visiting a cemetery on the other side. Their cheeks were smeared with mascara.

Inside the Portakabins at the other end of the bridge sat men and women who were clearly not Abkhazians. It took me a moment to figure out why their pale faces were such a surprise to me. I'd known that Russia was pulling the strings here, but I was taken aback by the openness of it all. The border officers were wearing the uniform of the FSB, the Federal Security Service of the Russian Federation.

At the sight of my German passport, they took me to their superior's Portakabin, where a large Russian flag was hanging on a wall behind a desk. The border official had the epaulettes of a first lieutenant and the undeveloped face of a child. He couldn't have been much out of his mid-twenties, and he seemed happy to have found someone to relieve his boredom at this remote frontier post. It turned into the longest and strangest interrogation I've ever experienced.

'Books, you say ... About Russia ...' His eyes sparkled with genuine curiosity. 'Tell me what Germans think about Russia.'

'About what exactly?'

'About our country.'

'That depends who you ask.'

'What do most of them think?'

'That it's a very big country.'

'What else?'

'That the winters are very cold. That it's the land of

Dostoyevsky and Tolstoy. That Russians like drinking vodka. That …'

'What do people think about Crimea?'

'That it's a peninsula in the Black Sea.'

'Do you think it's fair that sanctions were imposed on Russia?'

'Are you asking me?'

'The Germans.'

'The Germans view it in different ways.'

'How do most of them see it?'

'To be honest, I think most of them don't care.'

He nodded silently, as if scouring his mind for further questions. 'Tell me the titles of your books.'

'In German?'

'In Russian.'

'They haven't been published in Russian, only in German and English.'

'Then tell me the English ones.'

He typed a title on his computer keyboard.

'What's this?'

The website of an English daily newspaper had opened on his screen.

'A book review.'

'Praise or criticism?'

'Praise.'

He read it for a few seconds. 'Do I understand correctly that your books are in the artistic literature genre?'

'You ask some tough questions. They aren't novels. My literature is documentary.'

'Are you famous in Germany?'

'Not by a long stretch.'

'Do books about Russia bring in a lot of money?'

'I would guess there are other subjects that sell better.'

'Do you have any contact with Russian authors?'

'No. Although, one of my friends in Moscow writes poems.'

'What's his name?'

'You won't have heard of him.'

'Do you publish these poems in Germany?'

'Me? No, I'm not a publisher.'

'I mean, do you publish these poems in your books?'

'In my own …? No, not so far.'

It went on like this for almost an hour. The border official then made me wait in his office for another hour, while his superiors in Moscow decided on my fate. I stared at the white, blue, and red tricolour on the wall and wondered if, at some point, I had divulged too much or too little, and whether the FSB censors would shower my books with praise or criticism.

Eventually, the officer gave me my passport back and wished me a safe journey.

A few yards further on, a couple of Abkhaz border guards were standing in the shade of a tree, smoking. When I held up my passport, they wearily waved me through. It looked as if they weren't really sure what they were doing there.

The Mingrelian widows had long since moved on, and I was the only passenger on the next border bus.

'From Germany?' The Abkhazian driver was studying me in the rear-view mirror. 'I don't understand you Germans. Why do you let all these scum into your country? Sooner or later, there'll only be negroes living there. And gays!'

I let the familiar offensive monologue wash over me in silence. This was the first time I'd heard such remarks since leaving Russia, and it seemed as if, without noticing it, I had jumped over a magic border back into the area covered by Russian TV transmitters.

A few large bugs scuttled across the bus's dashboard. Their brownish-green carapaces had caught my eye back at the border, where I'd seen them crawling around on the glass between me and an unimpressed Russian female border guard.

'The Georgians have planted them here,' the driver said, 'to bring us to our knees!'

I'd heard about the invasion of insects that had devoured over half of Abkhazia's hazelnut and mandarin crop the previous year. *Halymorpha halys* originally hailed from East Asia, but the bug had developed a liking for the subtropical climate of the eastern Black Sea region, partly because it had no enemies here. After the insect's massed assault on plantations along the Abkhazian and Georgian coastline, the former warring parties had accused each other of deploying it as a biological weapon.

Essentially, the enmity between the Georgian and the Abkhazians revolved around the same question that most neighbourly conflicts in the Black Sea region revolve around: who was here first? I had stopped reading the mountains of polemic academic articles in which each camp dismissed the other's past. Etymological battles had run wild over the issue of whether the name of a specific tree or fish had entered Georgian from Abkhazian or vice versa, in a specious attempt to prove that one of the two had built houses from the trees and made soup from the fish long before the other.

The more plausible catalyst for the conflict was – yet again – Stalin. In the early years of the USSR, tiny Abkhazia had been an independent Soviet republic of equal rank to Georgia. It was Stalin who coerced the Abkhazians into a lopsided marriage with their neighbours in 1931. Their forcibly united republic was ruled henceforth from Tbilisi. At the same time, Stalin did what he had done with the institutions of so many

Soviet minorities and shut down Abkhazian schools, news-papers, and theatres. Other ethnic groups had later primarily directed their rage at the symbols of Stalin's machinery of power – the Kremlin, Moscow, the USSR, and its successor state, Russia. Abkhazia was different, though. To Abkhazians, Stalin was first and foremost a Georgian. Soviet repression handcuffed them to their neighbours, more and more of whom settled in Abkhazia after the forced merger. At the end of the nineteenth century, the region had been 85 per cent Abkhazian; by the end of the Soviet era, the proportion of Georgian immigrants had increased so much that Abkhazians accounted for less than 20 per cent of the total population.

All these pent-up grievances were released after the collapse of the Soviet Union. Within an incredibly short time, rifts emerged between neighbours, friends, and families who had for decades shared the streets, their houses, or their beds. Abk-hazia's interwoven fabric of nationalities was rent apart. The Georgians were expelled, and Russians, Armenians, Greeks, and other minorities fled too. By the time the smoke cleared, Abkhazia had lost over half of its inhabitants. For the first time in a century, the Abkhazians were more or less alone on their patch of the world.

For this they had paid quite a price. The landscape I saw flashing past the bus windows was still clearly marked by the war's legacy. Every second house was empty. Often the roofs had caved in, the walls were crumbling, and all that remained of doors and windows were soot-blackened frames, staring out blindly like the eye sockets of skulls. In depopulated Abk-hazia, there were not enough hands to maintain the houses, let alone people to live in them.

I got out in the capital, Sukhum, and flinched, as I made

my way from the bus station into the centre, at the sound of volleys of automatic gunfire close by. I looked around for help, but the old man I asked about the shots merely laughed.

'That's how we celebrate weddings here, young man.'

Sukhum's streets and gardens abounded with the same imported subtropical plants I had seen in Sochi 100 km to the north-west, but here they proliferated more extravagantly, more freely, more wildly. Eucalyptus trees lined the seafront promenade, each of them as magnificent in size as the specimen I had seen floating across the sea off Georgia. Palms, ferns, succulents, and cacti colonised the spaces between the trees. Vines, creepers, and convolvulus clung to every surface, and the entire city was awash with flowers of all conceivable colours.

When the Abkhazian Black Sea coast was transformed into a holiday paradise for the Russian upper class and later the Soviet proletariat, the architecture was dressed up in an imported Mediterranean style to match the plants, producing its most spectacular flourishes in Sukhum. The spa hotels were adorned with Roman columns and Moorish arches; the railway stations resembled Renaissance palaces. Many of these Russian-Soviet colonial mansions were practically ruins now, their crumbling facades overgrown with jungle-like vegetation. In conjunction with the guerrilla-like political climate, this conjured an image in my mind of Abkhazia as some kind of long-lost corner of Latin America. From the house fronts hung outsized portraits of the separatist leaders – ageing, saluting war veterans with grim faces that seemed to say, '¡No pasarán!' Even the green-and-white striped flag with a palm raised in warning on a red background in the corner looked vaguely South American.

In the Museum of the Glory of War, a guide proudly

showed me the list of countries that had recognised Abkhazia as an independent state. Alongside Russia, it included Nicaragua, Venezuela, and the two Pacific island nations Nauru and Vanuatu. I asked the museum guide if she had heard of Nauru and Vanuatu before they recognised Abkhazia. Narrowing her eyes in hostility, she shook her head.

On the landward side of the city, a footpath overhung with lianas wound its way steeply uphill. I saw the roofs of Sukhum recede below me and carried on climbing up through the thickening jungle until I heard the cries I had been waiting for.

The monkeys of Sukhum

On 1 July 1927, a steamer sets out from the west coast of Africa, bound for Europe. Among the passengers is an elderly grey-bearded man, a Russian. However, it is not his nationality that sets him apart on board but his luggage: Ilya Ivanovich Ivanov boards the ship with a dozen chimpanzees and two baboons.

Ivanov is particularly attentive to three apes named Babette, Syvette, and Chornaya. These female chimpanzees are part of an experiment none of the other passengers know anything about. Only a few weeks ago, Ivanov inseminated the monkeys with human sperm at a research institute in Conakry, the capital of Guinea.

The voyage north doesn't agree with the monkeys. The chimpanzees in particular suffer from the falling temperatures.

Chornaya dies at the port of Marseille.

Syvette doesn't survive the onward journey to the Black Sea.

Shortly after their arrival in Sukhum, Babette too succumbs.

Post-mortems are conducted on all three apes. To Ivanov's

great disappointment, the diagnosis is the same in each case: not pregnant.

A Russian exile newspaper describes Ivanov, who is fifty-six years old at the time, as 'a distinguished older gentleman with a long grey beard and a pince-nez on his nose – a typical Russian professor from the good old days'. What is neither typical nor distinguished, in the narrow sense of the word, is Ivanov's research. As early as 1910, at a congress in Graz, this biologist who specialises in animal breeding causes quite a stir by announcing that he thinks it is possible to cross primates and humans. Ivanov doggedly promotes his theory in the ensuing years, and at the Institut Pasteur in Paris he finds some backers, who arrange a research residency for him in West Africa.

The setback with the chimpanzees doesn't discourage him for long. At his behest, an ape research station is established in the late 1920s on the Black Sea coast, the only climatically suitable place in the Soviet Union. Ivanov hopes to be able to continue his experiments in Sukhum, but adopting the reverse approach this time. Instead of fertilising female monkeys with human sperm, he plans to mate female Soviet citizens with primates. Following press reports about his plans, the institute in Sukhum receives several letters addressed to Ivanov by young women volunteering to participate in the trials.

'I am taking the liberty of making you an offer,' one of them writes in March 1928. 'My request is that you take me on as a test subject. I beseech you not to reject me. I will submit myself to all the conditions the experiment requires. I firmly believe that fertilisation is possible.'

'Madam,' Ivanov replies without delay, 'I inform you post haste that I have received your letter and noted your offer. I shall be in touch as soon as necessary and possible ... The trials will doubtless take place in Sukhum.'

Ivanov stays in contact with this woman for about a year and a half. He even appears to have selected an ape mate for her, but then, in August 1929, he sends her an unexpected telegram.

'The orangutan has perished. We are looking for a replacement.'

There is no time for that, however. On 13 October 1930, Ivanov is arrested. Stalin's campaign of terror is in full swing, and the Soviet scientific community is suffering an ideological purge. Elderly gentlemen resembling 'professors from the good old days' hold very few trumps. An ambitious emerging scientist has allegedly denounced his colleague to the authorities to further his own career. Ivanov is deported under the standard charge of 'membership of a counter-revolutionary organisation' to Kazakhstan, where he dies from a stroke on 20 March 1932, a few months before his sixty-second birthday.

Ivanov's downfall also brings his ideas into disrepute. The cross-breeding experiments are discontinued, and the would-be mates are never heard of again.

The monkeys, however, stay on in Sukhum.

As I got closer to the former research site and passed institutional buildings that had half disappeared under creepers, I heard them screeching in the jungle. The sound swelled in ear-splitting surges, coalesced into polyphonic choruses, and then ebbed away and fell silent, before starting afresh.

Then, around a final bend in the footpath, the cages appeared before me. A few hundred monkeys were crouching behind long lines of bars, the majority of them rhesus and capuchin monkeys, but a few baboons and guenons too. Two Abkhazian families with small children were feeding the animals mandarins and lettuce leaves. Their progress from cage to cage was the cause of all the screeching.

A man in a checked flannel shirt was pushing a wheelbarrow across the compound. He gave a knowing nod as I enquired about Ivanov's experiments. 'Stalin wanted him to breed the perfect worker. As strong as a gorilla and as compliant as a robot.'

Ivanov's studies were kept under wraps in Soviet times. When scoop-hungry tabloid journalists discovered these old skeletons in the cupboard during perestroika, it triggered a spate of wild rumours. Ivanov's only goal had been to prove Darwin's theory about the evolutionary kinship of primates and humans through experimentation, but sixty years later the newspapers were full of reports of a 'Red Frankenstein' who had been instructed by the Party to create a new race – the socialist Übermensch, a proletarian superman, *Homo sovieticus*.

'Complete myths,' Zurab Yasonovich Mikvabia grumbled.

The institutional director's office was in an old prefabricated building a short distance from the cages. The concrete facade was riddled with bullet holes from the civil war. I had climbed the dark staircase to the third floor and had knocked on the door that the man with the wheelbarrow described to me. A low voice that seemed to come from a long way away had shouted, 'Come in'. Entering, I had seen a haze of pipe smoke at the very back of a long, narrow room. In the middle of this cloud sat Mikvabia, a man approaching seventy, in a white laboratory coat with a greying walrus-like moustache and sad St Bernard eyes.

'All myths.'

He hated these old stories. Ivanov, he told me, had only visited the institute once, and neither before nor after his unfortunate death had monkeys been crossed with humans in Sukhum. The institute had been established not as some covert Übermensch factory but as a medical research laboratory and the world's first centre for experimenting on monkeys. And that, Mikvabia said, is precisely what it had remained throughout all the upheaval and warring. For over ninety years, medical drugs and treatments had been tested on primates in Sukhum.

Mikvabia's voice was a deep bass that set the whole room aquiver, and his words resonated with a survivor's pride. Just under three decades earlier, when his moustache was still black, he had fought in the civil war. Twice in quick succession, the front line had ploughed through the research compound – once when the Georgians had marched into Sukhum, and a second time when the Akhazians, with Mikvabia in their ranks, had retaken the city. More than 2,500 monkeys had lived in the cages and a nearby open-air enclosure before the war; by the time the war ended, there were fewer than 150 left. Most of them had escaped from the institute's ruined facilities during the fighting and were unable to find any suitable food in the wild. Years after the war, hikers in the Abkhazian mountains were still stumbling across the bones of starved primates.

It had taken a long time to rebuild Sukhum's monkey population. In the first few years after the war, when even Russia had yet to recognise the separatist republic and its economically isolated inhabitants lived entirely on what they were able to produce for themselves, many of the remaining monkeys had succumbed to malnutrition. Supplies only started to flow into the region again later, when the Kremlin began to see Abkhazia as a means of applying diplomatic pressure to Georgia. By then, only a few dozen monkeys were left alive. The institute's scientists mated them with newly arrived primates from Vietnam and Mauritius, smuggled into the country via the Black Sea in breach of international trade embargos.

Now there were something like 600 monkeys living in Sukhum. With gritted teeth, Mikvabia and his colleagues had opened the research site to private visitors, as the admission fees covered part of the institution's costs. There weren't many attractions in war-scarred Sukhum and, as a result, the primate zoo was popular. It didn't appear to bother the visitors that the monkeys their children were feeding lettuce leaves through the bars of their cages were quite likely to die during animal experiments. Mikvabia's customers were predominantly Russian pharmaceutical firms, for whom his institute had in recent years tested such things as flu jabs and cancer drugs.

In the course of the afternoon, Mikvabia introduced me to some of his colleagues, a few of whom were even older than him. I looked on in astonishment as a ninety-year-old veteran scientist patted the director on the cheek with a trembling hand.

'Zurab Yasonovich,' he croaked, 'the institute is in good hands under your leadership. It's a good thing that the young generation is taking the helm now.'

It was not only the war that had bonded the 200-strong staff together. Many here had been part of the institutional furniture for so long that they had experienced the glory days when monkeys had been readied for space flight at Sukhum.

An ancient researcher let me leaf through her PhD thesis. She had trained the six rhesus monkeys that had travelled on space rockets in the 1980s. I saw black-and-white photos of little monkeys in warm kiddies' playsuits with their tummies fastened to the seats of their space capsules by iron clamps, electrodes on their shaved heads, button eyes wide with curiosity. The animals had been sent into space in pairs, so that they could keep each other calm during the voyage. They had been given names whose initials were ordered according to the Cyrillic alphabet.

Abrek and Bion launched on 21 December 1983.

Verny and Gordy followed on 17 July 1985.

Dryoma and Yerosha lifted off on 12 October 1987.

All six rhesus monkeys had returned to Earth in good condition. After landing, they had been taken to Moscow for medical examination, and five of them had remained there. Only Verny had ended up back in Sukhum, and he lived in the institution's compound until war broke out. They lost track of him after that. Maybe he had caught a bullet. Maybe he had starved to death. Maybe, I thought, he had somehow managed to survive in the forest, maybe Abkhazian mandarins had saved his life, maybe …

'The Georgians probably took him home as a war trophy.' Mikvabia's bass voice shook me out of my optimistic thoughts. 'The Georgian army pillaged half the country when it withdrew. We've heard that lots of monkeys were later sold into Turkey as pets.'

Whenever Mikvabia talked about the Georgians, his bass voice sounded even deeper than usual. Before we said goodbye at the end of the day, he gave me a long and impassioned speech about the Abkhazians' right to self-determination, about their vendetta against their neighbours, about the thousands of years of Abkhazian civilisation, and the equally ancient barbarism of the Georgians.

Silently, I watched the trails of pipe smoke that Mikvabia left hanging in the air as he gesticulated. His monologue was depressing. The Abkhazians had made themselves hostages of Russia, and their self-determination therefore had all the solidity of a soap bubble. The country was poor, broken, and without prospects, and one thing that was preventing it from moving on was the hatred of the war veterans, who were blocking the later generations from building themselves a future.

Cautiously, I tried to draw Mikvabia's eye to what might lie ahead. 'Maybe some time needs to pass, Zurab Yasonovich. Maybe your children and grandchildren will find a path to reconciliation, maybe a few generations from now the Abkhazians and the Georgians will—'

'Be normal neighbours,' he cut in. 'Definitely, but no more than that. We'll never be part of Georgia again. Not after everything they did to us. My children won't forget it either, even though they were only small during the war.'

'Then I hope Abkhazia will find another way out of its unhappy isolation …'

Mikvabia shrugged indifferently. 'It took Israel a long time to be recognised too.'

Before I left, I took a look at the institute's small museum. The display cabinets were full of pale monkey skulls and black-and-white photos of primate scientists. In one corner of the room stood a discarded Lenin memorial, in the opposite corner a monkey skeleton. The museum guide explained to me that it was the skeleton of an orangutan – the only orangutan that had ever lived in Sukhum. I wondered if it was the ape that Ivanov had selected for the willing woman, but no one at the museum could tell me.

The bony orangutan had extremely long arms. Even though the skeleton was erect, its bleached knuckles dragged on the wooden floor. It stared at Lenin with large empty eye sockets. Lenin's bronze eyes squinted back.

The return of the Circassians

Paintings of the Caucasus by the Russian Romantics feature a recurring figure on horseback: a warrior in a black felt coat, with cartridge belts crossed over his chest, a rifle slung at an angle across his back, a dagger and sabre in his belt, his mouth a cruel slit, and his eyes under a felt hat proud, hard, glowing like coals.

Of the many mountain tribes against which tsarist Russia waged its bloody nineteenth-century war of conquest, it was the Circassians who epitomised the Caucasus in the Russian imagination. Over half a million of them lived in the mountain villages to the north and west of the mountain range's spine at the time, making them the most populous group in the regional ethnic mosaic. When Russia, still drunk on victory from Catherine the Great's conquest of the Black Sea coast, pressed southwards into the Caucasus from the late eighteenth century onwards, the Circassians put up the most stubborn resistance to its advance. In alliance with the other mountain peoples – including their close relatives, the Abkhazians – they ensnared the tsar's troops in a gruelling guerrilla war that went on for several generations.

Nowadays, there are three autonomous republics in the Caucasus named after the Circassians and their ethnic subgroups: Karachay-Cherkessia, Kabardino-Balkaria and Adygea. In the most recent censuses, around 700,000 people there described themselves as Circassians.

There are, however, a far higher number of Circassians who no longer live in the Caucasus.

When Russia temporarily broke the mountain peoples' stubborn defiance in the mid-nineteenth century, it was clear to the army high command that war could flare up again at a moment's notice as long as the Circassians were able to entrench themselves in their inaccessible mountain villages. A plan took shape, bluntly referred to by officers as *ochishchenie* ('cleansing').

The Circassians were given an ultimatum: they could either be resettled in the more easily controlled foothills on the northern flanks of the Caucasus or leave the Russian Empire, which now extended beyond the mountain range. Emissaries of the tsar travelled to Istanbul and put the Ottomans, who had recently been defeated in yet another Russo–Turkish war, under pressure to open their empire to Circassian 'emigrants'. There is debate about how many people were forced to leave the Caucasus around the fateful year of 1864. The Russian high command talked about a good 400,000; some people say it was two or three times that number.

There is also debate about how many people did not survive the deportation. At least 50,000 people, or maybe even more than twice as many, perished as the Circassian villages emptied and the homes of displaced families were razed. Some died of hunger; others didn't survive the forced marches into the Ottoman Empire; others again were driven onto overloaded refugee ships, some of which never reached the Turkish coast. Virtually no other people has drowned in the Black Sea in such large numbers as the Circassians. There are individuals living along the coast who will not touch seafood to this day on principle; they refuse to eat fish whose ancestors have gnawed at the bones of their own forefathers.

The Circassians who did make it to the Ottoman Empire were mainly resettled within the borders of modern Turkey, and various sources have estimated that between 1.5 and 2.5 million of their descendants currently live in the country. Others moved farther afield. There are about 100,000 Circassians in Syria and approximately half that number in Jordan, where they still form the king's bodyguard in their traditional battle garb. A few thousand live in Israel, Europe, and the United States, and a few hundred in Egypt.

'My grandfather still spoke Circassian to me,' Bassel said, changing up a gear as he drove me southwards out of Sukhum, 'back home in Damascus.'

It was shortly after six. The evening sun hung low over the sea, and the palm trees cast long oblique shadows over the coast road. Southern light came in through the side windows, tingeing the glass of Bassel's spectacles red. Sticklike arms as thin as a teenager's protruded from the sleeves of his checked shirt, even though Bassel was nearly thirty. He had an introverted face, and I often wasn't sure whether his smile was directed at the outer or the inner world.

It was five years since Bassel had fled Syria. He had just completed a computer science degree when the civil war broke out. Had he stayed any longer, he would have been conscripted into the army.

'Some people here ask me why I didn't want to fight,' he said, turning to look at me. 'If Syria had been attacked, maybe I would have done. But kill my own people? Brother against brother?'

With a silent shake of his head, he went back to concentrating on the traffic. My eyes were drawn to his wrists, which must have been even more slender back then, soon after his twenty-third birthday. I was glad he hadn't ended up on the front line but in Abkhazia instead, however weird it was for a Syrian to end up in Abkhazia.

But Bassel wasn't alone. Twelve miles south of Sukhum, we turned off the main road and drove through a small place called Dranda, on whose outskirts there were a few nine-storey prefabricated buildings. This was where the workers from a collective farm growing citrus fruit had lived before the Georgian–Abkhazian war. Now most of the residential blocks stood empty, apart from one, where a few hundred refugees from the Syrian war were living. All of them had Circassian roots. A century and a half after their ancestors had been driven out of the Caucasus, they had unexpectedly returned – unexpectedly for the Caucasus, even more unexpectedly for themselves.

Bassel led me up the bare staircase to a flat on the fourth floor. His mother, Fadia, who looked surprisingly young, invited us into the living room. She had baked Circassian dumplings stuffed with white cheese. I sank into the depths of a Soviet armchair. On the sofa next to me sat Sami, Bassel's younger brother, and Mohammad, a neighbour of about seventy. Bassel's father, who usually lived here with the rest of the family, had gone back to Syria for a few weeks to check in on relatives.

In Damascus, they had led the life of an average middle-class family. Fadia was a technical draughtswoman, and her husband managed a factory that manufactured doors and windows. Shortly after the war began, an envoy from the Abkhazian separatist government had appeared in Damascus and started canvassing for Syrian Circassians to return to their historical homeland. He promised housing and subsidies to all takers. His offer was not entirely altruistic: there was a surfeit of empty houses in Abkhazia, and the depopulated region could really do with new inhabitants indebted – and thus loyal – to the separatist regime.

Time was shortest for Bassel, and so he went first. He had never been to the Caucasus before, or even close. He learned the Cyrillic alphabet by heart on the plane to Moscow and then, on the bus to Abkhazia, googled the few available scraps of information in Arabic about his new home. His younger brother, who was also living under the threat of conscription, followed soon after turning eighteen. Their parents came not long afterwards, when gunfire could be heard in the streets of Damascus.

Bassel, Sami, Fadia, and Mohammad told me in faltering English about the time before the war. The Circassians who had ended up in Syria after their deportation in the nineteenth century had originally settled on the Golan Heights. Old Mohammad, who could still remember living there, counted off the names of a dozen Circassian settlements on his fingers. It was only when Israel occupied the Golan Heights during the Six-Day War that the Syrian Circassians fled to Damascus almost as one. Even though they no longer lived as a distinct diaspora community within the city, they continued to regard themselves as Circassians.

'There are small differences between us and the Arabs.'

Bassel made to carry on, but Mohammad cut in.

'Small?' He spread his arms wide as if to demonstrate how big the differences really were. 'Huge, more like! Circassian men and women live together. They don't sit in separate parts of the house like the Arabs.'

Bassel nodded. 'But younger Syrians had given that up too. The whole country was slowly becoming more liberal. Until the war started.'

Bassel and Sami spoke of the Circassian cultural centre in Damascus to which their parents had sent them every week. There, they had been taught the language and songs of their ancestors. The brothers had also learned the mourning dances with which the Circassians kept the memory of their deportation alive – Bassel enthusiastically, Sami somewhat less so. However, their grandfather's stories made a greater impression on them both. Fadia's father was the Caucasian patriot in the family. His own grandparents had been part of the Circassian exodus in the nineteenth century, and he had passed on what they had told him to his grandsons.

The love that Bassel and Sami's grandfather had for his ancestral homeland was so strong that he had visited Abkhazia for the very first time shortly after the fall of the Iron Curtain. He had travelled regularly to Sukhum in the chaotic post-war years, and when he got home, he would give long and rapturous accounts of his rediscovered Caucasian paradise to the rest of the family. Fadia and her sons had quietly eaten the Abkhazian honey her father brought back from Sukhum, but however patiently they listened to him, the Caucasus had never really taken root in their hearts.

'And now, here we are.'

Fadia's smile spread to her sons' faces too. Less than five years after her father's death, all of them were gathered in Abkhazia. It was a quirk of fate that had nested itself deep inside their family mythology.

Bassel was one of the few residents of their block in Dranda to have found work in Abkhazia. A mobile communications company had employed him as an IT engineer soon after he arrived, even though he could barely speak any Russian at the time and had to rely on the shape of the icons to find his way around the company's operating system. He could speak the language now, albeit less fluently than his younger brother, who was studying tourism in Sukhum. In the daytime, when her two sons were out, Fadia often sat alone in the flat, zapping back and forth between Russian, Abkhazian, and Georgian TV channels, understanding precious little of what was being said.

The one who had it hardest was Mohammad, because he was too old to start learning Russian. He was the artistic type, with dreamy eyes, and had worked as a writer and journalist in Damascus. In rambling, lyrical English, he told me about a poem he wrote shortly after arriving in Abkhazia.

'I have a dream. I dream that I'm doing a painting of a boat. The boat comes free from the paper and carries me around the world. I visit the Louvre and see the paintings of the Impressionists. I go to the Bolshoi Theatre and listen to Beethoven. I sit under sugar cane palms in Cuba. My boat is small, and the world is big. Then I wake up. The boat is gone, and my world is small again. I sigh and tell myself, "You are a prisoner of geography."'

Given the choice, none of them would have picked Abkhazia as their safe haven, but all four knew that things could have turned out much worse. Bassel and Sami had escaped the civil war. They hadn't drowned in the Mediterranean, they weren't trapped in a refugee camp, they had enough to eat and could sleep in a bed at night, even if it was a Soviet plywood bed. They even seemed to have got a better deal than the Circassians who had fled from Syria to the Russian part of the Caucasus. Bassel had heard that Russians were not always friendly towards refugees – which came as little surprise to me after my recent experiences.

None of them knew how things would pan out. As we talked, I sometimes caught Fadia's gaze wandering to her two sons and thought I saw unexpressed concerns there. Bassel and Sami weren't married. What would happen if they fell in love here? Would they ever go back to Syria? And with each passing day in Abkhazia, did it not grow ever more likely that they would lose their hearts here?

Later, as Bassel drove me back to Sukhum along the dark coastal road, I asked him whether the Circassians in Syria married within the community.

He nodded. 'People take a dim view when Circassian girls get involved with Arabs.'

'And the other way around?'

He looked at me in astonishment. 'The other way around? You mean, Circassian men with Arab women?'

'Yes.'

Bassel grinned the way you only grin about someone hopelessly naive. 'Why would any Circassian man do that? Circassian women are a thousand times more beautiful. Every woman in Syria envies them.'

I met up with Bassel again a few days later, on the eve of my departure from Abkhazia. Like half the city on a summer evening, we walked up and down the promenade. Every now and then, we bumped into other young Circassians from Syria, people Bassel knew, who were wandering around just as aimlessly as we were. We would walk along together for a while, chatting in Russian and cracking open the sunflower seeds that Bassel's friends offered us from their paper bags. During these conversations, I noticed how their eyes tracked the young Abkhazian women strolling in the opposite direction.

Late in the evening, we crossed paths with an elderly man whom Bassel knew because he worked for one of the separatist government's agencies. The man's expression was stern and distrustful. He was one of an earlier generation of Syrian Circassians that had emigrated to the Caucasus as volunteers to fight on the Abkhazian side against the Georgians.

The man asked me where I had crossed over into Abkhazia. This wasn't the first time I'd been asked this question, but only now did it hit me that its primary motivation was not curiosity but ideology. Many people here regarded anyone who entered from Georgia with suspicion.

'Why didn't you come in from Russia?'

'I—'

'A writer, huh? What does that mean? Are you here to extract information from us?'

'No, I—'

'Are you working for the Georgians?'

'No.'

'Why do your newspapers always say life is bad in Abkhazia? Why don't you write about Georgia being full of criminals and junkies?'

'How—'

'Tell me why the Georgians refuse to accept Abkhazia's independence, even though they lost the war? You Germans, too, had to come to terms with your country being divided!'

'Because of all the displaced people.' For once I managed to get a word in edgeways. 'Because of the Georgians who had to flee from Abkhazia. How are they supposed to accept that they cannot go back to their homeland?'

He gave a contemptuous snort.

'Abkhazia was never their homeland! However long they lived here. Just as Syria was never my homeland.'

When the man said goodbye after delivering his furious monologue, Bassel and I stared after him for a long time.

'Once a warrior, always a warrior,' Bassel said by way of apology. 'These veterans cannot change their ways.'

I nodded silently. Once again, I was glad that Bassel hadn't ended up on the front line. That evening, I promised myself never to forget that, when in doubt, it is easier to live with the stigma of the deserter than with the psychological damage of the victor.

'Come and visit me in Berlin,' I said, as our walk came to an end by Bassel's car.

Our smiles were bitter as we shook hands because we were both aware that Bassel had the world's worst possible combination of papers for a trip to Berlin: a Syrian 'terrorist' passport and an Abkhazian 'Mickey Mouse' passport. For the foreseeable future, Bassel was trapped in his distant ancestors' homeland, to which he had had little connection before a twist of fate transformed the past into his future.

My thoughts necessarily turned to Bassel when, a few weeks later, a sixth country unexpectedly joined the ranks of the states that acknowledged Abkhazia's independence. The motives were transparent: the Kremlin had brought a wartime ally onside.

That country was Syria.

Turkey

Karadeniz

I have no religion, and at times I wish all
religions at the bottom of the sea.

Kemal Mustafa Atatürk, interview with British
journalist Grace Ellison, ca. 1926

Fırtına the falcon

Some people call the Georgian city of Batumi 'the Las Vegas of the Black Sea' – which is more flattering than the older nickname French sailors once gave the rain-drenched coast on the Georgian–Turkish border: *le pissoir de la mer Noire* ('the urinal of the Black Sea').

Over the course of its history, Batumi never remained on one side of the border for long. The city was Georgian, then Ottoman, in the Russian Empire, in the Turkish republic, and then in the Soviet Union, before finally reverting to being Georgian again. In the years since independence, it has developed into a neon-flashing casino metropolis, which explains its present-day nickname. Tourists come across the nearby border from Turkey to gamble and drink. From farther afield come groups of Arab men, seen skulking in the shadows of newly built office blocks around Thai massage salons. A small exile community of young liberal Russians who have ventured south, aiming to sit out the Putin winter under the palms, gathers in the bars of the old town.

Batumi has never completely thrown off its Turkish past. It is visible in the mosques and kebab houses of the city centre, and above all in the huge bazaar filling the corridors of the bus terminal and the adjacent streets – a maze of stalls packed with imported Turkish goods. The only Georgian product I saw there was tobacco grown in the surrounding mountain villages and sold on the market by farmers with nicotine-stained fingers. All the other stalls were piled high with goods supplied by travelling salesmen from Turkey: socks, caps, bras, babygros, rubber boots, gardening gloves, flashing plastic toy swords and guns, carpets, leather jackets, and spices.

The bus station's parking bays resembled loading areas. The traders heaved their boxes out of the collective taxis in which they had travelled across the nearby border. Taking a seat with my rucksack in one of the vans, I found myself in the company of a gang of Georgian smugglers. The front two rows of seats were occupied by plastic bags bulging with bottles of brandy and cartons of cigarettes. As the bus set off, ten men began hastily dividing up the goods between sports bags with fake brand logos. Their leader – a green-eyed, aquiline-nosed film star lookalike, who in a wealthier country would definitely have had a choice of alternative careers – studied my rucksack and asked me something in Georgian. I tried Russian, English, and finally my sketchy Turkish, but none of them worked. Eventually, the man shoved two cartons of cigarettes and a bottle of Ukrainian vodka into my hand without a word. I shrugged and stuffed them into my rucksack.

It was less than half an hour's drive to the border. When we reached it, we had to get off the bus, which drove through the customs zone without any passengers. The footpath led directly along the sea, with only a fence between us and the rocky coastline. The water was pale grey that day and merged almost seamlessly into the blanket of cloud at the horizon, but I was the only one looking. A few hundred border-crossers stood in a closely bunched queue outside the customs containers, staring straight ahead. I was pushed to one side, and briefly lost contact with the smugglers, but a sudden hand on my shoulder confirmed that the men were keeping an eye on their newest courier. Abruptly, the waiting people perked up and, as if on command, the entire human mass rolled forwards. We passed through Georgian and then Turkish customs. No one was remotely interested in our luggage, even though the smugglers' sports bags were clearly full to bursting.

On the Turkish side, the mountains dropped precipitously to the sea. A small mosque clung to the slope, and surf crashed loudly on the rocks below. While we waited for the bus, the smugglers tossed their luggage into one big heap and signalled to me to do the same. They pushed me towards the mosque and into a low outhouse, where there were some toilets. Coming out, the Georgians stopped at the mosque's fountain, a little water source for ritual ablutions before prayers. Two of the smugglers turned on the taps, cupped their hands under the jet, and began to drink.

An old man who had obviously been observing us appeared from inside the mosque. Yelling angrily, he advanced towards the Georgians and shooed them away from the taps. I couldn't understand what he was shouting, but his body language was unequivocal: unbelievers were not to drink from this fountain. Rarely have I had such a clear sensation of crossing a boundary.

As we drove on, a warm June rain began to fall, the heavy drops blurring the view of the sea through the bus window. I gave the smugglers their cigarettes and vodka back and tried to find out where they were heading, but their only response was to point straight ahead, along the coast road.

Little did I know at the time that this four-lane highway, built right along the shore, runs almost without interruption to Istanbul, brutally cutting off almost every town and village from the sea on its way. I could already feel during that rainy bus journey, however, that the Black Sea has a different status in Turkey from the one it enjoys in the northern coastal states. Suddenly, it no longer seemed like the warm southern waters for which the Russians and the Ukrainians feel such nostalgia, but like a third-class inland sea paling into insignificance beside the Mediterranean and the Aegean. Of all Turkish waters, it is the coldest, the murkiest, and the least popular with tourists – a northerly, utilitarian sea: good for fishing, bad for swimming. Every settlement we passed had a concrete fishing port on its seaward side, but nowhere did I see a beach, a marina, or even a waterside cafe. It was as if the only interest in the sea here were professional.

'Black Sea Turks don't know how to have fun.'

Yaşa, on the other hand, had a pretty good idea of how to have fun. I got to know him in Ardeşen, a town of 40,000 just the other side of the border, where I got out after saying goodbye to the smugglers. Yaşa owned a grill room. He was the long-haired surfer type, fluent in English, and he looked out of place in Ardeşen. The two happiest decades of his life had been spent in Bodrum on the Turkish Aegean coast, where the Istanbul glitterati have their holiday homes and their yachts. Yaşa had come back to his hometown on the Black Sea three years ago but regretted his decision every single day. He missed the beach bars, the discos, and the forthright glances women used to flash him. He also missed the beer, which wasn't on his menu or that of any other restaurant in Ardeşen.

I looked at him curiously. 'Black Sea Turks don't drink?'

He nodded sadly. 'Only in secret. When they send for whores. But …' He cast around for a second for the right words. 'Believe me, those parties are no good.'

I asked him why he had returned home. He considered this for a moment, as if he couldn't properly remember himself, before giving a shrug. 'This is my homeland. I'm a Lazi.'

Every Turk in Berlin had told me about the Lazi people. They were looked upon as weird bumpkins and misfits, as

Turkish hicks and the butt of jokes all over the country. Gags about the Lazi tended to involve two men called Temel and Dursun who come up with the most complicated solution imaginable to a very simple problem. The more popular these Temel-and-Dursun jokes became around Turkey, the less popular the names Temel and Dursun became on the Black Sea. No Lazi parents wanted to make their sons a national laughing stock.

When Turks talk about the Lazi, they are generally referring to the entire population of the eastern coastal region, who have visibly intermingled with the peoples of the neighbouring Caucasus; I saw blond and red-headed Black Sea Turks, with blue eyes and green. However, despite their name having become a synonym for the entire region, the real Lazis are an ethnic minority living in only a small number of towns and villages around Ardesen. They are distantly related to the Georgian Mingrelians, but the Lazi converted to Islam under Ottoman influence. At first sight, there is not much to distinguish Lazi Turks from Turkish Turks. Not much apart from falcons.

Barış, a friend of Yaşa's, dropped into the restaurant later with one of his birds. The falcon sat on his right shoulder, majestically calm, its eyes yellow and pulsating in its disconcertingly motionless head. Whenever Barış raised or lowered his shoulder, only the falcon's body followed the movement, not the head, which always seemed to float in the same spot in the room. It looked as if the falcon were moving the shoulder rather than the shoulder the falcon.

Barış, who was paying for his testosterone-fuelled athletic physique with early onset baldness, had taken the falcon from its nest three months previously. It was one of two methods the Lazi used to capture falcons, the other being the net technique, which involved tying a sparrow to a convenient branch and spreading a net so fine as to be virtually invisible in front of the tree. The hunter would then lie in wait until a falcon fell upon the sparrow. No sooner was it trapped in the net than the hunter grabbed it. Barış was more of a fan of the nest method than of using a net, because, he said, baby falcons adapted to humans better than grown birds. He tracked down the nests by flying a camera drone up and down the cliffs and rocks around Ardesen. As soon as the young hatched, he would abseil down and steal one of the babies from the nest. Only ever one – a matter of falconer's honour.

Barış didn't know why the Lazi loved falcons, but his brother, his father, and his grandfather had all been falconers too. Further back in their ancestral history, the Lazi had trained falcons to hunt, and they still did, though for fun now rather than out of necessity.

Fırtına – the falcon on his shoulder – was the best hunter he'd ever had, Barış said. 'Agresif! Çok agresif!'

Barış liked to set Fırtına on chickens. With a knowing smile, he drew his right thumb across his throat. That was how it looked when Fırtına tore chickens' heads off. 'Valla agresif!'

The falcon widened and narrowed its pupils as we drank tea. Tea in tiny glasses, tea with sugar lumps, tea the kind of which I would drink pints and pints over the coming weeks. Tea the colour of amber, grown on the slopes around Ardesen.

During the evening, we were joined by Mithat, a regular and one of Yaşa's friends. Later, when the kitchen closed, Ömer, the chef, sat down with us too. The four of them talked in Turkish. From the snatches of conversation that I understood, and others that Yaşa translated for me, I gradually built up a picture of just how typical this motley gathering was for the Black Sea region. Yaşa and Barış were Lazi. Mithat was a member of the Hemşinli, a different regional minority related to the Armenians. And Ömer ...

Yaşa slapped his chef on the back. 'Ömer is a Kurd. A baddie.'

Everyone laughed. Barış laughed so hard that his shoulders shook, and once more it looked as if it weren't he who was directing his movements but the falcon's unmoving head. Only Ömer's laughter was a little more restrained.

'And Turks?' I asked. 'Aren't there any Turks in Ardesen?'

The laughter ceased abruptly.

'We're all Turks,' Yaşa said with utter seriousness.

I was often reminded of that crew at the restaurant as I drifted west along the coast over the following weeks. Experience had taught me to be wary of solidarity between Black Sea peoples. I had seen in Abkhazia how, at the drop of a hat, neighbours who had shared restaurant tables for decades could become strangers, and how shoulder-slapping wind-ups could quickly degenerate into real aggression when the political wind turned.

Turkey's Black Sea coast had experienced such changes in the weather too. Little remained of the old ethnic diversity of Ottoman times after the empire had first collapsed in the First World War and then shrunk drastically before finally being violently remoulded into a nation. Not all peoples had come through Mustafa Kemal Atatürk's new beginning unscathed. This applied to the Kurds, who wanted to go back to the abolished caliphate; the Armenians, who demanded a state of their own; and the Pontic Greeks, who flirted with their Hellenic relatives' expansionist schemes, which is why they were struck by what the exiled still describe with the Greek word *Katastrofe*. In 1923, a fateful year, Atatürk agreed on a forced exchange of population with the regime in Athens. Half a million Muslims were driven out of Greece into Turkey, and more than a million Pontic Greeks were deported to Greek territory.

The few Pontic Greeks who still live in the north-eastern part of Turkey are Muslim, Turkish-speaking, and fully assimilated. Like the Lazi, the Hemşinli, the Armenians, and all the other minorities, they have internalised the phrase that Atatürk coined as his state's motto: 'How happy is the one who says, "I am a Turk."'

An icon falls from the sky

On my way west, I allowed myself a few detours south into the Pontic Alps. I soon began to see why the sea obviously didn't impress the people here – in every respect, it lay in the mountains' shadow.

The Lazi in Ardesen had taught me the most important word in the Black Sea Turks' vocabulary: *yayla* ('plateau', 'wold', 'upland'). The word seemed to describe both the landscape itself and the feelings it inspired in the hearts of its inhabitants. Every time I heard it, it was pronounced with a glow in the speakers' eyes and a lilt in their voices: 'Yaaayla …'

This mountain range runs virtually the whole way along the Turkish coast. From the shore, it climbs rapidly to altitudes of 2,000 m, 3,000 m, and 4,000 m furthest east. The never-ending rain blowing in off the sea – *le pissoir de la mer Noire* – keeps its northern flanks moist, and on the lower terraced slopes tea grows on plantations large enough to satisfy the entire country's gargantuan thirst for tea. I saw the knee-high bushes stretching for miles in every direction, broken only by small family graveyards whose white surah-inscribed headstones poked up out of the glowing green of the fields. Women in headscarves kneeled among the plants to harvest the first crop. Their plucking shears fitted with bags went *snip-snip-snip* in time to my footsteps.

Higher up, closer to the snow-capped peaks, was where the true *yayla* landscape began, the upland grasslands more like Switzerland than anything I had ever associated with Turkey. The clanking of cowbells carried across the mountain meadows. Dense coniferous forests stretched from one summit to the next, interspersed with vast flowering carpets of yellow and purple rhododendron. Birds of prey circled over the slopes, signs warned hikers about bears and lynxes, and had it not been for the Atatürk portraits fastened to the eaves of the wooden huts, I would never have dreamt that I was in Turkey.

I saw swarms of bees buzzing around hives, bringing to mind the stories I had heard about the hallucinogenic effects of Black Sea honey, which was won from the blossoms of a specific type of rhododendron containing minute quantities of a neurotoxin. It was first reported in antiquity: Xenophon describes how half of his army suffered collective intoxication during the return march from his Persian campaign after the soldiers had eaten honeycomb in a mountain village; Strabo writes that Roman legionnaires were murdered here after being incapacitated with honey. Every Turk living in the highlands who I asked about *deli bal* ('mad honey') gave a knowing nod. Some claimed to know someone who knew someone whose mind had been addled by the rhododendron honey. However, no one I spoke to had actually tried it, and when I asked about it in grocery stores, my question prompted only horrified head-shaking.

In the year AD 385, an icon fell from the sky into the middle of these enchanted forests abuzz with bees and myths. It was an image of the Mother of God – the work of St Luke the Apostle, according to legend – that had mysteriously vanished from a church in Athens shortly before. On the night of the picture's disappearance, the Virgin had appeared in a dream to two Greek monks by the names of Barnabas and Sophronios, announcing that she had had enough of the Athenians' pagan delusions and would therefore have angels carry her icon east to the Pontic Mountains. The monks set out to investigate, and they found the image in a cave 30 km inland from the coast, among black cliffs, where it appeared to have arrived without human assistance. Barnabas and Sophronios established a cave shrine to *Panaya tou Melas* ('Our Lady of Black Mountain'). The shrine became a monastery known in the Pontic dialect as Sumela. The monastery buildings still cling to a practically sheer wall of rock in the mountains south of Trabzon, but its last monks were driven out of Turkey in 1923 along with the rest of the Pontic Greeks. Almost a century passed before the first pilgrims from Greece tentatively returned to Sumela to sing mass for the most important Pontic icon on 15 August, the feast of the Assumption. However, the monastery was closed for renovation when I visited – for the third year in succession. There were rumours that not everyone in Turkey had appreciated the growing stream of Greek pilgrims.

From the monastery, a narrow road winds through mountainous ravines, above which the sky tapers to a frayed blue strip. A van was following the hairpin bends north to the coast, and it took me to Trabzon, into the former heart of the world of the Pontic Greeks – a heart that suddenly stopped beating in 1923.

This wasn't the first ending that the city had witnessed.

A few centuries before, unbeknownst to most of the rest of the world, the last outpost of the Roman Empire had sunk into oblivion here on the Black Sea coast. Emperor Constantine had moved the seat of his empire to the Bosporus in the fourth century, replacing the ancient city of Rome with Constantinople. This second Rome survived the demise of the first, and the Byzantine empire – with a Greek imprint now, but still referred to by its inhabitants as 'Romania' – endured into the Middle Ages.

An old Pontic Greek folk song relates how news of the fall of the Byzantine capital reached Trabzon after the Ottomans captured Constantinople:

> A bird, a good bird, left the City,
> it settled neither in vineyards nor in orchards,
> it came to settle on the castle of the Sun.
> It shook one wing, drenched in blood,
> it shook the other wing, it had a written paper.
> Now it reads, now it cries, now it beats its breast.
> 'Woe is us, woe is us, Romania is taken.'

Yet Trabzon had been ruled since the thirteenth century by the Comnenians – a side branch of the Byzantine ruling dynasty – who now regarded their small Black Sea empire as the last bastion of ancient Rome following the fall of Constantinople. For eight brief years, Trabzon was the centre of a dramatically reduced empire until, in 1461, the Ottomans invaded it too.

It was the start of high summer when I arrived in Trabzon. The humid maritime climate transformed the city into a giant sauna. I felt as if I were breathing in more water than air, and even though the temperature was still below 30 degrees centigrade, my senses were telling me that it exceeded 40. Every step along the hilly streets brought beads of sweat to my brow.

The city had spread unsentimentally over the ruins of the old Comnenian Empire. New houses had been squeezed into the gaps in the collapsed sections of the gigantic medieval fortress – simple, low-rise constructions with walls that had been partially cobbled together from fragments of the old bastion. From the better-preserved chunks of citadel hung satellite dishes and washing lines, and between them goats grazed in vegetable patches.

The only cool spot in Trabzon was inside the New Friday Mosque, one of many Byzantine churches converted into Muslim places of worship after the Ottoman conquest. Sultan Mehmed II had celebrated the first Friday prayers ostentatiously here in 1461, giving the former Hagios Eugenios Church its new name. I sat down cross-legged, felt the coldness seep up into my limbs from the floor and allowed the carpet patterns to mesmerise me until I almost nodded off.

A loud wail made me start and raise my chin from my chest.

'Allaaaaaaaaaaaaaaaaaaaaaaaaaaaaaaaaaa-hu ekber …'

I watched drowsily as the mosque filled with the faithful. There was something about the way they took up their positions on the carpet that struck me as odd, but I only realised what it was when afternoon prayers began. The men did not bow towards the front of the rectangular mosque hall, but in the direction of the side wall. I was the only one who had instinctively sat down on the carpet facing east, respecting the logic of the nave of the old church, not the position of Mecca.

The church walls had once been adorned with frescoes of orthodox saints and portraits of Comnenian rulers. Presumably the pictures were still there, but a layer of plaster had covered their eyes for half a millennium. I read about them in an old American travel guide whose author implied that he found the way the Turks treated Christian churches barbaric. I had to laugh when, a few pages further on, I read why St Eugenios of Trabzon, after whom the original church was named, had been proclaimed a saint and martyr. An early Christian, he had been executed in the third century AD by the city's pagan rulers for destroying a statue of the sun god Mithras out of religious fervour.

The city's capture by the Ottomans in the fifteenth century put an end to the imperial Roman tradition but not to its Greek legacy. Pontic Greeks continued to make up the majority of the population, and shaped public life in Trabzon, into the twentieth century. Some of them dreamed of the resurrection of the Greek Black Sea empire when the Ottoman Empire disintegrated in the aftermath of the First World War. That dream died in 1923. Trabzon's Greek newspaper offices, schools, banks, groceries, brothels, and bars emptied in one fell swoop as the Pontic Greeks gathered up the few belongings they could carry, hauled them to the harbour, and stowed them on the deportation ships.

Some of their descendants in modern-day Greece still sing that old Pontic folk song about the fall of Constantinople:

The churches lament, the monasteries weep,
and St John Chrysostom weeps, he beats his breast.
Weep not, weep not, St John, and beat not your breast.
Romania has passed away, Romania is taken.
Even if Romania has passed away, it will flower and bear
    fruit again.

The love story of Gabi and Yusuf

Our gazes met by chance, but there was something in his eye that caused me to slow my pace. He, too, seemed to quicken inside – as if both of us sensed that a conversation lay in store. Tea glass in hand, he was sitting on a shady street corner, a man with white hair swept back behind his ears and the watery blue eyes of a Black Sea Turk. After we had stared at each other for a moment in silence, he addressed me in fluent English, which was unusual not only because of his age but also for the region – I hadn't met anyone for days with whom I could talk in anything but my halting Turkish.

Yusuf Ziya Çakır was, it turned out, the owner of a small family shipping company in Trabzon's harbour, and he had set up his folding chair outside its door. He had learned English in conversations with the crews of foreign ships. He had picked up Russian the same way and, to my surprise, spoke it equally well. He had celebrated turning sixty-seven the day before our chance meeting.

He showed me around his shipping company offices. The walls were covered with paintings and photographs of old ships: sailing boats and steamers, passenger ships and freighters, warships and crane ships, as well as fishing vessels. Business was fine, Yusuf said, even if the port of Trabzon had seen better days. The construction of the new coast road to Istanbul a good ten years earlier had led to most of the two main Pontic commodities, tea and hazelnuts, being transported by road rather than sea.

Later, as we sat outside drinking tea, I told Yusuf about my trip, and suddenly there was a glimmer in his eye. It was as if something had stirred deep in his memory and was striving to get out. He put his glass down on the tarmac and leaned back in his folding chair.

'I'm going to tell you a story. You'll like it.'

This story had taken place four decades earlier. On 3 November 1978, when Yusuf was twenty-seven, a freighter had dropped anchor in Trabzon's harbour. The flag on the stern symbolised the socialist cooperation of workers, intellectuals, and farmers: a hammer, a pair of compasses, and a wreath of ears of corn on a black, red, and gold background. The *Rosenort* was from the German Democratic Republic.

Yusuf went aboard to negotiate with the East German captain about 2,850 tonnes of hazelnuts, which the ship was supposed to load in Trabzon and transport to Rostock, the home port of the *Rosenort* on the Baltic Sea. The two men sat down at a table in the ship's mess. A young stewardess brought them some coffee. The stewardess's name was Gabi. She was eighteen years old. Sparks flew as Yusuf looked into her eyes.

In the eight days during which Gabi's ship lay at anchor in Trabzon, Yusuf learned the one and only German phrase that still rolled off his tongue to this day: *Ich liebe dich*.

Gabi and Yusuf knew that their love was politically delicate. During the Cold War, Yusuf told me, a party security guard travelled on every ship from the Eastern Bloc to make sure that none of the crew defected. This was also the case on the *Rosenort*. One evening, Gabi and Yusuf got the party guard drunk on raki. Once he was snoring soundly with his head on the table, they snuck off the ship and went to the cinema. That same night, Gabi decided that she would not go back to her ship or to her hometown of Rostock, or to East Germany at all.

The apparatchik yelled, the apparatchik threatened, the apparatchik begged, but Gabi refused to be intimidated or persuaded. When the *Rosenort* set sail again on 11 November, it had lots of hazelnuts on board but no stewardess. Gabi and Yusuf were married in Trabzon within the week.

Yusuf got up from his chair, disappeared into his offices, and returned with a dog-eared pad on which all his clients in the 1970s had been noted. He took my pen and copied the details of the *Rosenort*'s harbour stay into my notebook, and I realised he must have made the entries himself – the slightly left-slanting capital letters were identical.

'Your eyes have grown in size,' Yusuf said as he wrote. 'You do like the story.'

'Very much so.'

'It goes on.'

Gabi and Yusuf had been married for eight months when a few relatives from Trabzon arranged a business trip to Ankara. Gabi decided to go along because she wanted to see the capital. Yusuf accompanied his wife to the bus. Her hand waving through the bus window was to be the last he ever saw of her.

A few days later, his relatives rang from Ankara in great agitation. They told him that Gabi had left the hotel the evening before without saying anything. They had seen her get into an unknown car out in the street, and she hadn't reappeared since.

Gabi didn't turn up the next day or the day after that. Her whereabouts were still unknown when the relatives arrived back in Trabzon. *It must be a misunderstanding*, Yusuf thought. *There must be some explanation.*

A few weeks later, a letter arrived from Rostock. Gabi begged Yusuf for forgiveness. Her parents, she wrote, hadn't been able to stand the pressure; the East German secret police had made their lives hell after their daughter's defection. They had sent desperate letters to Trabzon, beseeching her to come home. After a while, Gabi couldn't bear it any more and had written to her parents that she was willing to be smuggled back into the GDR. The East German embassy in Ankara had sent the car for her. *I know how much I've hurt you, Yusuf, but I had no choice*, Gabi wrote.

'I wrote back,' Yusuf said, 'but I don't know if my letter ever got through to her.'

All of this was over four decades ago, but for a second Yusuf's voice cracked and his eyes glittered. He had never heard from Gabi again.

The story had a prosaic ending. A few months after Gabi's letter, a freighter from Vancouver had docked in Trabzon. When Yusuf sat down with its captain, a young Canadian stewardess served them coffee.

'The only way to forget a woman,' Yusuf said, 'is another woman.'

When we spoke, he'd been married to a Turkish lady for many years.

Amazon island

Some 100 km west of Trabzon, a hilly promontory juts out into the sea. On top of it, high above the port of Giresun, stand the ruins of a Byzantine fortress. Grass has grown over the ground among what remains of its walls. The local council has sunk small concrete firepits marked *barbekü* into the gently rolling grassland. I reached this grill area shortly after sundown and, as I glanced at my watch at precisely 7:45 p.m., several things happened at once.

A cannon shot rent the silence.

The streetlamps came on, bathing the ruinscape in a warm orange glow.

At the foot of the hill, a staggered series of prayer calls rang out seconds apart, an echoing hail of tinny Arabic syllables.

All the Turkish families sitting on their picnic blankets simultaneously began to eat.

These were the final days of Ramadan. I walked quietly across the barbecue area, observing this collective breaking of the fast. I must have looked as hungry as the begging cats and gulls also skulking around the ruins, because one of the Turkish patriarchs suddenly beckoned me to his family's folding table. A chair was pushed under my backside, a plate set down before me, a tea glass pressed into my hand, and nine pairs of eyes stared at me, friendly and attentive. I counted four generations. The old lady at the head of the table must have been the patriarch's mother, the younger women his daughters, and the small kids his grandchildren. I made gestures expressing my thanks, gave my name, and stammered where I had come from and where I was heading.

'Almanya?' the patriarch asked. Was I German? His grin bared a gold tooth as he fished his phone from his pocket. 'Almanya!'

He rang someone, yelled a few sentences in Turkish at the screen, and handed me the phone. I spied a man who did not look dissimilar to the patriarch and, in the background, a barbecue party like our own.

'Hello,' the second patriarch said in German, 'this is Nuremberg.'

He was the first man's cousin and had emigrated from Giresun to southern Germany. He and his guests were sitting on the balcony of a post-war building under a striped awning that immediately struck me as typical of a German suburb. We exchanged a few bewildered niceties. When this was over, the first patriarch took the phone from my hand and dialled the next number. I spoke to two more family men breaking their fast in Hanau and Dresden respectively.

We ate, we chatted, we laughed at my mistakes, and we ate some more. At some stage, when my plate was clean and my Turkish exhausted, I merely watched the others talking, without the remotest sense of being a stranger. I exchanged silent glances with the patriarch's mother, who spoke even less than I did – maybe because she had no teeth – and relaxed into the embrace of a family with members even on the outskirts of German cities.

The next morning, I went down to the harbour. The greenish water was teeming with barrel jellyfish. With their mushroom-shaped bodies, they hauled themselves through the waves in slow motion, infinitely lazily and without any apparent goal. As our ship cast off, a swirl of tumbling jellyfish formed in our wake.

The ship's name was *Altın Post* ('the golden fleece'). I was sharing the upper deck with about 100 tourists, most of whom spoke Arabic. They were from the Gulf – from Qatar, Bahrain, and the Emirates.

To my left sat a Saudi, who was gazing with delight at the forested mountainsides along the waterfront.

'We don't have anything like this at home. We have nothing but desert!'

But it wasn't only the scenery that had brought him and his three sons – all lanky boys in their acne phases – on holiday to the Black Sea coast.

'The Turks respect us and have the same god as us. Europeans believe only in their freedom. I don't want people looking at me oddly because my wife wears a niqab.'

Only then did I notice the woman standing behind her three sons. The black veil covered her entire body, with only a slit for the eyes. When I smiled at her, I thought I saw her eyes smiling back, but I couldn't be sure.

Many women on board were wearing niqabs. The veils made it hard to guess their age or how they were related to the men beside them. Were the men their sons, fathers, brothers, or husbands? I had been struck by these groups of Arab tourists in all the towns at the foot of the Pontic Mountains, but I didn't know if the Turks really welcomed them as heartily as that Saudi thought they did. A few days earlier, in Trabzon, I had met a young aviation engineer from Istanbul. As we drank tea, he had stared grimly at the female tourists at the neighbouring tables as they poked drinking straws under their niqabs.

'Look at them,' he hissed. 'What are these penguins doing here? Rich Arabs have popped up all over the place since Erdoğan came to power, buying houses, hotels, even whole villages. Eventually they'll take over the country and impose their rules on us. I don't want to live in a prison!'

A couple from Jordan were sitting next to me on the ship. The man spoke English and told me that his son was studying medicine in Dortmund. It was his and his wife's first time on the Black Sea. When the island that was the objective of our boat trip appeared, I asked the Jordanian what he'd heard about it.

'Nothing,' he said. 'Only that it's an island. Should I have heard something?' He looked at me expectantly.

There was a lot to hear. I had no idea where to start.

If you believe the ancient Greek myths, then this island was home to the strangest and most outlandish of peoples, the most barbaric of barbarians – the Amazons. Women who refused to subject themselves to men. Women who lived without men, who neither needed nor respected men, who made war on men and killed men. Women as cold and cruel and merciless as … well, men.

Fear of the Amazons led Jason and his Argonauts to keep out of their way on their voyage along the southern coast; they stayed far out at sea, stopping only on Giresun Island because the blind seer Phineus had instructed them to do so. There they found an altar of black stone 'where once the Amazons prayed together'. The warrior women, Apollonius writes, did not come together 'to burn on this altar offerings of sheep and oxen, but they used to slay horses, which they kept in great herds'.

The Amazons are bogeywomen galloping through the world of Greek myth. They are said to have only consorted with the men of neighbouring races to produce children, and to have rejected the babies if they turned out to be boys. They allegedly burned off their daughters' right breasts so that they could tense their bows in the saddle without impediment. It was this custom that explained why the Greeks called them the *a-mazos* ('breastless ones').

All of this must have been very hard to swallow for the Black Sea Greek settlers, who offered their own women-folk precious few freedoms. The ubiquitous depictions of Amazons from those times openly betray what ambivalent feelings must have been aroused by the idea of a caste of self-sufficient women warriors. Painted vases and reliefs show the Amazons wrestling in half-erotic, half-terrifying poses with the male heroes of the ancient world: alongside Hera-cles, who kills the Amazon queen Hippolyta after a tough struggle in order to steal her girdle; locked in combat with Theseus, who abducts Hippolyta in another version of the myth, prompting the Amazons to attack Athens in revenge; with Achilles, who unwittingly slays Penthesilea in the Trojan War and falls in love with her as he removes the helmet from the dying Amazon's head.

The Amazons come across as made-up characters in the myths, but they were by no means fairy-tale creatures to the Greeks, whose historians portrayed them as a real tribe that lived in the wider vicinity of the Black Sea long ago. Strabo situates their lost capital of Themiscyra at the mouth of the Thermodon river, not 150 km west of Giresun Island. Other historians refer to different Amazon settlements on the shore of the eastern Aegean, in Egypt, and in the northern Caucasus. As always, the most complex account is provided by Herodotus. He describes how the Amazons were taken prisoner by the Greeks during a failed raid on Athens, and overpowered the guards on their slave galleys, but then, for lack of any nautical knowledge, drifted aimlessly across the Black Sea. They were eventually washed up in the Cimmerian Bosporus, from where they marched inland and settled to the north-east of the Sea of Azov. There, they supposedly met the Scythians, with whom they entered into a strange symbiotic alliance. They formed a warrior society based on equal rights, with women and men bringing up children and fighting side by side. The custom among these Amazons, in Herodotus's telling, was that a woman could only marry once she had killed a man in battle.

Later Western historians viewed all of this as utter nonsense, naive fairy tales, a transparent retrospective attempt to embed a myth in reality. The Amazons, it was claimed far into the nineteenth century, were the spawn of the Greek imagination, invented not least to legitimise the inequality of gender relations in antiquity. After all, the barbarically twisted world of the Amazons illustrated what would happen if power were ever invested in women rather than men.

But then something unexpected happened. In the nineteenth century, a generation of Russian archaeologists better schooled in anatomy than their predecessors took a closer look at the skeletons found in the northern hinterland of the Black Sea underneath kurgans, the burial mounds of the ancient peoples of the steppes. It had been instinctively accepted that all of these warrior graves contained men, for why else would the dead be inhumed with weapons, with battle-axes and swords, bows and quivers, with their horses? But now, the archaeologists were astonished to come across the first warrior skeletons that were incontrovertibly female. Sometimes there were other, male skeletons lying sideways at their feet in the classic sacrificial position familiar to the archaeologists from other graves. Executed men as an adjunct to women's tombs – the finding stretched credulity, but very soon these early discoveries set a pattern. It is now estimated that underneath every fifth or perhaps every fourth kurgan in the northern Black Sea region lies not a male but a female warrior.

The Amazons really did exist. Maybe not in the way presented by Greek myths, but they were real. A society of mounted women warriors once lived on the shores of the Black Sea, and they must have given the heebie-jeebies to those Greeks who heard of them, or perhaps even met them in combat.

I gave the Jordanian on the tourist boat a slightly potted version of these tales. The Amazons, I said, were women warriors who had ridden into battle against men, killed men, and buried their war dead with sacrificed men.

The Jordanian stared at me with an expression of feigned horror that looked more like actual horror. 'I hope that there are none alive today.'

The island was tiny. About a mile from the shore, a series of grey rocks rose up from the sea, a green canopy of laurel and locust trees arcing over the hilltop. In the densest spot in this grove stood the remains of a Byzantine monastery. A second, older ruin dated back to ancient times, but the fragments of that temple were so weathered that no one could clearly say which gods had been worshipped there. It took less than half an hour to walk around the island. The rocks and trees and ruins were all encrusted with white bird droppings. Hundreds of cormorants – bat-like black birds drying their outspread wings in the sun – crouched on dead branches around the edge of the island. They brought to mind the birds that attacked Jason and his crew in the legend of the Argonauts as they approached the island, unleashing a hail of quills as sharp as arrows on the *Argo*.

The tourists toured the island in two groups. The guide of the larger group spoke Arabic, the other Turkish. Neither spoke any English. I would have given my right breast to understand what the two men told the veiled women about the Amazons.

Inside the ruined monastery, a woman warrior was waiting. Sitting on a throne that had been cobbled together out of rough-hewn wooden planks was a young Turkish woman dressed up as an Amazon. The tassels of her leather bodice dangled down over her crotch, and the thongs of her sandals were wound up to the knee around her bare legs. She was holding a spear in her left hand and staring at us with earnest, unmoving eyes, as stiff as a dummy in a shop window. The entrance to her niche in the wall was cordoned off to keep visitors at a distance. One after another, the tourists stepped up to the cord and snapped photos of the warrior. I watched in fascination as Arab women pulled selfie sticks from the folds of their niqabs and took pictures of themselves with the half-naked Amazon in the background.

On the boat back, I asked the Jordanian what the Arabic guide had said about the Amazons.

'The same as you. That they kill men.'

I pressed him. Had he portrayed the Amazons as good people or bad?

'Bad, obviously. They kill men.'

I asked the Jordanian to translate the question for his wife, who didn't speak any English. She was wearing a red headscarf that hugged her cheeks, and she had a mocking glint in her eye. She listened to the question and answered with a dry chuckle.

'The Amazons are good,' her husband translated. 'They kill men.'

As the ship made its way back to Giresun, I saw the Arab women standing in their niqabs at the bow. They were snapping selfies in the famous pose from *Titanic*. I wondered if they smiled under their veils, if they pursed their lips and sucked in their cheeks like women without veils did – or if they had a different eyes-only selfie language that outsiders like myself couldn't interpret.

That evening, I happened upon a bar called Amazon in a dark corner of Giresun city centre. It was the first bar I'd seen on the Turkish coast; I hadn't drunk a drop of alcohol since leaving Georgia. I sat down gratefully at one of the dark wooden tables, ordered an Efes beer, and kept track of the horse racing on the bar's TV with one eye – and on the patrons with the other.

It slowly dawned on me that the Amazon pub was completely Amazon-free. Not one of the drinkers was a woman.

Atatürk's eyes

The *Bandırma* was forty-one years old when she made her entrance onto the world stage. She had been built as a steam freighter in Paisley on the west coast of Scotland, from where she did the rounds of North Sea ports for five years under her original name, the *Trocadero*. She passed through the hands of two Greek owners before being acquired in 1894 by an Ottoman shipping company and deployed to the Black Sea under her new name. The *Bandırma* had an eventful career. She capsized in an accident, and it took a major effort to refloat her. During the First World War, a submarine tore a hole in one of her sides, and she was later hit by a torpedo. By the time she ended up in the Turkish Black Sea port of Samsun on 19 May 1919, she was an old, battered, and only passably seaworthy vessel.

Behind her lay a rough four-day voyage which could well have proved her last, given that her compass had given up the ghost on the way across the Black Sea from Istanbul. The sailors must have been glad to see the passengers make it ashore safe and sound. On board were four dozen Turkish officers and soldiers, a few administrative officers, and the unit's commander – an army inspector tasked with dissolving the remnants of the defeated Ottoman army in Anatolia in accordance with the Entente Powers' decree to the vanquished Ottoman Empire.

The inspector had no intention of executing this order. Mustafa Kemal Paşa, who was thirty-eight when he landed in Samsun, had other plans. He made his way across Anatolia, gathering together what remained of the war-weary army and ignoring the telegrams summoning him back to Istanbul, then proclaimed his own government – to which his superiors responded by sentencing him to death in absentia; made war on the Greeks – who were trying to annex the western part of the decaying Ottoman Empire with the approval of the victorious powers; drove their troops out of the country; seized control of the executive; forced the sultan to abdicate; disempowered the caliph; founded a republic; became its president; remoulded the empire into a nation; schooled his subjects to become citizens; put education before religion, elections before dynasties, the hat before the fez; chose Sunday over Friday, the Swiss Civil Code over sharia law, the Latin alphabet over the Arabic, the Christian calendar over the Islamic one; and eventually, after shaping the Turks in his image, allowed them to adopt surnames in the Western style. They responded by bestowing upon Mustafa Kemal the honorific title under which he took his place in history: Atatürk ('father of the Turks').

A year before the landing in Samsun, Atatürk had noted in his diary:

> Should I one day exercise great influence or power, I think it would be best to change our society in one fell swoop – immediately and within the shortest space of time. For unlike some others, I do not believe that this change can be achieved by leading the uneducated only step by step towards a higher level … It is not I who should move closer to them, but they to me.

Similarly to Peter the Great in Russia two centuries earlier, and as Lenin did with the Soviet Union after the October Revolution, Atatürk completely overhauled his country. What he and the two Russian reformers shared, regardless of their many ideological and historical differences, was a reversal of the old mirror-game between civilisation and barbarism. Peter

the Great modernised Russia through a violent Europeani-
sation of his empire. Lenin destroyed the tsarist system and
replaced it with imported Marxism. Atatürk broke with an
Islamic legacy and established a nation-state in the Western
mould. All three looked abroad for civilisation – and regarded
their own peoples as barbarians in need of radical re-educa-
tion, against their will if necessary.

When Atatürk summed up the great exorcism of barbarism
in front of the members of his party in 1927, he did so in a
marathon thirty-six-hour speech spread over several days. Its
first sentence was short: 'On 19 May I landed in Samsun.'

The day he came ashore from the *Bandırma* is still a Turkish
national holiday, and Atatürk, who did not know his precise
birth date, later symbolically declared himself a child of 19
May.

That day also marked a watershed moment for the Black
Sea. From the late fifteenth century to the early nineteenth
century, the Ottoman Empire and its vassal states had more
or less encircled the entire body of water, from the Caucasus
in the east through Anatolia in the south, the Balkans in the
west, and Crimea and the northern steppes. It was Catherine
the Great and her successors who gradually pushed the sultan-
ate back from the coast until, following its defeat in the First
World War, the weakened Ottoman Empire was in danger
of vanishing not just from the Black Sea but from the map
altogether. Before Atatürk took the lead of the Turkish liberation movement, its heads had dreamed of winning back
and reviving the lost empire. Atatürk imposed his vision of
a republican nation-state confined to its present dimensions,
and this undoubtedly saved Turkey from extinction. At the
same time, this process definitively reversed the balance of
power on the Black Sea. The Ottoman Empire was replaced

as the decisive power by the Soviet Union, which extended its influence to the henceforth-socialist Balkan states on the sea's western shore after Stalin's victory in the Second World War. For half a century, the coast of the Black Sea was red.

The *Bandırma*, whose landing in Samsun had set all this realignment in motion, had already been consigned to history by the time Atatürk held his party conference speech. A few years after that famous 19 May, the age-worn ship was retired from service, and its carcass was broken up for scrap at the docks on Istanbul's Golden Horn in 1925.

South of Samsun city centre, roughly where Atatürk came ashore that day, a scale model of the ship stands on the shore. Its black-painted hull contrasts with the non-blackness of the sea, which was metallic blue the day I arrived. Turkish families were posing for souvenir photos on the replica freighter. I climbed the iron staircase to the bridge to find Atatürk sitting in consultation with his closest confidants – wax-faced dummy officers in combat uniform decorated with red lampases and gold aiguillettes. Atatürk was presiding along one side of the planning table, his unbuckled pistol holster lying in front of him. His familiar face stood out from the rest of the group: the high forehead, the severely combed-back hair, the hard mouth, the piercing eyes as blue as the Black Sea.

Those eyes had followed every step I took after crossing the Georgian–Turkish border. Whenever I entered a hotel, Atatürk was staring at me from the wall behind the reception counter. Each time I paid for a room, his gaze met mine on every lira note and coin. In every restaurant, every cafe, every grocery store hung at least one of his canonical portraits. I saw his likeness on badges on elderly men's lapels; on stickers on cars and motorbikes; as busts outside government offices, libraries, and hospitals; tattooed on the biceps of young waiters.

The old administrative building in Samsun in which Atatürk had taken up quarters in 1919 had been converted into a museum. The display cases showed hats, shirts, and gloves Atatürk had worn; his shoes, cufflinks, ties, braces, and walking sticks; as well as teacups that had touched his lips. On the wall next to the toilet there was even a golden plaque engraved in Turkish and English:

ATATÜRK'ÜN KULLANDIĞI BANYO
RESTROOM USED BY ATATÜRK

I had often asked myself whether omnipresent Atatürk wasn't slowly getting on the Turks' nerves. On the bus from Giresun to Samsun, I had cautiously posed this question to my neighbour, a middle-aged engineer who had spent half his life in Zurich. He answered in fluent Swiss German that, during his student years in Ankara, he had witnessed the timid beginnings of a debate about Atatürk's mistakes, his authoritarian traits, his attitude towards minorities and dissenters, and his personality cult. But then ...

'You know what happened next.'

He cast a suspicious eye over the people nearby and, although none of the other passengers seemed to be listening, he mouthed the syllables silently.

'Er-do-ğan.'

Ever since the new autocrat had started to roll back the founding father's democratic reforms, Atatürk had become a symbolic figure for the opposition, as he usually was when one part of Turkey's soul was at loggerheads with the other. It wasn't the right time to discuss his mistakes. Those who disliked the present strongman instinctively harked back to the strongman of the past, and there was little room for manoeuvre between the two.

I could understand that liberal Turks preferred Atatürk's state to Erdoğan's. I was conscious that the country was virtually inconceivable in its current form without Atatürk, and that in Turkey's darkest hour he had almost singlehandedly dragged it out of the mire. I knew that it was still officially an offence to insult the memory of the founding father. And yet I repeatedly caught myself thinking that Turkey would only truly be free on that still-distant day when his portraits lay alongside the religions he had vociferously wished at the bottom of the sea.

In the wake of the *Argo*

The Pontic Mountains flattened out west of Samsun. As a more or less continuous range, they still screened the coast from the Anatolian hinterland, but their peaks were no longer capped with snow, their slopes were less steep than further east, the flat coastal strip was wider, and as the humid greenhouse climate gradually gave way to drier midsummer heat, the ubiquitous tea plantations were also gone. The more the mountains faded into the background, the more dominant the sea became. The first bathing beaches and seaside cafes appeared. The quotient of bars in the towns increased, and the headscarf count fell. From somewhere like Sinop onwards, halfway along the Turkish coast, I even saw the occasional woman drinking raki. My own surprise surprised me more than the sight itself.

It was the summer holidays, and my path increasingly crossed that of German Turks spending their vacation in their second homeland – or first, depending how you tally these things.

Ali had emigrated in 1972 from Giresun to Mönchengladbach, where he had worked in the textile industry until the textile industry was kaput. After losing his job, he moved to Gladbeck and worked down the mines until his back was kaput. At the time he got his disability certificate, the coal industry too was long since kaput, and Ali took early retirement. Now he spent the summertime in Giresun and the winters in Gladbeck.

We met at Samsun bus station, where Ali was waiting for a bus east and I for one heading west. He told me that his children seldom visited him in Giresun because they worked as hard in Germany as the Germans did, and when they did have some holiday, they preferred to go to Antalya on the Mediterranean, where the sunshine was more reliable than on the Black Sea coast. Ali showed me a photo of his family's allotment in Gladbeck. It had a small cherry tree in the middle. Every cherry tree in the world, Ali said, originally hailed from Giresun – or Cerasus, as the city was known in ancient Greek times. This was the root of the German word '*Kirsche*', the Turkish word '*kiraz*', the English word 'cherry', and names in many other languages. I'd heard about this theory before, but I had started to doubt it, because I hadn't spotted many cherry trees in Giresun. True, Ali said, nodding. Giresun's cherry trees had died off long ago; no one quite knew why. He used two fingers to zoom in on his allotment until the cherry tree in Gladbeck filled the entire screen. He examined it with a gentle, almost loving eye. Ali and the cherry tree: two exports from Giresun.

Şevki came to my attention in a harbour pub in Sinop, because he was making a phone call in German with an audible Cologne accent. His father had wound up in Stuttgart in 1969 as one of the first wave of *Gastarbeiter* ('guest workers') and had helped shunt trains there. Only later, after relocating to Cologne, did he send for his wife and children.

Şevki had come of age by then and had been working as a bookkeeper in Turkey, but all he could find in Cologne was a temporary job in a cosmetics factory. It was there that he met his wife, also a child of migrant workers. The two of them had later run a newsstand together on the right bank of the Rhine. Now, Şevki was longing to retire. He wanted to spend the autumn of his life in Sinop, the city of his birth, where, 2,500 years before him, Diogenes had come into the world – the blissfully happy philosopher who lived in a barrel and asked Alexander the Great to step out of his sunlight. His memorial stood by the road into the city, a tatty-bearded marble Greek on a capacious wooden barrel, holding in his left hand the lantern he supposedly shone in the faces of market-goers in Athens in broad daylight as he was unsuccessfully 'looking for a human'. Sinop, Şevki told me, had been found to be the Turkish city with the most satisfied inhabitants in a recent nationwide survey. Şevki had been coming here every summer for twenty years to drink his beer in the harbour pub. A few years ago, the pub's old owner, a biker with a goatee and shades whose photo was above the counter, had died. Şevki had asked the owner's sons if they would sell him the pub – he could imagine taking it on – but the sons wanted to keep it in the family. Şevki was now glad that they had rejected his offer. He had the modest smile of a philosopher who had come to understand that lifting a beer glass was less strenuous than lugging a beer barrel.

Beyond Sinop, the buses no longer ran along the coast but took a larger highway on the southern side of the mountains. I didn't want to lose sight of the sea, though, so I plonked my bag down beside the coast road and put up my thumb. No one ever took me very far, because most drivers were only travelling from one village to the next, but I rarely had to wait longer than five minutes for the next lift. For the next two days, I exchanged one passenger seat for the next.

I met Erol and Birol, two brothers who produced T-shirts in Istanbul and exported them to Russia. They had been visiting their parents in Inebolu but were so bored with their family by the second day that they'd skived off and were heading to the beach in their van. The three of us, all wearing shorts, sat on the connected front seat of the car. Erol was in the middle and would underscore every sentence he uttered by slapping our bare legs, mine to the right and his brother's to the left. He talked in English about his children. His wife had only wanted one child, but Erol thought one was too few – he'd heard that everyone who was an only child had psychological problems. So they'd had a second, but neither of them wanted any more – especially his wife, who had six sisters. The Turks, Erol said, were only slowly learning that more children didn't mean greater prosperity.

I met a second Erol who had fifty chickens, twenty-five cows, and an uncle in Berlin. He took me along on his tractor and bought me a cup of tea at a petrol station on the way. The Turks drink a lot of tea, I said in Turkish; the Germans drink a lot of beer. Erol held an erect index finger against his crotch and let it wilt before my eyes until it hung down, sad and bent. *That*, his grin said, *is what happens to men who drink beer. That*, I thought, *is how to persuade men to stay off beer.*

I met two taciturn youngsters who drove frantically, and smoked frantically as they drove, though they looked too young to be doing either.

I met the captain of a freighter on home leave. He spoke English, though he chose to answer all my questions about the Black Sea with colourful tales about the oceans.

Further west, the mountains curved back closer to the coast. The road wound its way in sharp bends along rock faces that fell steeply into the sea to our right or ended in cliffs with conifers sprouting from them. Islands of foam floated in the turbulent waters by the shore. Whenever the waves broke on the rocks, I would see fountains of spray shoot skywards as if in slow motion, hang there in the air, and then collapse in on themselves again.

In every coastal village, livestock was being sold at improvised markets. Kurban Bayramı, the Feast of the Sacrifice, was just around the corner. As if they knew what lay in store for them, cattle and sheep cowered in the corners of rough-hewn wooden enclosures strewn with sawdust.

On slaughtering day, I arrived in Cakraz, a village of 200 souls halfway between Sinop and Istanbul, surrounded by crags. Ten cows had been put to death on the market green that morning. Shortly after sunrise, the butcher had cut their carotid arteries, and when I reached the slaughter ground at 3 p.m., Cakraz's inhabitants were still hacking up the cattle. The corpses were spread out all over the green. Most had by now been reduced to a head in a swarm of flies, a hide, a heap of innards, and a puddle of blood in the grass. The stomachs were lying in the sun, all swollen, enormous green bubbles with sunlight shining through their transparent membranes.

Mustafa the butcher was a mountain of a man. His blood-soaked vest strained over a colossal belly that encircled his body. Sweat streamed from every pore of his massive head, to be absorbed by a towel wrapped around his bull-like neck. This was Mustafa's big day, and he was enjoying himself. He was directing the slaughter with barked instructions, hopping from one assistant to the next, yelling at the men who were cutting up the last carcass with a chainsaw, making a revolving gesture to the woman at the meat grinder to encourage her to up the tempo, and snatching a knife from a man's grip to show him how to scrape the meat from the dangling halves of cattle. He shouted, urged, stamped his feet, rolled his fat-garlanded eyes, and occasionally lapsed into a sort of dance that involved him throwing his huge arms – lobster-red on top, white under his armpits – into the air and wobbling his belly with a wiggle of his hips. He wasn't a butcher; he was a conductor high on blood.

I carried on watching as the cows were transformed into ever smaller pieces. No one took umbrage at my curiosity. One of the men handed me a knife and pointed with a grin to the scaffold from which the cattle halves were hanging. I scraped as well as I could.

At the end of the day, the last meat parcels to be distributed were stacked high on a large sheet of plastic. The butcher's wife, of similar stature to her husband, was slicing up the innards with a long knife and slapping a chunk of every heart, liver, lung, and kidney onto every pile. The villagers hauled their sacrificial meat home in plastic tubs.

Not long before I left, I saw the butcher suddenly grab his throat and disappear around the corner of a house. He was coughing, retching, and gasping; it sounded horrible. I wanted to go after him, but a smiling villager held me back. After a couple of minutes, the butcher reappeared, pale-faced but buzzing as if nothing had been amiss. I never found out what had happened to him. Maybe he was a vegetarian at heart.

'Barbaric!'

Zafer Türkmen was less than enthusiastic when I told him about the slaughter in Cakraz. He didn't think much of the Feast of the Sacrifice.

'Why would Allah want us to sacrifice animals to him? Mohammed would have done better to instruct humans to plant trees!'

Zafer was a doctor, an anaesthetist, and head of an Istanbul eye clinic, a successful guy in his sixties and the sort of Turk who doesn't leave you uncertain for long about which of his country's two national souls most closely resembles his own. First and foremost, though, he was – as he assured me in English – a yachtsman.

We were sitting in the small fishing port of Amasra, a little west of Cakraz, on a sailing boat that had immediately caught my eye because I'd seen so few of them on my journey. Wealthy Russians preferred motor cruisers, the Georgians didn't have any money, Turkish sailors preferred the Mediterranean, and the Black Sea was still considered the back of beyond by Western yachtsmen.

Zafer aimed to change that. He dreamed of filling the Black Sea with white sails. To tempt boats to the Turkish coast, he had organised a voyage on the trail of the Argonauts. He and fifty other sailors had set out from the Aegean two months ago. They had passed through the Bosporus together and then, like Jason before them, had stuck close to the southern shore as they headed for Georgia. After reaching Poti, they had turned around and were now on their way back to Istanbul.

Spying the yachts in the harbour, I had walked along the quay until by chance I heard someone on one of the boats making a phone call in German. Suat, who was from Lake Constance, had introduced me to Zafer, and the three of us were now sitting together on his boat. I won Zafer's affections the moment I produced my old German edition of the legend of the Argonauts from my rucksack. Excitedly, he went over the route with me. Did I not agree with him that the *Argo* must have put in at Amasra, as there was no other natural cove far and wide? Was I not struck by how exactly the descriptions of the landscape in the legend matched the actual coastline, and how precisely Apollonius had depicted the sea? Zafer didn't read the tale of the *Argo* as a myth but as a travelogue, despite knowing that its author was not an ancient yachtsman but a writer who had compiled his knowledge from a variety of texts.

'Philosophy is the origin of science,' Zafer philosophised, 'and myths are the origin of all travel.'

I got up the next morning after a short night at my hotel and carried my rucksack down to the harbour in the dark. The sailors wanted to set off early towards the Bosporus, and Suat, the man from Lake Constance, had offered me a lift on his boat, a yacht named *Mandolin Wind*.

We swung out of the harbour onto the open sea just as the sun came up between the water and the sky. As the sun rose, the colour of the sea shifted from anthracite through violet to deep blue. Suat steered the boat a few hundred metres northwards before setting a course parallel to the rocky coast. A dozen boats preceded us; a dozen followed behind. At a radio signal, each raised its sails simultaneously. A gentle crosswind propelled the Argonauts forwards.

Suat was in his early sixties and had the calm and introspective features of a man who would rather say a word too few than one too many. He had left Turkey for Germany at the age of eight and spent the majority of his life in the same small southern German town. That was where he had met Marga, the quiet German woman with whom he shared his life and the boat. Since retiring, they spent more time on the water than on land.

Suat's mother had split up with her husband at an early stage, back in Turkey. She explained to her children later that, in the 1960s, Turkish men had viewed almost any divorced woman as fair game, which is why she had emigrated to Germany with Suat and his three older sisters. For a few years, she had sewed men's suits in a textile factory, then she switched to a place that manufactured toilet cisterns. As she brought her four children up on her own, she banned them from having anything to do with other Turkish children. They were to learn German.

Suat, who spoke fluently in the Baden dialect, had worked as a sales rep for chemical products. Business had been good enough for him to finance the boat and early retirement. He had two passports and made liberal use of them. Like the other German Turks I had met on my travels, he lived in two worlds, but in his case there seemed to be a wider gulf between them – perhaps because his mother had brought him up as she did; perhaps due to his German wife; perhaps because his own children had, as he told me, never learned Turkish properly. That morning, as he chatted with the other Turkish sailors, I had got the impression that Suat was considered a Turk here, but he revealed that this wasn't entirely the case. The others called him *Almancı*, a Germanised Turk – someone who had lived over there for so long that he had more in him of there than of here. Suat didn't appreciate the word – just as he didn't appreciate being called a Turk in Germany.

My thoughts turned to Scyles, the Scythian king whose mother had raised him so thoroughly in the Greek tradition that Herodotus described him as becoming half Greek, someone who crossed over between cultures; spoke Greek; took a Greek wife; and, dressed in Greek costume, passed in and out of the Black Sea colonies without being identified as a barbarian. Eventually, both sides hated him: the Scythians because he was no longer a Scythian, and the Greeks because he blurred the boundary between them and the barbarians.

I had to think of all the Turks in Berlin, of the ties that still bound second- and third-generation immigrants to Turkey. Ties that generally remained imperceptible to Germans.

And I had to think back to The Admiral of my childhood, the émigré who in my imaginings had made a ship his home.

Just like Suat.

A BLACK SEA LEXICON
Entry no. 3: *Bosporus*

The sailors dropped me off in Zonguldak, where they were going to spend the night. I travelled on along the coast by bus. I stayed overnight in Eregli, where I saw the cave from which Heracles supposedly once dragged the hellhound Cerberus; got on the next bus; saw passing coastal villages where the hazelnut harvest was drying in the late-summer sun; stayed overnight in Şile; caught a third bus; felt the roads increasingly drawn away from the coast and sucked south-westwards into Istanbul's cobweb of traffic arteries; and, after a few further bus journeys, I finally stood at the northern mouth of the Bosporus.

Freighters were waiting all around for the signal to proceed through the straits. They were followed by other ships converging from the horizon, the Black Sea's entire traffic moving as if through a funnel into the narrow İstanbul Boğazı, the gullet of Istanbul. Marking the eastern and western banks of the entrance were two lighthouses, Anadolu Feneri and Rumeli Feneri – the lights on the Anatolian and the 'Roman' sides. Nowhere are Asia and Europe so dramatically separated as here, and nowhere are the two souls of Turkey so symbolically juxtaposed.

A hippie couple from Istanbul had opened a small cafe on the rocks above the eastern side, having dropped out of the music business after running a concert venue on the other side, the European shore. Both of them said that Istanbul had drained them of life. The traffic jams, the smog, the chaos, the never-ending influx of people whose exact number no one knew any more – fifteen million, seventeen million, or more. They had turned their backs on the city when their daughter was born. Efsun, whose name meant 'magic', crawled in her nappy through the cafe that her parents had named Efsunlu Bahçe ('the magic garden'). I sat beneath dreamcatchers and looked out at the sea until the sun set and the lighthouses on either side of the Bosporus came on.

Legend has it that Heraclius, the seventh-century Byzantine emperor, had one of his enemies decapitated and thrown into the Bosporus. It is said that the body floated south on the current into the Sea of Marmara, while the head sank immediately. However, the skull, picked bare, allegedly washed up months later on a Black Sea beach north of the Bosporus.

This tale sounds like fiction, but it suggests that the Greeks knew – at the very latest in Byzantine times, but probably earlier – the solution to an enigma which Europeans of the early modern era struggled to crack. The enigma went like this: why, if the salt water of the Black Sea flows out through the Bosporus into the Mediterranean, and at the same time dozens of rivers fill the Pontic basin with fresh water, is the Black Sea still a sea? Shouldn't its salinity steadily decline until at some point it is just a lake?

The scientific explanation for this mystery was discovered

in 1679 by a twenty-one-year-old Italian by the name of Luigi Ferdinando Marsigli, who steered his boat out into the middle of the Bosporus and dropped anchor. He paid out a long lead-weighted line that was marked at regular intervals with white bits of cork. Marsigli watched the line drift south with the current towards the Sea of Marmara. However, as the lead weights gradually drew the end of the line down into the depths, what Marsigli had been anticipating actually happened. He noticed that the cork markers a few yards under the surface of the water altered their direction of travel. The line curved back from south to north like a bow until the Italian researcher saw the first pieces of cork glowing deep in the water under his keel.

This confirmed what Marsigli had heard from fishermen in the Bosporus, who had long observed the phenomenon by how their nets moved without being able to express it in scientific terms. There was not one current but two opposed currents running through the straits. At the surface, water flowed south out of the Black Sea into the Sea of Marmara, through the Dardanelles and on into the Mediterranean. Yet Mediterranean water was simultaneously streaming north through the deeper regions of the Bosporus into the Black Sea. These two currents were kept apart by their differing levels of salinity. The water from the Black Sea, lighter and less salty due to the inflow of rivers, stayed on the surface, whereas the heavier salt water from the Mediterranean flowed along the bed of the Bosporus.

At the time, Marsigli knew nothing of the theory of how the straits had been created approximately 8,000 years earlier as a result of a land-splitting deluge, which is also when the two-level fluid dynamics must have originated. Ever since, the Black Sea has been filled and drained through the Bosporus, both at the same time, both without pause.

It is not just the water that flows in both directions: the Bosporus has also been a bottleneck for migratory movements between the Mediterranean and Black Sea regions. When the Greeks pressed north with their war galleys and merchant ships, they had to row against the surface current, as did the Argonauts, whose laborious progress through the Bosporus is described by Apollonius. Other invasive species found it easier – they could simply ride the undercurrent, like all the fish, crabs, snails, jellyfish, and plankton species that have immigrated into the Black Sea from the south over millennia.

Other passengers negotiated the Bosporus in more subtle and current-free ways. When Vladimir the Great, ruler of the pagan Kievan Rus princedom, was looking for an appropriate religion for his realm north of the Black Sea in the tenth century, he sent out a host of envoys to gather information about the beliefs of the surrounding peoples. The prince immediately rejected the Islam of the Volga Bulgars when his scouts informed him of the Muslims' abstinence. 'Drinking is the pleasure of the Rus!' Vladimir thundered. 'Without it we cannot exist!' The Khazars' Judaism bothered him due to circumcision and their nomadic lifestyle, and the Europeans' Catholic churches were reportedly drab and dull. On the other hand, Vladimir's scouts praised to the skies the Orthodox church of Byzantium, the seat of the Greek patriarch on the Bosporus. And so the prince ultimately decided in favour of the Christian God from the other side of the Black Sea. Vladimir was baptised in Crimea, and his subjects were forcibly converted not long afterwards via mass bathing in the Dnieper in Kiev.

Orthodox Christianity was introduced via the Bosporus into present-day Ukraine, before spreading from Kiev to all parts of the Russian Empire over the ensuing centuries. In the meantime, the Ottomans captured Byzantium and used the Bosporus as a channel to export their own religion. Imams, Qur'anic teachers, and construction materials for mosques were shipped northwards as Islam spread around the coasts of the Black Sea.

Twice during my travels, I witnessed how the Bosporus continued to wash all kinds of jetsam into the Black Sea.

A few days after arriving in Istanbul, I was walking along the Golden Horn, the narrow, watery appendix jutting inland from the western shore of the straits. The Greek patriarchate still has its seat, the official centre of the Orthodox Christian Churches, in Fener district on the southern bank of the Golden Horn. It withstood the population exchange of 1923 and also survived the 1955 Istanbul pogroms, which caused many of the remaining Greeks to turn their backs on Turkey.

It was a Sunday morning. A few dozen people sat praying in the gilded interior of St George's Cathedral, most of them pilgrims and tourists from Greece. Polyphonic choruses rang out, and through the altar door strode a grey-bearded priest, holding in his right hand a sceptre in the shape of a two-headed snake and flanked by train-bearers keeping the ends of his vestments off the floor; he looked like a bride being guided to the altar. For the next two hours, I listened to the Orthodox liturgy that had been sung here, almost unchanged, for millennia.

Even while I was in Istanbul, the patriarchate next to St George's Cathedral must have been polishing the document that would, a few months later, send shockwaves through the Christian world north of the Black Sea. The annexation of Crimea and the war in Donbass had also widened the religious rift between Russia and Ukraine. Although the Orthodox clergy in Kiev were still officially under the authority of the Patriarch of Moscow, the more bitter the hostilities had become, the more insistently the Ukrainians had demanded their religious independence. The patriarchate in Istanbul finally granted their wish: in January 2019, a plane flew across the Black Sea carrying the Tomos, a decree that officially separated the Ukrainian Orthodox Church from its Russian counterpart, triggering outrage in the Kremlin.

Also during my stay in Istanbul, I heard that a Turkish Black Sea fisherman had found the first ever pufferfish in his nets that summer. A tropical fish species in the Black Sea: what any marine scientist would have relatively recently taken for a joke now sounded like the plausible starting point of a horror scenario. For a long time, the low temperature of the Black Sea had been one of the major barriers preventing Mediterranean invaders from swarming through the Bosporus. Over the previous three and a half decades, however, the sea's average temperature had warmed by a good 2 degrees centigrade, and scientists were expecting that its surface temperature might rise by a further 5 degrees by the end of the century. Climate change had cleared the way for the pufferfish to enter.

Day after day, I took Istanbul's ferries from one shore of the Bosporus to the other, from continent to continent, from Asia to Europe and back, constantly astonished that no one other than me was astonished. Only after a while did I realise that only tourists talked about the 'Asian' shore – Istanbulites referred to it as Anatolian. For people here, taking a ferry across the Bosporus was not an intercontinental journey but a routine commute.

Still, I couldn't wipe the grin off my face whenever I stood in the bows of one of the ferries and fed the gulls sesame-sprinkled pastries. It was half a year since I had stood by the Cimmerian Bosporus on the opposite side of the sea, beside the straits between Russia and Crimea at the beginning of the Asian half of my journey. This was where it ended. The rest of my travels would lead me through Europe. Whatever that meant.

Bulgaria

Cherno more / *Черно море*

If the De'il was minded to get us into the Black Sea
quick, he was like to do it whether we would or no.

Bram Stoker, *Dracula,* 1897

The renamed

Autumn had set in by the time I left Istanbul behind. To the west of the Bosporus, in Thrace, Turkey's tiny European tip, the air was full of the scent of mushrooms. Everywhere in the forests I saw people creeping through the undergrowth with baskets. Young men with vans waited on the roadside to buy the mushrooms from the gatherers on behalf of a vegetable exporter near the Bulgarian border. Huge, fat, highly fragrant porcini filled the backs of the vans; I'd never seen so many of them in one place before.

Just over a mile from the border lay a tiny seaside village called Begendik, which consisted of a hundred houses, a mosque, and a teahouse. I saw more stray dogs in the streets than humans. The spartan teahouse was empty apart from a glowing wood-fired oven, a few chairs, and the obligatory Atatürk portrait on the wall. The landlord was a toothless old man whose grandparents had been expelled from Bulgaria into Turkey in 1935, like most people's grandparents here, with the exception of those whose grandparents had been expelled earlier, in 1927, or later, in 1954. The old man reeled off the dates without thinking, the details of a long litany of suffering etched into his memory.

When the ethnic patchwork of the Ottoman Empire was brutally unpicked in the aftermath of the First World War, the governments of Bulgaria, Greece, and Turkey drove their minorities in the tri-border region of Thrace into the others' arms. The Greeks and Bulgarians disappeared from the villages on the Turkish side of the border, and into their abandoned houses moved Turks who had been simultaneously expelled from Bulgaria and Greece. The region's Albanians, Bosniaks, Macedonians, and Armenians were also caught up in this giant game of musical chairs.

The hardest nut for the ethnic jigsaw-puzzlers to crack was the Pomaks – Slavic Muslims whom no one knew quite where to banish to because they were too Turkish for the Bulgarians, too Bulgarian for the Turks, and not Greek enough in any respect for the Greeks. A few miles inland from Begendik, in an even smaller border village called Sislioba, I found a woman whose ancestors had spoken Pomak, but that was long ago, and the Pomaks in Atatürk's Turkey had been smart enough to forget their Slavic language as quickly as possible, just as the Pomaks in socialist Bulgaria had been smart enough not to exhibit their Qur'ans.

The woman with the Pomak ancestors was sitting in the deserted market square with her son at a stall piled high with honey, jams, and herbal teas. It looked as if the two of them were waiting for tourists, although it was inconceivable that any would turn up – the village lay in the depths of the Thracian forest, close to the EU's external border that ran to the north and whose nearest crossing point was dozens of miles away.

The honey-seller had a jolly face, which was framed by a green headscarf. She didn't know for sure on which side of the border her Pomak ancestors had lived, but she knew a great deal about the people who had sneaked through Sislioba in recent years on their way to the border – people with scared eyes and whispering voices, without passports or money, dressed in flimsy jackets and carrying no luggage. For a time, the Thracian forest had been full of them, until the Turkish army reinforced the border fence and sent patrols out into the woods two years previously. Since then, very few refugees had been sighted in Sislioba.

The honey-seller's son, who must have been around thirty, was tall and thickset and somewhat slow. He had gentle and girlish black eyes, which looked as if they might at any moment burst into tears, and his lower lip quivered when he spoke.

His mother asked with a smile if I couldn't find her son a German wife. 'Then, at long last, I'll be rid of him.'

She drew her son's head against her shoulder and patted his cheek.

The son looked at me. His lip quivered. 'Can you find a wife for me? In Germany?'

'I'll try, but aren't there any women in Sislioba?'

The son's eyes went all watery. 'They're all related to me. Can you find one in Germany? Please? In Germany?'

The mother told me about a group of Syrians who had appeared in Sislioba a few years previously.

'Zdraveyte!' they had shouted to the Turks in Bulgarian. 'Zdraveyte!'

The Turks understood enough to grasp that the Syrians thought they were on the other side of the border. When they made it clear to the refugees that they were in Turkey, the Syrians broke down and cried. Their smugglers had led them through the forest for days and eventually assured them that the EU border was behind them before vanishing. The Syrians had been swindled out of all their money.

The Turks gave the weeping Syrians some food, as Turks tend to when someone weeps. Then the police had turned up and driven the refugees away to a camp. The mother didn't know what had become of them. They had never been seen in Sislioba again.

The son was still going on about a German wife as we said goodbye.

'Write down my number, so you can call me when you find her ...'

I hope he isn't still waiting for that call from Germany.

On a coach full of red-eyed early risers, I travelled towards Bulgaria on a leaden autumn morning. The route to the border crossing led not along the coast but in a wide arc through the countryside. The turbulence created by the coach sent the rain streaming horizontally across the side windows. V-shaped flocks of birds headed south under a grey October sky.

In the seat next to me was a man who addressed me first in Bulgarian and Turkish before we agreed on Russian. His name was Gürcan Güneş and he was on his way to visit relatives in Bulgaria. His Turkish surname meant 'sun'. Of all the names Gürcan had had in his fifty years of life, this one was his favourite; he wouldn't have chosen it otherwise.

Gürcan had narrow, clever, agile eyes, and he dressed like a man without the remotest interest in style. Under the chequered pattern of his short-sleeved shirt bulged the chest of an athlete. He explained that he had played football in his youth and had been well on the way to turning professional when he was laid low by a knee injury. He had become an engineer instead. Gürcan now sold metal hoses for a Turkish machine engineering company and had built up a side business in satellite dishes. He had a few hundred clients at a small profit, but the volume made it worthwhile. He owned a five-storey house in Istanbul, where he lived with his wife, his two children, and his elderly parents.

Gürcan had spent the second half of his life in Turkey and the first half in Bulgaria, where he was born in 1969 as one of just under 800,000 Turks whose forefathers had escaped the expulsions of the early twentieth century. Later, in the socialist era, Bulgaria had been suspicious of its Muslim minorities but, for cynical reasons, expulsions were no longer the political weapon of choice. During the Cold War, the Turkish–Bulgarian border had hardened into the Iron Curtain, the stated objective of which was to keep the proletariat in the country. This meant that the Bulgarian Turks were trapped in the Eastern Bloc alongside the Bulgarians themselves.

Nevertheless, they remained a thorn in the side of the regime in Sofia. Centuries of Ottoman dominance in the Balkans had not been forgotten, and the mere presence of a Turkish minority stoked old fears. Nearly one in ten inhabitants of socialist Bulgaria was a Turk, and the ratio was rising slightly because the Muslims had more children than the rest of the population. This led the authorities to hatch a dastardly plan in the mid-1980s: they might not be able to get rid of the Turks, but they could make them disappear, make them invisible, by destroying their identity.

Gürcan was sixteen when soldiers appeared one day in his hometown of Kurkariya. They made their way through the factories, the collective farms, and the schools, taking the Turks aside in each one. The soldiers had a simple request: the Turks were to choose new names. Bulgarian ones.

Gürcan's father, who had been called Enver Süleymanov all his life, was known as Encho Stanishev after the renaming campaign. Gürcan's own new identity card was marked Gensho Stanishev.

He was still at school at the time. It was clear, he said, that his Bulgarian teachers were embarrassed by the campaign. 'From one day to the next, they had to get used to calling us by different names. They were obviously ashamed, but not one of them dared not to go along with it.'

What made matters worse was that it was customary in

Bulgaria to use patronyms in addition to first names and surnames. Gürcan's full name, when his father was still called
Enver, was Gürcan Enverov Süleymanov. Now he was called
Gensho Enchev Stanishev. The situation was more complicated for Gürcan's father, whose own father was long dead
when renaming began. He and hundreds of thousands of
other Turks were nonetheless compelled to adopt Bulgarian
patronyms, which meant that they had to give their dead
fathers posthumous new first names.

'They forced us to change dead people's names. Can you
believe it? People long buried in the cemetery! What kind of
a person thinks up such things?'

Gürcan's expression was so indignant that it was as if the
matter had occurred mere days back, not three and a half
decades ago.

The official designation of this campaign harked back to the
name chosen by the nineteenth-century Bulgarian resistance
movement against Turkish domination: the regime spoke of
a 'process of renaissance'. In macabre fashion, this was quite
apt for a scheme to rename the dead. Above all, however,
it brought home to Turkish Bulgarians what the state really
thought of them. Concurrently with the renaming campaign,
they were banned from using their language. There was also
a more severe crackdown on their religion, which had never
been welcome in socialist Bulgaria.

Individual Turks who were not willing to be reborn as Bulgarians resisted the directives in the late 1980s. Riots broke
out and people died. Ultimately, when communism's imminent collapse seemed nigh, the regime decided to sort out the
problem in the traditional fashion after all. For a three-month
period in the summer of 1989, the Iron Curtain was raised
exclusively for Muslims, and party secretary Todor Zhivkov

proclaimed that the path abroad was open to anyone who wished to take it. The Turks understood that this was not an invitation but an ultimatum. That summer, around 350,000 of them packed up whatever they could lash to the roofs of their Soviet cars, and the roads south were black with people. It was Europe's largest ethnic cleansing campaign since the end of the Second World War.

Gürcan was lucky enough to escape almost unscathed. When the great expulsion took place, he was serving in the Bulgarian army, where he got to know a Turkish businessman who offered him a job in Turkey. He arrived in Istanbul in 1990 with only a suitcase in his hand. A year later, he brought his wife over, then his parents. Things had turned out well for Gürcan, better than for most of the displaced, who quickly realised that, after four decades behind the Iron Curtain, they were very different Turks to the Turks in Turkey. When Bulgaria's communist regime crumbled shortly after that fateful year of 1989, around 150,000 Turks returned to the villages and towns from which they had been expelled.

Gürcan's path had been stony at first too. Not all Turks in Istanbul had immediately accepted him as a Turk, he said. 'They were often Anatolians who had themselves emigrated to Istanbul. It's the same old story: uneducated people don't like migrants, even if they themselves are migrants.'

When the Turkish authorities issued him a new passport, they asked Gürcan which of his many names they should print in it. His Bulgarian passport contained the completely wrong surname, Milanov, which had been given to him on leaving the army by a bureaucratic error that Gürcan had never bothered to correct because he wanted to limit his dealings with the Bulgarian authorities. He was looking for a completely fresh start altogether; he didn't want any of his old names back. Gürcan was dreaming of a career as a businessman and he longed for something clear, memorable, and positive. A little earlier, he had seen a billboard in Istanbul with the name of an insurance company emblazoned on it in large letters: Güneş. Sun. Gürcan Güneş. That was what he needed.

When I met Gürcan on the bus, the Turks in Bulgaria had long since recovered their old names. The successors of the communist regime had distanced themselves from the 'process of renaissance' and condemned the eviction of the Turks. What had happened was far in the past, and when Gürcan talked about his life in Turkey, he did his best to make the story sound like not a victim's monologue but an account of voluntary emigration, an émigré's tale of rags to riches.

But what was done was done. When we reached the border, two Bulgarian customs officers climbed onto the bus. Gürcan had worked himself into a lather – he had been telling me about the renaming of the dead – but the closer the officers came, the quieter his voice became. When they took our passports, he fell silent. I could only see his jaws grinding together.

Frogmen

At the mouth of the Rezovo river, which separates Turkey from Bulgaria, three men were trying to pull a motorboat out of the water with an old Mercedes. The Mercedes was screeching and smoking, but still the boat wouldn't budge. Two of the men began to push the car from the back, and I joined in. We wedged our heels into the ground and threw our whole weight against the car, but the tyres just kept spinning. The bank was too steep, and the boat was too heavy. The air smelled of burnt rubber.

The men decided to come back the next day with a tractor. I

was about to leave, when the water by the motorboat rippled. A harpoon rose from the water, followed by an arm, a snorkel, and a head. At last, a whole man stood before me in a camouflage-patterned diving suit. He waddled ashore on long flippers and eased the neoprene hood off his head. His white hair was cropped short, and water dripped from his bushy eyebrows.

In English, I asked the timeless question you always ask men by the sea. 'So? Caught anything?'

He shook his head. 'No fish out there today.'

I looked out over the sea and wondered if the harpooneer had been poaching in Turkish waters. On the far side of the river mouth stood a watchtower under a flag bearing the red crescent. The man laughed when I asked him if the border guards didn't get jumpy when they spotted a diver.

'Not any more. Communism is over.' He brushed the drops from his hair with his left hand. 'You couldn't even get close to the border in the past. All of this was an exclusion zone.' With the side of his hand, he hacked two trenches in the air. 'First border. Second border. Between them, no-man's land. Where are you from?'

'Germany.'

He nodded grimly. 'Lots of Germans died here.'

'So I heard.'

About 4,000 East German citizens are estimated to have tried to flee through the Iron Curtain into Turkey while holidaying on the Bulgarian Black Sea beaches. Very few made it across, and not all of them were captured alive. Other inhabitants of Eastern Bloc countries – from Poland, Hungary, Czechoslovakia, and the Soviet Union – also launched escape bids from here. The archives of the Bulgarian foreign ministry recorded 415 foreign tourists whose trails went cold along this green border between 1961 and 1989.

The old man put the harpoon to his shoulder and pretended to shoot. 'Lots. Lots and lots.' He lowered the harpoon in embarrassment. 'I'm sorry.'

I looked at him in surprise. 'It wasn't your fault.'

I noticed that something was playing on his mind. He seemed to be trying to formulate a sentence, and his lips opened several times, but nothing came out. Eventually, he shook his head abruptly. 'I don't like talking about it.'

'I understand.'

'Sorry.' He shouldered his flippers and harpoon. 'Enjoy the rest of the day.'

I watched him walk up the bank, stow his diving gear in the boot of a parked car, and drive off without looking back.

The following morning, after a night in the border village of Rezovo, I slung my rucksack over my shoulder and set off north on foot, along the seashore.

The coast was rocky, rugged, jagged, and dotted with bushes that the wind had sculpted into bizarre slanted shapes. Stony headlands encrusted with brightly coloured lichen – turquoise, purple, orange, and pink – projected far out into the water. Cormorants dried their outspread wings on isolated rocky islets.

After a few miles, the dense forest of the Strandzha mountains descended to the water's edge. Beneath some tall oaks, my path was suddenly blocked by a fence that stretched back inland from the shore – vertical concrete posts, lines of rusty barbed wire. Metal bars had been attached to the tops of the posts, so that the wire was tilted to one side, obviously to make it harder to climb over the fence from the north. The entire structure had clearly fallen into disuse and, noticing which way the barrier sloped, I realised that these must be the old border installations from the Cold War era – a section of the Iron Curtain. I had known before the old guy with the harpoon mentioned it that a second fence had run a few miles away from the actual border, the boundary of no-man's land, designed to fool people who had crossed it by making them think they were free so they would drop their guard.

My mind immediately went back to the story the honey-seller on the Turkish side had told me about the Syrians who believed that the EU border lay behind them because their traffickers had deceived them. The direction of escape had been reversed between Turkey and Bulgaria. Once, the path to freedom had led south; now, the route to safety led north.

I followed the fence a few hundred metres into the forest. There was no end in sight – the concrete posts reached as far as my eye could see. The barbed wire was torn in many places, the Iron Curtain was no longer an obstacle, but the mere fact that it was still standing, that in thirty years no one had taken the trouble to tear down this infrastructure of terror, was hard to comprehend – for me, in any case, with Berlin in mind.

As I walked on, suddenly I couldn't get the man with the harpoon out of my head. What had he wanted to tell me? Who was he? I recalled his broad neoprene-clad shoulders, the well-built body that was unusually fit for a man of his age. Had he been a diver during the Cold War? Maybe an army frogman, an elite soldier, a border guard? Was the shot he simulated with his harpoon the echo of a real shot? Did he have a human life on his conscience? Was that what he'd been burning to say?

When a road appeared a few miles further on, I positioned myself on the verge and raised my thumb. A man named Petko drove me to the next town, Sozopol. His wet hair hung low on his forehead, he was driving barefoot, and the car's heating was turned up to full blast. He made an apologetic hand gesture as I peeled off my jacket.

'I've just got out of the water. I need to warm up a bit.'

On the back seat lay a harpoon, and in the boot was a neoprene suit.

Petko was a car accessories salesman. He spoke hectic English and held sombre views about Bulgaria.

'We can't dig ourselves out of our hole. The whole country is ruined and corrupt, and the old Russian cliques have their fingers in every pie. In the nineties, a few foreign investors were brave enough to come here, but they all got fleeced, and everyone's avoided us ever since. We've been totally left behind. Even the Romanians have overtaken us. Get that – the Romanians!'

After a few minutes' drive, a village appeared on the left-hand side of the road, but it looked more like a slum than a village. Windowless bare-brick huts flashed past, with bare-footed children, mountains of rubbish, and smouldering fires between them. A smoky haze hung over the entire place.

'Gypsies.'

Petko's voice now sounded even more sombre than before. 'Stupid, dirty gypsies. They steal, they booze, they have ten children while drunk, claim allowances for large families, the children don't learn anything and start stealing and drinking, and then it starts all over again. What do you mean, integrate them? You don't know these people. They won't integrate! Give them flats in the city and they just torch the floors and go back to their filthy villages. They'll kill you for a few lev, they'll bury an axe in your skull because they like the look of your phone, and when the battery's empty, they'll chuck it away. It's impossible to change them. Even if you killed a couple of thousand of them, it wouldn't make any difference; there are simply too many of them. Stupid, dirty, hopeless gypsies …'

As I contemplated how to jolt Petko out of his monologue, an idea suddenly occurred to me. I asked about the harpoon hunter I'd met in Rezovo.

'An older man?'

'Yes.'

'Bushy eyebrows?'

'That's right!'

'I know him. Comes to the coast regularly. A professor from Sofia.'

'A professor? Professor of what?'

Petko thought for a second. He didn't know precisely, but his answer gave me the feeling that my speculations couldn't have been much wider off the mark.

'Literature, I think.'

The Sozopol vampire

I saw many familiar things in Bulgaria that I hadn't seen by the Black Sea for a long time. Prefabricated socialist residential blocks. Icons on dashboards. Women in leather miniskirts and stilettos on the arms of men in tracksuits. Cyrillic lettering.

At the same time, there was no overlooking the fact that I had arrived in the EU. In the small coastal town of Sozopol, blue signs were attached to the facades of renovated old buildings, detailing the amount of funding received to the cent. The museums had wheelchair ramps, the exhibition texts had been translated into English, and Sozopol's past as a trading colony in ancient times was presented in a systematic and comprehensible fashion, unlike in Turkey or Georgia, where

Black Sea history lay around in large unsorted chunks under the open skies.

A former Greek school hosted a museum of maritime painting. I walked past any number of white sails against blue backgrounds until I stopped in one room, electrified. Hanging on the walls were square pictures reminiscent of Picasso, and in their cubist melee of figures I identified elements of Black Sea myths.

As I tried to decipher one of the motifs, a man suddenly stepped between me and the picture. He was wearing a white sailor's sweater and must have been in his mid-sixties. Without a word, and much to my surprise, he stepped up to the painting, lifted it off the wall with both hands, and turned it clockwise through 90 degrees before hanging it back up.

The effect was astounding. All of a sudden, details I hadn't noticed before emerged from the background because they were now at the correct angle, whereas other motifs that had previously caught my eye were tilted horizontally and vanished from my field of vision.

The man shook my hand. 'I'm Ivan.'

Only now did I recognise him: he was the artist. I had seen Ivan Bakhchevanov's photo on a poster at the entrance.

He rotated the painting a second, a third, and a fourth time, until it was back in its initial position. Each time, fresh details came to the fore, making the composition more and more complex.

Bakhchevanov spoke Russian and explained that the idea had come to him while he was diving in the Black Sea. The underwater world was completely different from the world above the water, but the two belonged together – two aspects of the same sea. Bakhchevanov loved the moment of immersion and resurfacing when your perspective twisted, and he had wondered how he might capture these two halves of the world in one picture. Conventional seascapes were one-dimensional. They showed only the top of the water: waves, ships, cliffs, gulls. Once Bakhchevanov started thinking about the limits of these pictures, he was struck by a whole host of other dimensions of the Black Sea he shouldn't omit from his paintings: the present and the past, myth and reality, day and night, the cycle of the seasons, the displacements of peoples around its shores, the rise and fall of empires, the emergence and failure of human designs.

And so Bakhchevanov guided me from one picture to the next, rotating the Black Sea. Every turn set stories in motion, made figures appear in the paintings, young one moment, old the next, in love with other figures, then falling out with them and mourning for their lost loves. Ships sailed across the sea, sank, rested on the bottom; the sun came up, dipped below the waves, and rose again on the far side as the moon. Fish and birds swapped positions, the water froze and thawed. Mythical heroes turned into mortal humans, history became personal, beauty faded, hope sprouted, death was not the end, and a thousand years were like a single day.

Bakhchevanov's small studio was on the upper floor of the school building. It was covered in plaster dust, as he was currently working on a sculpture. Hanging on the wall was an old diving suit that he had outgrown – in girth, not height. He had replaced it many years ago with another one that he kept, along with his harpoon, on the sailing boat he had built with his own hands. I was amazed. He was the third harpooner I'd met in just two days.

Before we said goodbye, Bakhchevanov revealed to me that he had originally intended to hang the exhibition's two dozen pictures up on small electric motors. They would have rotated automatically through 90 degrees every ten minutes. Unfortunately, it would have cost too much; his finances didn't stretch that far. Now he was the motor that moved the Black Sea.

The most famous voyage in Black Sea history begins on an October day in late nineteenth-century London. A black-clothed man, tall, gaunt, and pale, arrives on the banks of the Thames in a horse-drawn carriage and arranges for the loading of a long, heavy wooden box onto the *Czarina Catherine*. The merchant ship, named after Catherine the Great, sets sail the next day for Bulgaria. It proceeds along the Thames estuary, turns west into the English Channel, rounds France and Spain, advances through the Straits of Gibraltar, crosses the Mediterranean, and finally reaches the Bosporus. Its captain, a man called Donelson, is struck by the consistently favourable winds that have blown the *Czarina Catherine* from England to the Black Sea in less than four weeks. He is even more surprised by the persistent fog that seems to dog the ship. Beyond Istanbul, it becomes so dense that the crew loses its bearings. A few Romanian seamen are convinced that the inexplicable weather conditions are somehow related to the wooden box from London, and they beg the captain to throw the piece of cargo overboard. Donelson gives the superstitious sailors a good thrashing and sails blindly on.

When the fog clears, it becomes apparent that the *Czarina Catherine* has missed its destination, the Bulgarian port of Varna, and has instead landed in Galati in Romania; unbeknownst to the crew, the ship has entered the Danube and sailed upriver into the heart of the country. Even Donelson is now slightly relieved when a man turns up unheralded in Galati harbour and takes reception of the mysterious wooden box in order to transport it overland, through dense forests and gorges teeming with wolves, to a castle in the Carpathians.

The Romanian sailors were right. The wooden box, which is packed with Transylvanian soil, contains a stowaway, a zombie passenger who took the same maritime route from the Balkan coast to England a few months earlier and has left a trail of horror behind him in London. His name is Count Dracula.

Bram Stoker wrote his vampire novel without ever having set foot by the Black Sea. He pieced together his image of the Balkans in the libraries of Victorian England and embellished it in the final years of the nineteenth century for a reading public greedy for horror stories – and, in particular, for tales of barbaric creatures that posed an external threat to the United Kingdom. Stoker populated the Black Sea region with the figments of a fearful British imagination, just as Athenian dramatists had frightened the ancient Greeks.

Many inhabitants of the Balkans hate the old vampire stories, because they are often the only thing Western Europeans associate with their homelands. Others welcome the vampire tourists who come to the Balkans on Dracula's trail. It is therefore with mixed feelings that archaeologists must have greeted the skeleton of a vampire during excavations in Sozopol in the summer of 2012. Lodged in the ribcage of the man, who was buried in the fourteenth century, was an iron wedge. His contemporaries appear to have driven a stake through his heart when he was already in his grave.

I had read about the Sozopol vampire, but it took me a while to find out what had become of him after the dig. The custodian of the archaeological museum was certain that his remains had been transferred to the historical museum in the capital, Sofia. One of her colleagues confirmed this, but she had heard that the vampire had not been kept there. It took a third colleague to tell me where to find the remains.

'They're in the castle.'

I flashed the three women a questioning look. 'What castle?'

The castle lay a short way outside Sozopol, on the outskirts of a place by the name of Ravadinovo. From a distance, it looked like the seat of a family of Central European nobles, a gloomy building with Romanesque towers and a large, steeply pitched roof. Close up, it looked like what it really was: a folly, not even three decades old. It had been built by a Bulgarian wrestler called Georgi Tumpalov, a medieval enthusiast who had come into money and fulfilled a childhood dream with this palace. In the spacious grounds stood a memorial Tumpalov had erected to himself – a white knight with a broad marble chest, brandishing an outsized sword.

No one, Tumpalov included, seemed to know what to make of the castle. The lord of the manor lived elsewhere. Of the interior, only a small museum in the basement was open to the public, while the rest of the gigantic building stood empty. A few tattered peacocks roamed the gardens. The gatekeeper told me that the castle was occasionally hired out as a set for Bollywood films. The wrestler's long-term project was to turn it into an international meeting place for global peace, but no one knew when this plan was to be implemented. Maybe when peace had finally settled over the world.

The vampire skeleton lay in a glass case in the basement museum. The rusty iron wedge between the ribs looked like the head of an axe or the tip of a ploughshare. The women at the archaeological museum had told me that the dead man must have held a prestigious position, might even have been the town headman, because he had been buried in the part of an abbey church reserved for dignitaries. But something – a crime, a character flaw, a sin – must have persuaded his contemporaries that the man's soul could not ascend to heaven, that it would restlessly haunt the earth and assault the living until it was rendered harmless. Hence the wedge in his chest. Something like a hundred similar vampire graves had come to light in Bulgaria in recent decades.

I stood beside the glass case for a long time, trying to picture the misstep that had turned this man into a vampire in the eyes of his fellow citizens. Whatever it might have been, his maltreated bones surely did not deserve to be put on display in this phony castle.

A BLACK SEA LEXICON
Entry no. 4: *Hydrogen sulphide*

Half a year had passed since I'd witnessed the start of the holiday season on the Russian coast. Now, on the Bulgarian coast, I saw it end. As if a film were rewinding, I watched the reverse of the metamorphosis that had awakened the Caucasian seaside resorts from their winter sleep. The windows of the cafes and hotels went dark, shutters came rattling down, beach huts were boarded up, leaves fluttered to the ground and were blown on the autumn wind through streets that were gradually falling silent.

In Nesebar, a town north of the Gulf of Burgas founded by Greek traders in antiquity, only one hotel remained open. That evening, I wandered for a long time through the dark streets of the old town in search of something to eat.

'This is just the beginning.' Zdravka Georgieva, who had

grown up in Nesebar, loved the suspended time of winter. 'In January, nothing moves here at all.'

She was a young archaeologist, a woman who expressed her thoughts carefully, who wasn't inclined to grand pronouncements, and whose professional and private lives were closely intertwined with the history of her hometown. Her mother's grandparents came to Nesebar in 1924 as Macedonian refugees. All they brought with them was a horse-drawn cart full of household possessions rescued from their home north of Thessalonica before it was razed to the ground during the great game of ethnic musical chairs in the 1920s. Meanwhile, the Greek houses of Nesebar were emptying. Yet Zdravka's father's family was Greek; her great-great-grandfather had stowed away in the hold of a ship from the Marmara region of Turkey at the end of the nineteenth century for reasons that no one in her family knew.

Zdravka's Macedonian-Greek ancestors had eked out a modest immigrant existence in Nesebar. Her father had been the skipper of a fishing vessel until his retirement, and her mother had worked as a telegraphist at the post office. Zdravka grew up in the historic part of town, among descendants of other immigrants, on the half-mile-long peninsula that is connected to the mainland only by a causeway at its western end. For millennia, the sea had been eating away at the coast of the town, and its oldest buildings had long since slipped below the surface of the water. When Zdravka developed an interest in Nesebar's history, she soon realised that there was no chance of investigating the past without getting her feet wet. And so she became an underwater archaeologist.

She and the rest of her research team had been diving in the waters around Nesebar and documenting the town's sunken structures for years. Few people were more intimately familiar with the Black Sea than she was. This unique sea made life both easy and difficult for divers at the same time, she said. Easy because the relatively unsalty water spared one's eyes and skin more than the Mediterranean did; hard because it was less translucent, which impeded vision and photography.

Zdravka was also more familiar than most with the strange peculiarity that distinguishes the Black Sea from every other sea on the planet. Some 90 per cent of its water volume is clinically dead. Although it is absolutely teeming with life near the surface, its depths are an utter void.

What causes this are the different levels of salinity separating the two layers of water from each other. The heavy Mediterranean water streaming in through the Bosporus stays at the bottom, while a lighter, far less salty mixture of sea and river water floats on top. Since there is virtually no exchange between the two, no oxygen percolates down to the bottom from the top. This effect is exacerbated by organic waste – the residue of dead flora and fauna – which is carried out into the Black Sea from the river estuaries and strips even more oxygen from the water when it rots. Below a depth of about 200 m, the sea is anoxic: it contains neither oxygen nor life that requires oxygen. The only thing that can survive in these conditions is extremely well-adapted bacteria that feed on the organic waste of the seabed. As the bacteria break down the plant and animal remains, they produce hydrogen sulphide, a highly toxic gas that stinks of rotten eggs and is lethal for humans even in small doses. The depths of the Black Sea contain the world's largest occurrence of this fatal substance.

Discovering the world beyond the Bosporus, the seafarers of antiquity were astounded by the sheer abundance of life in the sea, its gigantic shoals of anchovies and its profusion of bonito, mackerel, bluefish, and turbot. They could only appreciate the thin, densely populated surface layer, not the lifeless, toxic-gas-filled abyss beneath their keels.

This anoxic layer was only identified in the nineteenth century. Ever since, it has been a subject of panicked analysis in many scientific publications. In the 8,000 years or so since the sea took on its present form, its complex water architecture has proved stable, but the consequences of a potential catastrophe that might churn up the hydrogen sulphide from its depths to the surface would be devastating. Any denizens of the sea relying on oxygen – that is, all flora and fauna – would, at a stroke, be deprived of the basis of their existence. A deluge of fish carcasses and lethal gas would pour through the Bosporus and stream through the megalopolis that is Istanbul.

And yet, the same chemical effects that make the sea's sediment so dangerous have been a blessing for archaeologists. In the 1990s, the first remotely operated underwater vehicle ever to penetrate the sea's anoxic layer came across a Byzantine shipwreck lying almost intact on the sea bottom; it looked as if it had sunk only a few months earlier, not one and a half millennia ago. Due to the lack of oxygen, the deep water is entirely free of all organisms that decompose the wooden hulls of sunken ships in other seas. Some of the rigging was even still hanging between the masts. Other diving expeditions soon turned up even older ships – such as galleys of Roman origin, carrying amphorae in which archaeologists found vestiges of wine and preserved fish.

Zdravka was involved in the biggest haul so far. She had been on board a research ship off the Bulgarian coast in the autumn of 2017 with the aim of collecting soil samples from the deepest parts of the sea. During the weeks-long expedition, the crew had happened upon a variety of shipwrecks, mainly Ottoman gunboats, though there were also some ancient Roman ships.

The wreck that showed up on the scientists' monitors on one of the final days of the expedition looked Roman at first sight too. Yet as the robot vehicle approached it 2,000 m down, Zdravka and her colleagues realised that this was something different, something exceptional. Judging by its rudder, it was a Greek galley from the fifth century BC, which had sunk during the period when the Black Sea was being colonised. It bore a remarkable similarity to the ship on the famous Odysseus vase in the British Museum – the galley to whose mast the hero has himself bound upright in order to resist the sirens' song. The ship was half buried in the bottom sediment, and a few planks had become detached from the hull, but none of the wooden components showed much more than a scratch from the two and a half millennia they had spent on the bottom of the sea. It was the oldest ship-wreck any archaeologist had ever seen.

Zdravka's eyes shone as she recounted this discovery. She spoke of the sleepless days and nights of the expedition's final week and of her amazement and incredulous speechless-ness when she grasped that before her eyes lay a ship dating back to the distant days when her hometown of Nesebar was founded.

My mind turned to Ivan Bakhchevanov, the painter in Sozopol, and the historical simultaneity his paintings depicted. The ships of ancient times weren't gone; they were simply lying on the other side of the sea.

North of Nesebar lies Slanchev Bryag, Bulgaria's most famous seaside resort, better known as 'Sunny Beach' to the foreign tourists who come here in search of sunshine. It was raining when I arrived. The concrete hotel complexes were completely deserted, the beach desolate, the restaurants closed, and all the shops boarded up. For mysterious reasons, the only thing open was a sex shop, perhaps to raise the spirits of the lonely watchmen hunkered down in small plastic sheds outside the empty hotels.

When I decided to continue north towards Romania after half an hour of aimless wandering, I discovered that there were no more buses. No tourists, no public transport. I took up position by the main road in the rain.

A few minutes later, a white Toyota pulled up.

'Get in!'

Lynn and Wayne were from Wakefield in northern England. They were actually heading in the opposite direction, but then Wayne had spotted me standing by the road and since the two of them had no particular place to go, he had done a U-turn and said to Lynn, 'We'll go wherever that guy's going.'

Wayne's lower arms were tattooed with skulls, and his bull neck was sunburnt. Lynn was very blonde and a chain-smoker. Both were in their late forties. In their teens, they had had two kids, who had long since grown up and moved out. They'd done a bit of this and that in their lives, delivering food, working on building sites, and running a sandwich shop. They had slowly grown fed up with Wakefield, but they couldn't make the break. Then Lynn's elderly father, who'd been living in an old people's home for years, doing nothing but operating the remote control from his armchair to watch horseracing, had been diagnosed with cancer. All of a sudden, he had been desperate to catch up with everything he'd missed out on in life, though it was far too late for most things. Lynn and Wayne realised that plans mustn't be put off, and so they had sold their house, their car, and their furniture and googled 'cheap property in Europe'. And that is how they came to be in Sunny Beach, where, three weeks ago, they had bought an apartment complete with a terrace, a garden, a view of the sea, a swimming pool, and a stray cat called Pebbles for €18,000. They had no idea what they were going to do in Bulgaria, but things were bound to work out somehow. Maybe a bike rental business. Maybe a fish and chip shop.

I asked them why they'd got sick of Wakefield.

Wayne spat out of the car window. 'Too many immigrants.'

Romania

Marea Neagră

Alas, how close I stand to the world's end!

Ovid, *Tristia*, first century AD

The wrong horse

Lynn and Wayne dropped me off in Varna, the last Bulgarian city before the Romanian border. I covered half of the remaining 100 km or so by bus, but I got stuck in a coastal backwater called Kavarna; the next bus to the border went the following day. I walked to the edge of town and stood by the roadside.

The car I got into smelled of cigarettes and musk. Ceiling lights bathed the interior in a dim pink glow, and funfair techno pounded from the loudspeakers. Spying the faces of the two men in the front, I could hear in my head the voices of all the Bulgarians in the past few days who had said as a parting warning, 'Don't get into a car with gypsies!'

It was too late now.

The two of them drove that car like people with nothing to lose – terrifyingly fast, seatbelts off, not concentrating, half a hand on the wheel, half an eye on the road, and overtaking so madly that my heart skipped a beat. When they spoke, they had to compete with the music and only occasionally turned it down to shout questions I didn't understand over their shoulders. We didn't share a language.

And yet, they let me out in a village just before the border without having slit my throat, which is what everyone had predicted would happen.

I crossed the border on foot, and in the twilight I reached Vama Veche, a hippy community on the Romanian side that looked just as dead as every other resort I'd been through in recent days. High over the sea rode an almost-full moon, its reflection on the water a quivering silver ribbon. The sea was black – but, then again, all seas are black at night.

Monica, the owner of the only hotel still open, was in her mid-forties and could remember how all the Roma children disappeared from her class at the end of the socialist era.

'As soon as the system started to slacken its grip, their parents stopped sending them to school. I remember ringing one boy's mother and asking why he wasn't there. All she said was, "It's better for us like this."'

That night I mulled over all the Roma I'd met around the Black Sea coast. I thought of the little girl in Abkhazia, perhaps ten years old, who went from table to table in the seafront cafes of Sukhum, annoying all the patrons by reciting the same Pushkin poem over and over again until they pressed a few roubles into her palm. I thought of the mouth of the Terme river in Turkey where, instead of the Amazon capital that Strabo had claimed once lay there, I found a Roma camp with women changing their babies' nappies under scarlet canopies. I thought of the Roma families I saw begging outside the mosques of Istanbul and of people's glances as they anxiously swerved them. I also thought back to Gürcan Güneş, the Bulgarian Turk who had laid out his accumulated knowledge about the Roma before me on the bus journey we took together.

'In Bulgaria,' he had said, 'there are Romanian, Turkish, Greek, Yugoslavian, Macedonian, and Bulgarian gypsies. The Turkish gypsies sit outside toilets – a very profitable business; they make a killing. The Yugoslavian ones are the best musicians. The Macedonians are the dirtiest, and the Greek gypsies steal the most. If a Greek gypsy hasn't stolen anything all day, he gets so jittery he'll throw his axe into a neighbour's garden just to be able to steal it back ...'

What all Roma everywhere on the shores of the Black Sea had in common was that everyone disliked them. They were the barbarians everyone here could agree on, the last nomads in a thoroughly settled world.

It had increasingly rankled me on my travels that I hadn't been able to strike up a conversation with a member of a Roma community anywhere – sometimes due to the language barriers, sometimes because they were wary of my approaches, but mostly because I caught myself instinctively dodging their begging groups.

Before I continued my journey the next morning, I asked Monica where I might find Roma along the Romanian coast.

'Where? Everywhere! It's better to ask where you won't find any!'

She suggested I try my luck in Mangalia, the next town on my way north. She had heard a radio report about a Roma settlement where the inhabitants were protesting against the demolition of their dilapidated houses.

The settlement comprised two short streets on the northeastern edge of the town. One glance took in where it began and where it ended. The gardens of the surrounding detached houses were barricaded off with high opaque fences, and there wasn't a soul in the street. The Roma had neither fences nor gardens, and they were all outdoors. I saw a few dozen people gathered around a row of concrete shacks that looked as if the bulldozers had already been at work.

'Don't do it.' The taxi driver who had brought me here from the bus station shook his head for the umpteenth time. 'Why do you want to talk to them? I can tell you everything you need to know about them. They rob, they drink, they don't work, they're dirty, their kids don't go to school ...'

We agreed that he would keep my rucksack in his car until I called him to retrieve it.

Eyes followed me as I walked along the street. I saw people of all ages standing and crouching on the pavement, all dressed in the same cheap synthetic clothes as those strewn in piles in the dust by the shacks. In the middle of the road stood an almost man-sized disco loudspeaker playing crackly Balkan pop. A man in a pair of chunky sunglasses, obviously the village DJ, ostentatiously blew me a kiss as I passed. I wasn't sure how I was supposed to understand this gesture.

Halfway along the street, I realised that it wasn't going to be easy to make friends here. It was then that I spotted the horse. It was standing outside one of the concrete huts, next to an unglazed window, its reins tied to the middle strut. Without any clear plan – in fact, simply because I was casting around for a reason to stop for a moment – I pulled my phone out of my bag and took a photo of the horse.

In a flash, I heard shouting from behind me. I span around to see two young men running towards me, their expressions a nasty omen. They shook their fists angrily and yelled at me. I couldn't understand a word, but I did realise that I'd bitten off more than I could chew. I listened nervously and tried to look as unthreatening as possible. The taxi driver had told me that the people in the settlement spoke Turkish. I pointed at the horse with a stupid smile.

'Çok güzel,' I said. Very nice.

The men were briefly startled, but then asked something I didn't understand and carried on yelling at me. I smiled until the corners of my mouth ached. It was only when a third, slightly older man sidled up to us on his bike that the atmosphere relaxed a bit. I stammered my name in Turkish, said something about my journey, and praised the horse's beauty again. After a while, the two younger men calmed down and moved on.

Zafet, the older guy, offered me a cigarette. His eyes wavered between curiosity and mistrust. He kept asking if I was travelling alone. Truly alone? It was beyond his comprehension. He nodded when I asked if all the people here were Turks, if they were Muslims, if they went to the old mosque I'd seen in the town centre. I then asked about the huts. 'Problem,' Zafet said. 'Problem.' But I didn't catch the details, because his Turkish wasn't the Turkish I knew from Turkey.

When we said goodbye, Zafet pointed in warning to my shoulder bag. 'Zapzarap!'

I nodded in acknowledgement and clutched the bag tightly to my side as I started to walk back down the street.

An old woman came walking towards me and extended an open palm. 'Para!'

Smiling, I shook my head.

Another old woman, who had obviously overheard my conversation with Zafet, asked me if I was looking for the mosque. I nodded, grateful to have a goal, and walked off in the direction she was pointing, followed by the gazes of curious children and suspicious adult eyes. Suddenly, two teenage girls appeared on my left, and another two approached me from the right. I felt as if all four of them were ogling my bag and, whichever way I turned, one of them always seemed to be directly behind me where I couldn't see her. As I quickened my pace and clasped my bag more tightly, I suddenly sensed that I was one of those people with something to lose, and that here I had come up against walls that could not be breached in one fleeting afternoon, and so I hurried on sheepishly, past the man with the loudspeaker, who blew another irritating kiss at me, and when I nervously glanced back, three blocks further on, I was relieved to see no one following me.

Ovid's last metamorphosis

On the way from Mangalia to Constanta, I watched the scenery change through the bus windows. The woods retreated, the hills flattened out, the perspective expanded, and the entire countryside pushed outwards, widening until the land dissolved entirely into flat earth and high skies, clearly divided by the horizon all around. I was back on the steppe, the same northern landscape I had seen at the start of my journey on the Russian side of the sea. The road was lined with parched wormwood bushes, strawlike grass, and quivering thistles. Harvested fields stretched out in a brown-on-brown checkerboard pattern in every direction. Here and there, small scrub-covered hillocks rose out of the arable land, their outlines spared by the tractors' ploughs. Kurgans – the burial mounds of the ancient peoples of the steppe.

On the bus, I listened to the other passengers' hubbub of Romanian, fascinated to suddenly come across a language so clearly from different climes in this absolutely Slavic corner of the Black Sea. It sounded like an Italian dialect, Portuguese shaken and stirred, or drunken Latin.

There is much debate about how the Romanians, inheritors of a Romance language, ended up in this corner of Europe. Some people believe that a derivative of Latin clung on here since the days of the Roman Empire, whereas others think the Romanians only arrived from the western Balkans in the Middle Ages. Whatever the correct answer, I wondered what Constanta's most famous Roman would make of the fact that a variant of his mother tongue was spoken today in his former place of exile.

His memorial stands in the centre of the town on the expansive Piata Ovidiu, the square that bears his name. His ageing body is wrapped in a bronze toga, his chin is propped on his right fist, and his downward gaze is pensive.

The decree ordering Ovid to leave Rome hit him like a bolt from the blue. Publius Ovidius Naso was at the height of his fame after the publication of his *Metamorphoses* a few years earlier; there was no greater poet in the whole empire. Yet none of this could prevent Emperor Augustus from personally banishing him for life in AD 8 from the capital to the port of Tomis, an outpost in the north-easternmost corner of the realm.

There is no record of what provoked the emperor's ire. Officially, Ovid was to atone for the lubricity of his early work *Ars Amatoria*. Ovid himself suggested that there was a different, more concrete reason: through no fault of his own, he had seen something not intended for his eyes. It is rumoured that he witnessed a moral indiscretion by Augustus's granddaughter, Julia.

Present-day Constanta is one of the most charming towns on the Black Sea coast, a curious yet curiously harmonious mix of Central European, Ottoman, and socialist elements. If one is to believe the letters Ovid sent from his exile to friends and relatives in Rome, however, there was no more godforsaken place in the entire empire. Ovid's *Tristia* and *Epistulae ex Ponto*, his laments and letters from the Black Sea, wallow so epically in the hardships of his banishment that it is hard to understand why the Romanians have erected a monument to this gloomster in their most beautiful Black Sea city.

'There's no more dismal land than this beneath either pole,' Ovid claims. The icy winter climate doesn't appeal to him; the landscape of the steppes pains his eye, accustomed as it is to southern scenery; and he finds the food, the local wine, and even the water unfit for consumption. Worse than anything else, however, are the people. The Greeks there hurt the poet's ears with their feral Greek, which is intermingled with the vocabulary of the barbarian tribes living around Tomis – the Sarmatians and the Scythians, the Getae, the Bessi, and the Thracians: 'names unworthy of my talent'.

Virtually no one speaks Latin in Tomis. Ovid, the master bard of Rome, finds himself in the role of a stammering fool whose words produce no meaning in the ears of his listeners. 'Here *I'm* the barbarian, understood by no one, and these stupid peasants mock my Latin speech.' Why, he wonders, should he bother writing in his mother tongue? 'What's the point of such labour – will the Sarmatians or Getae read my work?'

Generations of later exiled writers took inspiration from Ovid's laments, even authors who were not banished abroad but went into internal exile – for example, the Russian Osip Mandelstam, who retreated into his shell after the October Revolution and called one of his poetry collections of the early Soviet era *Tristia*. Others reacted with ambivalence to Ovid's later works. Patrick Leigh Fermor carried the poet's letters from exile with him when he wandered the Black Sea coast on his great trans-European hike in the 1930s. Enthused though he was by their language, Ovid's whingeingly egocentric tone irritated him. 'If only he had written more about his surroundings!'

Ovid's principal concern, however, was that his surroundings were gradually permeating his soul. 'Believe me, I feel you may find my Latin diluted with Black Sea usage.' By necessity, the poet learned the language of the barbarians, to be able to communicate in Tomis, and it soon took up more room in his head than he cared for. 'I blush to admit it, I've even composed in the Getic language, bending barbarian patois to our verse: among the uncultured natives I'm getting a reputation as a poet.'

Ovid arrived in Tomis with a fixed view of the world, but on the Black Sea coast it gradually softened. When looking from the centre of the empire, there appeared to be a clear dividing line between the civilised part of the world and the uncivilised remainder. But here on the barbarian fringes of the empire, the blurring and fraying of that border was tangible to Ovid. At first, this thought confused and horrified him, but then he seemed to yield to his fate. Shortly before his death – which is estimated to have occurred in AD 17, because that is when his letters fall silent – and after ten years of banishment, a gentler tone creeps into his elegies. 'But now the place is less odious than before'. This shift in tone is mild – after all, the primary audience of these letters are still readers in Rome – but he is kinder to the inhabitants of Tomis than before. 'Men of Tomis, I've committed no crime: you I love, although I loathe your land … and against the place – not its people – I've brought true charges.'

In case he were to die in exile, Ovid had instructed his wife in an earlier letter to at least have his ashes returned to Rome and have them interred there under a stone, for which he simultaneously provided the inscription. The Latin words are engraved on the base of the monument to him in the centre of Constanta.

I WHO LIE HERE, SWEET OVID, POET OF TENDER PASSIONS,
FELL VICTIM TO MY OWN SHARP WIT.
PASSER-BY, IF YOU'VE EVER BEEN IN LOVE, DON'T GRUDGE ME
THE TRADITIONAL PRAYER: 'MAY OVID'S BONES LIE SOFT!'

We know no more about the final resting place of the poet's bones than we do about the precise date of his death. To the north of Constanta, a tiny uninhabited island lies close to the shore, and it is said that this is where Ovid was buried. But no one knows when and no one knows where; there is no gravestone, nothing but a myth.

Maybe, I thought, as the island slid past the windows of my bus in the autumn rain, maybe it all turned out quite differently. Maybe in AD 17 Ovid's Latin letters had fallen silent, but not the poet himself. Maybe he had finally settled in Tomis, no longer resisting the incursions of foreign words into his thoughts, composing poems in Getic, debating with Thracians, writing letters to Sarmatians. Maybe Ovid, the poet of metamorphoses, had eventually metamorphosed into a barbarian.

The Black Danube

On its almost 1,800-mile journey through Europe, the Danube grows wider and wider until it unravels into a thousand arms shortly before the Black Sea. To enter the Romanian part of the delta, you have to pass via Tulcea, a port set back 60 km from the coast, at a point where all roads end and a cobweb of waterways begins. Wait at the jetty, I'd been told, and a boat will turn up sooner or later. On the jetty, I ran into Daniel, Zsolt, and Marian.

The three of them were planning to fish. And drink. They were sitting on rucksacks full of angling kit and alcohol. We clinked glasses once, twice, thrice, by which time it was agreed that the free bed in their fishing hut was mine.

We shared the small motorboat with a few residents of the delta – rough-skinned men and women whose expressions changed little and lethargically. The boat cast off from the jetty, left Tulcea harbour behind, and swung into the canalised Sulina arm. Space was tight: we were perching on our rucksacks. Above us was a lot of sky, around us a lot of water, with little else between the two.

Daniel, Zsolt, and Marian worked for a mineral water company in the Carpathians. Once a year, they went fishing together. Daniel, the youngest, was in his late twenties and in management, an alpha male with a dominant voice and beefed-up muscles. Marian was obviously a gym bunny too, but he had warm, clever eyes and worked in sales – like Zsolt, the oldest of the three, a quiet Hungarian in his mid-forties with the narrow eyes of a man of the steppes and the physical serenity of a Buddhist monk.

They had rented accommodation halfway along the Sulina branch between Tulcea and the coast in a place called Crisan, whose low-slung wooden houses lined both banks. By the time we tossed our luggage onto the jetty, it was almost dark, as befitted an early November evening.

Dana, the landlady, had cooked catfish. As the guest of honour, I was given the head. It was huge, its barbels dangling over the edge of my plate. We drank red wine dispensed from silver bags that looked like cows' udders. After the catfish came fish soup, then crucian carp; never in my life had I eaten such quantities of fish. The wine flowed by the udderful, and between glasses we drained shots of fruit brandy and whisky.

A TV music channel was playing Romanian pop. Daniel turned up the volume.

'Manele! You don't know manele? Where have you been, man? Manele is the only thing gypsies are good at. They play it at weddings and at birthday parties. You slip them some cash to get them to call out your name on stage. A thousand lei from Daniel for his wife! Everyone wants to show how much money they have in their pockets – that's how it works in Romania. No money for rent, but the car has to be showy.

Empty fridge, full tank. You slip the manele singer your last banknote, and for one night you're the greatest, even if next morning you have no idea how you're going to feed your kids. The real manele stars are millionaires and drive Ferraris.'

He showed me a video of a birthday party. I saw a grinning Daniel up on stage, arm in arm with a singer who was chanting Daniel's name. The singer's jacket pockets were bulging with bundles of notes.

Daniel had little good to say of other Roma people. 'I'd nail them all to crosses if I could. They move around Europe begging and ruin the reputation of us Romanians. It says "Romania" in my passport. Wherever I show it, they treat me like dirt because they think it stands for Roma.'

Over the course of the evening, Daniel drew on my pad a chart of Romanian Roma society, a complicated diagram composed of circles, sub-circles, and arrows indicating the relations between them.

'Here on the left are the harmless gypsies. The ones who work, the ones who are married to Romanians, the musicians. To their right are the ones who don't work or do any harm because they keep to their own and have no major demands. The next level are the fucked-up gypsies – thieves, murderers, rapists. And here are the gypsy bosses, the worst of all. They aren't based in Romania but in Europe, where they blow the money they make from the other gypsies. The harmless gypsies are scared of the fucked-up gypsies, and all of them are scared of the bosses.'

Daniel glanced at Marian. 'Don't give me that look! You know I'm not talking about your wife.'

Marian was married to a Roma woman, a social worker who looked after disadvantaged families in Bucharest. He told me that his mother had taken a long time to reconcile herself to her daughter-in-law.

'When I was small, she would always say the gypsies would come and get me if I didn't eat up.'

Marian's view of the Roma was more nuanced. He said that they had a difficult status in Romania because no one had any interest in their integrating.

'The politicians bribe the gypsy bosses to tell the gypsies who to vote for, which makes a few hundred thousand votes up for grabs. If the gypsies were more educated, they wouldn't go along with it, and so it's to the politicians' advantage if the gypsies don't go to school.'

It was the first and last time on my journey that someone took the Romas' side.

We listened to manele bands far into the night. Daniel sang. Marian danced. Zsolt smiled his Buddha smile. We milked one wine udder after another, and I can't remember how I found my way to bed that night.

Early the next morning, Marian shook me awake. Down at the jetty, Mirca, a neighbour, was waiting with his motorboat. We stowed the fishing rods on board and set off.

The river was still shrouded in darkness to the west, while at its eastern end dawn was breaking. Mirca held the tiller in one hand and a bottle of beer in the other. A lopsided smile made a concertina of the creases on the right-hand side of his face. He was wearing dappled green army fatigues, as were Daniel, Zsolt, and Marian. I was the only one on board not in camouflage. The icy wind created by the moving boat blew in through the seams of my jacket.

We entered a series of progressively narrowing side channels. Whenever another boat came towards us, both skippers would abruptly cut the throttle so their bow waves wouldn't knock the other off course. Swaying reeds lined the banks, which would sometimes part unexpectedly and widen into lakes several miles across. We would plough our way through the open water, the engine roaring, past broken wood – thin twigs, thicker branches, and the occasional water-polished tree trunk – and islands of reeds, large and small, that had torn free of the banks. Various species of waterfowl perched on every last scrap of flotsam. I saw ducks, swans, gulls, coots, herons, cormorants, two pelicans, a kingfisher, and all kinds of other species I didn't recognise.

I had long since lost my bearings in the tangle of rivers and channels, when a wooden hut appeared on the bank before us. Three men in hip-length rubber boots were standing in the water emptying their nets. Silvery crucian carp covered the bottom of their boat, a plastic tub brimmed with crayfish, and two pikes were thrashing about in a submerged fish box.

The men were from a fishing village deep in the delta. Two of them – old Gori and his son, Florin – were Ukrainians. They called themselves *khokhly*, an old-fashioned word the Ukrainians of Ukraine don't like because the Russians employ it as an insult. The Ukrainians in the Danube delta were descended from the Zaporozhian Cossacks dislodged from the Dnieper by Catherine the Great in the eighteenth century, but that was a long time ago, and even the few *khokhly* who were mindful of their heritage had long since assimilated with their Romanian neighbours. Old Gori still spoke Ukrainian, but his tongue was half paralysed, rendering his words practically unintelligible. Florin, his son, had known a smattering of Ukrainian as a boy but had forgotten most of it over the years.

The third fisherman, a Romanian, climbed into Mirca's boat to guide Daniel, Zsolt, and Marian to a good spot for angling. I stayed with the two Ukrainians and, around noon, they took me to their village.

The village was made up of a few dozen simple wooden houses with some 500 people living in them. It was called Mila 23, because once upon a time it had been situated twenty-three miles up the local river arm, counting back from the coast. The coast isn't a fixed point in the delta, however. It doesn't stand still, as sediment is continually being swept out of the Danube and deposited around its mouth. Year by year, the delta advances a few more metres into the Black Sea. Which is to say that Mila 23 had long ceased to be at the twenty-three-mile mark and was instead a good distance further upstream.

The fishermen moored their boat to the village cooperative's landing stage and delivered their catch. A fat man in a rubber apron weighed the carp and pressed a few crumpled lei notes into Gori's hand. Then Florin led me to the Lipovan church.

The church was a modest little building with a yellow plastered facade. A small metal cupola crowned the pointed roof, and there was a wooden bell tower at the front. The whole thing had been consecrated ...

'In the year 7493 after Adam!'

An old man had suddenly appeared at my side in the churchyard. News had obviously travelled fast that there was a foreigner in the village who was interested in the Lipovans.

The man's name was Grigory, and he spoke Russian. He only came up to my shoulder, and he peered up at me with very blue, very alert eyes. His long beard was milky white, as beards that were once blond tend to be.

Grigory was a Lipovan, like almost everyone else in Mila 23. The Lipovans were from Russia – Christians whose ancestors had broken with the Russian Orthodox Church in the seventeenth century because they found the reforms of the

Moscow patriarchate unacceptable. They still maintained the old Russian religious traditions: they crossed themselves not with three fingers but two; in processions, they walked around the church not anticlockwise but clockwise; and they counted the years not since the birth of Christ but since the Creation.

The Patriarch had persecuted the dissidents mercilessly in the seventeenth century. Renegade priests were burned at the stake, raising two fingers of their burning hands to heaven in the sign of the cross until the bitter end. The persecuted Old Believers fled to sparsely populated regions on the margins of the Russian Empire, where they founded secret communes that kept to the letter of the righteous faith. Many of them ended up in the Siberian taiga, some in the Baltic forests, and others, including Grigory's ancestors, had hidden away in the depths of the Danube delta. Along the river banks, they built houses from linden wood, known in Russian as *lipy*, which is why people called them Lipovans.

Inside the church, Grigory showed me the centuries-old books that the Old Believers had carried with them during their escape from Russia – books in which the name of the Lord was still written the way it was written in Russia until the ecclesiastical reform, before the patriarch and his scribes had succumbed to Satan: Isus instead of Iisus, with one 'i' instead of two. The books were kept on a shelf next to the iconostasis, the wall of icons. Behind it lay the altar on which the Old Believers placed five loaves of bread during the service – five, not seven as the errant reformists did.

'And they sing three hallelujahs, not two as is proper …'

Grigory's late father, Kondrat, born in the year 7432 after Adam, 1924 after Christ, had been the priest of Mila 23 for forty years. Next to the church doors was his grave, a fenced rectangle with an Orthodox wooden cross at its head – one vertical beam and three crossbeams, the top bar shorter than the middle one, the bottom one at a diagonal.

Grigory led me into the vine-shaded courtyard of his house, which was cheek by jowl with the church. He showed me faded black-and-white photos of his father's ordination in 7465 after Adam, or 1957 after Christ. Next to his father stood an Old Believer bishop whose white beard came down to his chest. At his father's heel stood four-year-old Grigory in shorts: very small, very blond.

His wife bumped a wheelbarrow full of firewood across the courtyard. She was a tiny woman with a lime-green headscarf, her deep voice inconsistent with her stature. 'Tell him about the church!'

Mila 23's old church, where Grigory's father had served for so long as a priest, had been so damaged by flooding that the Old Believers were forced to tear it down. They wanted to build a replacement, but the socialist authorities refused to grant a construction permit. The people were to work, not pray.

Grigory grinned. 'So we came up with a ruse.'

The Lipovans applied for a building permit for a shed to be able to protect their old books and icons from the damp at least. When they received the permit, they built a small unobtrusive storehouse. At one end, they erected the icon-ostasis and, behind it, the altar. On Sundays, they laid their five loaves on the altar, gathered in front of the images of the saints, and crossed themselves with two fingers while Grigory's father sang the liturgy. They were only able to con-secrate their secret church-shed officially in the year 7493 after Adam, 1985 after Christ, when the socialist regime relaxed its grip. The storehouse formed the main structure of the present village church. The Lipovans had added the cupola and the belltower later.

Other than the business about the church, Grigory said that the Lipovans had seldom been bothered by the authorities. Romanian was the mandatory language used for teaching at the village school, but the teachers came from Mila 23 and were Lipovans, so they spared their pupils the anti-religious propaganda of the socialist curriculum. Bucharest was a long way away, the village lay in a remote corner of the Danube delta, and from centuries of persecution the Old Believers had learned a great deal about how to elude the state.

'We listened to everything the socialists had to say, replied yes to everything, and then did as we liked.'

Grigory had been an apprentice shipbuilder in Galati and worked for twenty years at a dock in Tulcea, 40 km upriver from Mila 23. He'd moved back to the village when his father became bedridden after a stroke. When Grigory was a boy, his father had taught him all there was to know about the Old Believers, read the old books with him, sung the liturgy with him, and taught him the prayers. Following the stroke, Grigory had spent seven years singing the mass in the shed-church as a lay priest until the village was assigned a new priest.

Grigory had also passed on the Lipovans' spiritual tools to his own four children. Only one of them still lived in Mila 23 – a daughter who worked as a sales attendant in the local grocery store; the other three had left the village in the nineties. The economic upheaval after the collapse of socialism had made it more difficult to earn a living from fishing, and there was no other work in Mila 23. Grigory's son and his other two daughters now lived in Turin. The language there was similar to their own, so in recent decades many Romanians had emigrated to Italy in search of work. His son worked as a carpenter, his daughters as carers for Italian pensioners.

Grigory told me the old stories he had heard from his father and grandfather about the Old Believers' escape from Russia, the centuries of persecution and their clandestine life in the delta. Listening to him, I couldn't help but wonder whether this external pressure hadn't been the main thing binding the Lipovan community together, and what would become of them now that pressure was gone. Their old religious certainties – *five* loaves, *two* hallelujahs – had provided them with a sense of security for as long as the patriarchs and the socialists had tried to exorcise those certainties. But would Grigory's grandchildren still count the years since Adam? Or might the Lipovans one day sing their old songs purely for tourists, for the amateur ornithologists from Western Europe who paid to be ferried around the delta in search of rare waterfowl and ethnic groups?

Florin, the Ukrainian, took me back to Crisan that evening in his motorboat.

Daniel, Zsolt, and Marian hadn't had much luck fishing.

'Not a single damn fish the whole day!'

Instead, they had bought a bucket of crayfish from the fishermen. Dana cooked them for us. The wine flowed freely to the booming sound of manele.

It only dawned on me that second evening that, unlike Zsolt and Marian, Daniel, the manager, wasn't a simple employee of the mineral water company but the owner's son. His father had taken over the firm in the latter days of the socialist era and embarked on an aggressive expansion drive. The company was now worth €50 million, his father was a member of the country's financial elite, and Daniel was being groomed to run the business. The role didn't sit easily with him.

'I shit my pants every day. It's dog eat dog in management. You need to be armour-plated to cope. My father is cut from different cloth to me. He grew up in the Ceauşescu era, when you learned at school that one and one was two, end of story. Now they tell you it might be three or maybe seventy-seven – no one knows what's true. People like my father no longer exist nowadays. The man's like a rock. He's a fucking Ceauşescu!'

Zsolt and Marian knew Daniel's father well. He used to be the one who brought them angling in the delta as a reward for their services to the company, back when Daniel was too young for the kind of work outing his father enjoyed.

Marian recalled those orgiastic fishing trips. 'Twenty-seven bottles of Jägermeister in three days!'

One time, Marian said, the boss had been so drunk that he'd accosted a woman villager in the street, a total stranger, and offered her money to have sex with him. Had he been more sober, he would've noticed that the woman was wearing a border guard's uniform.

'We spent the night in jail.'

After a few more such anecdotes, Daniel and I stepped outside for a breath of fresh air. We staggered over to the jetty, which was lit up by millions of stars. The silence was broken by regular bangs from a faulty power line that sprayed sparks into the darkness.

'You live like a gypsy, man! When was the last time you were home? I couldn't do that – wander the world all on my own. Romanians need their homeland. We want families, cars, houses, sons …'

He spat into the pitch-black water. 'Fifty million, man. Fifty fucking million. Take a payout and I could settle down tomorrow in Thailand, ten hookers on each knee, and never lift a finger ever again. But is that what I want?'

He gave me a quizzical look, as if I knew the answer.

'No idea, Daniel. Is it?'

'I don't know, man. I don't know.'

He held his head in his hands, as if it was suddenly too heavy for him. 'I was born with a silver spoon in my mouth. Always had money for everything I wanted. Parties, drugs, whores, anything. But I'm useless, man. My father built it all up, I've done nothing. Nothing, zilch. I don't even know if I have what it takes. No one in the company believes in me. Do I go for it? Do I show them, fuck them all? Or is it just going to turn my hair all grey and I'll be the one who ends up fucked?'

Again, he shot me a questioning look. I could see his eyes right in front of me in the dark, clouded with a self-doubt that didn't fit with his alpha physique. All money aside, I didn't envy him.

'Hard to say, Daniel. Listen to your heart.'

For a while we stared out into the darkness before Daniel threw back his head and let out a long, loud wolf's howl that echoed in the night.

The next morning, we parted company. Daniel, Zsolt, and Marian went off fishing, and I took a boat downstream to the coast.

Sulina, the port town at the river's mouth, looked dead. The hotels were empty, and the amateur ornithologists had gone home. Only occasionally did huge container ships inch their way across the scene, monsters with Latin, Cyrillic, and Arabic ciphers on their sides, heading up the canalised Sulina arm, towering over every house in that small place.

Sulina had become a town in the mid-nineteenth century, when the European powers resolved to make the central arm of the Danube navigable for freighters. A harbour was built and a planning commission established. Sulina became a melting pot of people from every Black Sea nation, a place where Greek pilots, Turkish sailors, Romanian stevedores, Jewish and Armenian traders, and Western European engineers and captains came together and mingled. Barely a trace of this diversity had survived two world wars, apart from in Sulina's old cemetery. It was divided into four sections: Muslim, Jewish, Orthodox Christian, and miscellaneous Christian. The Muslim part lay largely fallow, and only a few isolated gravestones stood in the Jewish area, but the other two were packed. I spent a long time walking along the deserted paths, pursued by a black-and-white cemetery cat that didn't leave my side as I filled my notepad with gravestone inscriptions.

IN AFFECTIONATE REMEMBRANCE OF
THOMAS BULLEN
LATE MASTER OF S. S. CONSENT
WHO DIED (SUDDENLY) AT SEA
BETWEEN CONSTANTINOPLE & SULINA
MAY 22ND 1887
AGED 39 YEARS

ERNESTINA BRAUNSTEIN
DECEDATA 5 IULIE 1924 IN ETATE DE 66 ANI
SIMON BRAUNSTEIN
DECEDAT 17 MAI 1924 IN ETATE DE 67 ANI

HIER RUHT FRIEDRICH MILICH
GEBOREN AM 10. JUNI 1825
ZU SCHWAAN, MECKLENBURG-SCHWERIN
GESTORBEN AM 24. JANUAR 1886

ALLA MEMORIA DEL CARO ED INDIMENTICABILE MARITO
GIUSEPPE GIURGEVICH
CAPITANO MARITTIMO
NATO A PERZAGNO, DALMAZIA
IL 20 MARZO 1851
DECESSO IL 1 SETTEMBRE 1909

À LA MEMOIRE DE
NOTRE CHER FILS
ALEXANDRE BERJEAUT
NÉ LE 8 NOV. 1893
DÉCÉDÉ LE 14 SEPT. 1894

PRÍNCESEÍ ECATERÍNA MORUZÍ
NEPOTA LUÍ ÍOAN STURZA VOEVOD MOLDOVEÍ
NĂSCUTÂ ÎN CONSTANTÍNOPOL ÎN ANUL 1836
ÎNCETATÂ DÍN VÍATĂ ÎN SULÍNA LA 29 DEC. 1893

HIER RUHT CHAIM BRUMBERG
GEST. 29. NOVEMB. 1888

TEODOROS GHEORGHITZIS
N 1842 – M 1919
ANDONACHI GHEORGHITZIS
N 1922 – M 1923

HIER RUHET IN FRIEDEN
UNSER UNVERGESSLICHER
ROLAND LEUKERT
GEB. ZU PILSEN 3 / VII 1909
GEST. 20 / V 1927

An entire corner of the miscellaneous Christian section was taken up by the graves of the drowned. Virtually all the epitaphs were in English. They read like a long necrology of the Black Sea.

SACRED TO THE MEMORY OF
CAPTN DAVID BAIRD
WHO WAS DROWNED AT SULINA APRIL 24 1876
AGED 46 YEARS
THIS STONE WAS ERECTED BY HIS SON DAVID

IN LOVING MEMORY OF
ISABELLA JANE ROBINSON
ELDEST AND DEARLY BELOVED DAUGHTER OF
E. A. & E. D. S. ROBINSON, SOUTH SHIELDS
AGED 28 YEARS
DROWNED OFF SULINA ON THE 27 SEPTEMBER 1896
BY THE FOUNDERING THROUGH COLLISION
OF THE S/S KYLEMOOR

IN MEMORY OF
ABRAHAM FARRAR
ENGINEER, OF HARTLEPOOL, ENGLAND
DROWNED JULY 21ST 1879
AGED 40 YEARS
ERECTED BY HIS SEAFARING FRIENDS

SACRED TO THE MEMORY OF
BENJAMIN CREBER
BOY
H. M. S. COCKATRICE
WHO DEPARTED THIS LIFE ON THE 30TH AUGUST 1880

AT SULINA
THIS TABLET IS ERECTED BY HIS SHIPMATES

SACRED TO THE MEMORY OF
WILLIAM SIMPSON
WHO DIED AT SULINA ON THE 28TH JULY 1870 AGED 46 YEARS
THIS STONE IS ERECTED
BY THE EUROPEAN COMMISSION OF THE DANUBE
BY WHOM MR. SIMPSON WAS EMPLOYED FOR 13 YEARS
AS FOREMAN OF THE WORKS

IN AFFECTIONATE REMEMBRANCE OF
MARGARET ANN PRINGLE
OF NEWTON-BY-THE-SEA NORTHUMBERLAND ENGLAND,
WHO WAS ACCIDENTALLY DROWNED AT SULINA
ON THE 21ST DAY OF MAY 1868
AGED 23 YEARS

IN MEMORY OF
WILLIAM WEBSTER
CHIEF OFFICER ON BOARD THE S. S. ADALIA
WHO NOBLY SACRIFICED HIS OWN LIFE IN ENDEAVOURING
TO SAVE
MARGARET ANN PRINGLE FROM DROWNING
AT SULINA ON THE 21ST OF MAY 1868
AGED 25 YEARS
HE WAS THE ONLY SON OF THE LATE JOHN WEBSTER
OF BISHOPWEARMOUTH CO. DURHAM ENGLAND

A narrow track led down from the cemetery to the shore. I walked to the outermost tip of a spit of land at the end of the Sulina canal and watched the brown earth-sated waters of

the Danube roll into the Black Sea. Around the river mouth
it kept its colour before, maybe 100 m from the shore, the
brown shaded into grey and the river dissolved into the sea.

Ukraine

Chorne more / *Чорне море*

This is what the foamy waves
of the Odessan sea throw onto the shore.

Isaac Babel, 'The King', 1921

The spring at Kyrnychky

There are many strange borders around the Black Sea, but that between Romania and Ukraine is one of the stranger ones. It coincides with the most northerly branch of the Danube delta, running along its length and dividing it into a Romanian half and a Ukrainian half. Russian Old Believers live on both sides, their villages separated in some places only by 200 m of water, so close that you can count the onions growing in the gardens on the other bank. It has long been impossible to cross over from here to there, however. The external border of the Soviet Union was drawn along the northern bank after the Second World War; nowadays, the south side marks where the European Union ends. Border craft patrol the river which has kept the Lipovan villages apart for more than seventy years. A man in Mila 23 told me that almost all the Old Believers in the delta had relatives on the other side, whom they knew only from stories recounted by their grandparents. The border had torn the Lipovan families asunder.

If you want to cross from Romania to the other side, you have to leave the delta and follow the Danube upstream to Galati – the nearest border crossing, a good 100 km from the coast. It does not lead into Ukraine, however, but into the southernmost tip of Moldova. Only 2 km further on comes a second border, this one with Ukraine.

An old Moldovan by the name of Foma, who had worked as a policeman in the Soviet days, took me to Reni, the first place on the Ukrainian side, which was where he lived.

On the way to the bus station, we drove past the base of a

monument with no monument standing on it. I pointed to the empty plinth.

'Lenin?'

Foma nodded.

This was not the first empty Lenin plinth I'd seen. Since the start of the war with Russia, the Ukrainians had toppled the old memorials to the Soviet leader all over the country.

'Is it Lenin's fault that life's bad?' Foma didn't wait for my answer. 'The goal of socialism was for everyone to have a house, a car, a dacha. What's so bad about that?'

The main street of Reni was pitted with enormous rain-filled potholes. We dodged these craters at walking pace like cosmonauts on a lunar expedition. Rarely had the gulf between the goals and the consequences of socialism seemed wider to me.

Foma didn't think much of Ukraine's new-found nationalism. 'Is it going to make our lives better if they send us hooligans who rip down monuments to Lenin? What are these nationalists even doing here? There are hardly any Ukrainians in Budjak! The villages here are Romanian, Moldovan, Bulgarian, and Gagauz. We all speak our own languages, and we communicate with one another in Russian. No one speaks Ukrainian ...'

He grumbled to himself for some time, shaking his head. Only when we reached the bus station did his face brighten up a bit.

'Are you going to Odessa?'

'Soon, yes.'

'The capital of crime! You know all the jokes, right? You don't? OK, I'll tell you one. A man returns to Odessa after many years abroad. Outside the station, he sets his suitcase down on the pavement, runs his eyes over the scene, and sees all the new houses that have been built while he was away. "Oh, Odessa," he sighs, "I don't recognise you." As he's about to walk on, he notices that his suitcase is no longer there. "Oh, Odessa," he sighs, "now I recognise you!"'

On the bus heading to the seashore, I met two women who were on their way to their home village. Natasha talked a great deal and laughed at anything and everything, most of all at her own jokes. Anya was quiet, and her facial expression was hard to fathom – both weary and panicky, as if she had just woken from a bad dream.

The village where they lived was called Kyrnychky and was halfway to the coast. It was a Bulgarian village. Natasha was Russian, though, from the Donbass region in eastern Ukraine. Anya was Moldovan.

My puzzled smile amused Natasha.

'Welcome to Budjak! Bulgarians, Romanians, Moldovans, Russians, Ukrainians, Gagauz – we have everything here! And we all get on well.'

It crossed my mind that everyone in Donbass had also got on well until they didn't any more, but I didn't want to reopen old wounds, so I avoided any comment.

Budjak, the small coastal stretch of Ukraine south-west of Odessa, had been part of Bessarabia until the Second World War, when Stalin carved off present-day Moldova from Bessarabia, throttling the newly established Soviet republic's access to the sea. Now, Budjak was the most ethnically mixed region of an ethnically mixed Ukraine. Of all its peoples, I was most interested in the Gagauz – Christian Turks of obscure provenance. I asked Natasha and Anya where I might find some.

'The next village to ours is Gagauz,' Anya said. 'Come and visit us, and we'll take you there.'

The bus dropped us off by the side of a country road. From that point on, everything very quickly went wrong. Natasha and Anya rang up a relative, Uncle Gena, who was supposed to drive us to the neighbouring village, but when he turned up at the bus stop in his old Lada, he was so drunk that we were relieved simply to get him and the car back to his home in one piece. Since we were then inside his house, though, he refused to let me leave without first drinking a glass of his homemade brandy with me, and we only managed to prise ourselves loose after one glass had become five. We walked to the other end of the village, to the home of Natalya, an acquaintance of Anya's who knew someone who knew someone in the next village, but it turned out when we got there that Anya had got two neighbouring villages muddled up. Since we were then inside the house, though, her husband, Vasya, refused to let me leave without first drinking a glass of his homemade wine with me, and after one glass had become four and I timidly enquired about the Gagauz, Natasha shook her head ruefully.

'It's late. People will be going to bed soon.'

It was five in the afternoon.

At some point, I gave up on that day and on the Gagauz and simply kept drinking. My disappointment must have shown, because Anya phoned up someone else she knew and invited her over; Tatiana had a Gagauz grandmother and was therefore a quarter Gagauz, which left me a quarter consoled. She didn't know much about her grandmother other than the fact that, despite only four years' schooling, she had spoken Gagauz Turkish along with fluent Romanian, Bulgarian, Ukrainian, and Russian. Tatiana herself spoke Russian, Bulgarian, and Romanian. Just like them, every single one of the now very considerable number of drinkers gathered in the kitchen were amazingly polyglot – apart from Natasha, the Russian, who in fine old Soviet tradition spoke nothing but Russian.

'Jens,' Natasha said, 'explain something to me.'

'What?'

'You lost the war, and we won the war, correct?

'Correct.'

'Then explain to me why you're doing so well now and we're doing so shit!'

I thought about this for a long time, but I couldn't come up with a convincing explanation.

Even from the bus, Budjak hadn't looked like the most prosperous place. I had been struck by cyclists at the sides of the road, transporting bundles of twigs on their luggage racks through the steppes. Natasha and Anya told me that this was firewood they had collected, as the houses here weren't connected to the gas mains and coal was expensive. Kyrnychky appeared to be one of the poorer of many poor villages in Budjak. There were no jobs here. Most local people lived on what they grew in their gardens and on occasional additional earnings abroad, in Russia or the EU, as cleaners, crop-pickers, carers for the elderly, construction labourers, babysitters, or smugglers.

Tatiana, the quarter-Gagauz, told me Kyrnychky's founding legend. A long time ago, supposedly, a man was walking with his blind son along the old country road where the bus had dropped us off. Discovering a spring on the verge, they pitched camp for the night. That evening, the son washed his face in the spring water, and the next morning he could see. Tatiana said that Kyrnychky was a Bulgarian word for 'spring', and since the miracle had taken place on 6 May, on that day every year the villagers walked in a procession to the spring to drink its healing waters.

'In any case, they used to, when the spring was still there.'

'It *is* still there.'

'Don't be stupid.'

'But it is. Next to the petrol station.'

'Oh, come on, it dried up long ago.'

There followed a long discussion as to the spring's present whereabouts, but no one was entirely sure what state it was in now.

At some stage, I realised that it was now far too late to leave Kyrnychky and look for a hotel. Natasha, who was sitting next to me, fluttered her eyelashes and offered me her sofa, but she was drunk and had dropped some earlier hints about a difficult ex-husband. I smelled trouble. Casting around for help, I leaned over to Anya and asked if I could stay at hers.

She nodded. 'We just have to be careful not to wake my son.'

On our way back through the village, my mind returned to Ovid, whose letters from exile contained epic accounts of the bitterly cold Black Sea winters – never-ending, sorrowful descriptions of tinkling ice, beards stiff with frost, frozen wine, ships ice-bound at sea. Reading these clearly overblown winter dirges, I had noticed only their self-evident intention: Ovid wanted to tug at the emperor's heartstrings in the hope that, out of pity, he would summon the poet back to Rome. Suddenly, though, I perceived the truth of every word. The temperature had fallen steadily during the past November days, and that night it dropped below zero for the first time. A chill wind came whistling in over the open steppe, funnelling the cold, damp sea air through every gap in my clothing. The frost stung my face so violently that it hurt. Even Anya, who must have been accustomed to this climate, swore in pain.

Her small house lay at the end of a track. Anya unlocked the door and raised one finger to her lips.

We tiptoed along the hallway and through a dark communicating room. Just as Anya was pushing me into the next room, I heard a noise. I spun round and saw someone leap up out of a bed in a dark corner.

'Who is this guy?'

The light came on. Anya's son was standing by the bed, a thin man in his mid-twenties with a shaved head. His outstretched hand was on the light switch. His eyes were red and full of hatred.

'Is there no saving you? D'you think I'm deaf? What's this guy doing here?'

'Calm down, Viktor.'

'You want me to calm down? You drag some guy home in the middle of the night and you tell *me* to calm down?'

'It isn't what you think.'

'Oh yeah? Has he come here to play chess?'

'Viktor ...'

I cleared my throat and tried to explain what had brought me to Kyrnychky, but even while I was speaking, I realised that my story sounded made-up. A German looking for Gagauz, a book about the Black Sea ... I saw Viktor's eyes narrow with suspicion.

'Do you think I'm stupid? The two of you?'

Anya pushed me back through the door into the hallway and ushered me into the kitchen.

'Sit down and I'll make us some tea. He'll cool down.'

A few seconds later, Victor's gaunt frame appeared in the doorway. 'He's still here?'

'Where's he meant to go, Viktor? It's winter. Am I supposed to send him out into the cold?'

'Send him wherever you like. To hell, for all I care!'

He let the door slam into the wall on his way out.

Anya made the tea. It was cold in the kitchen, and steam rose from the cups.

'What's wrong with him?'

She stared at me in silence, then shook her head. 'I can't explain it to you.'

'Should I leave?'

'No. Don't worry, he'll calm down.'

'Doesn't look like it.'

'It sometimes takes a while.'

'But what's up with him?'

Again, she gazed into my eyes for a long time without saying anything. Her brain seemed to be whirring. Finally, she put her teacup down on the table and crossed her arms over her chest.

'If you really want to hear the story, I'll tell it to you. But don't go saying afterwards that I forced you to listen to me.'

I nodded, and the story began.

Viktor was twenty-six, a child from Anya's first marriage, which hadn't lasted long. Shortly after the breakup, she had married again. Her second husband was from Kyrnychky, and that is how she and Viktor had ended up in the house we were sitting in.

Her second marriage was worse than the first, though it lasted longer. Anya's husband had beaten her without respite, without reason, without mercy. He beat her until she bled, broke her bones, kicked out her teeth, chased her around the house with his gun, fired shots near her feet out in the garden, and made her run for her life.

'I've no idea why I stayed. I wanted to leave, but I couldn't.'

Viktor grew up seeing his mother beaten black and blue. He went from being a boy to a teenager, and from a teenager to a man, as he watched his stepfather laying into Anya. It went on like this for twenty years until one day, shortly after he turned twenty-three, Viktor picked up the gun, held the muzzle to his stepfather's face, and pulled the trigger.

The police took the dead man and the murderer away. Anya was left in the house on her own, without a husband, without her son. She listened to the sirens fade into the distance, and when she couldn't hear them any more, she wiped the brains off the kitchen wall. That was three years ago.

For three years, they had been waiting for the trial to start. Meanwhile, Viktor was released from custody, as the judges saw no risk of his absconding. 'You should reckon with a fifteen-year sentence,' the lawyer said.

Anya used to work on a market stall in Kyrnychky for $100 a month. Now she took the bus nearly 1,500 km to Moscow every few weeks to earn slightly more looking after a Russian family's children. She had to pay the lawyer's fees.

Anya got up to fill our teacups. Her hands were trembling. The longer we sat in that kitchen, the colder we got. The only small stove in the house heated the bedrooms.

Next to the sink, by the door, lay a long kitchen knife, the sight of which made me more and more anxious. It reminded me of Chekhov's dramatic principle about the gun hanging on the wall in the first act and being fired in the final act. That was exactly what had happened here before. The longer I stared at the knife, the more it looked like a prop just waiting to be put to use.

'Anya, maybe it'd be better if I left?'

The idea of wandering the dark steppe in below-zero temperatures was scary, but I didn't know how to assess Viktor's anger.

Anya shook her head. 'Don't worry, he'll calm down. Sons want their mothers to put meals in front of them, and wash their clothes, and otherwise not to have a life. That's all he's bothered about.'

She blamed herself for everything that had happened. It was all her fault, because she was asleep when Viktor took the gun and because she came running into the kitchen only after hearing the shot, when it was too late. It was her fault, because she hadn't left her husband. It was her fault, because she'd turned her husband into a wife-beater and her son into a murderer.

'Anya …' I said, staring at her in horror. 'It's not your fault. How can you even think such a thing?'

She shrugged her shoulders wearily. 'Tell me it isn't my fault. Tell me so I believe it. Just try. You won't be the first.'

I did try, but my words merely bounced off her. She'd heard it all many times before, and she believed none of it. It was her fault.

Her husband's family blamed her too. Half the village blamed her. She'd lost count of all the men who had come to her door drunk, wanting sex, because they saw her as easy prey, a desperate woman who'd never find another husband in Kyrnychky.

Anya looked me in the eye. 'I'm trash.'

She sounded neither doleful nor cynical; it was a sober diagnosis.

All of a sudden, Viktor was standing in the doorway again, his lips twisted into a sarcastic smile.

'So? Told you about her terrible fate, has she?'

It took me a moment to come up with a riposte. 'You don't think it's a terrible fate?'

His smile turned even more sinister. 'It is. But she should have thought about that earlier.'

I realised that even Viktor blamed his mother.

He turned to Anya. 'When's this guy finally going to get lost?'

As he walked out of the kitchen, the knife caught my eye again. I had the feeling that he and I needed to talk things through, so I followed him out.

He was sitting on his bed, his legs folded in the lotus position, his face bony and focused, his ascetic features like a monk's.

Once more, I explained how I came to be in Kyrnychky. This time he believed me.

'Have they shown you how to drink?' He laughed his sinister laugh. 'They know how to drink here. Just don't know how to do much else.'

We chatted for a while, and I quickly realised that in a different life we could have found a common language. In this life, though, I groped for words, desperately trying to say something that would build bridges between mother and son, even though it became more and more apparent as I spoke that I was the last person who would be able to mediate between them.

When Anya appeared in the doorway to see what we were up to, Viktor sneered at her. 'Don't worry, we've concluded our own Molotov–Ribbentrop pact.'

I cracked up like an idiot. Rarely had I found a joke so liberating.

All the same, I barely slept that night. At some point, I heard through the wall the sounds of Viktor getting up and pulling the front door shut behind him. He'd told me he had to leave early; he worked on building sites. When the first light of dawn seeped in through the curtains, I got up. Anya was still asleep. I put my hand on her shoulder. Slowly, she opened her eyes and looked at me the same way she had done on the bus the day before, both weary and panicky, as if she were awaking from a nightmare she could never shake off.

She wanted to accompany me to the bus stop, but I talked her out of it. For a few moments, we gazed into each other's eyes silently, helplessly. There was nothing to say.

The steppe was crusted with frost. A few geese waddled ahead of me along the village track, until I overtook them and they scattered, hissing, in front of my feet. Leaving the houses behind, I was alone in the flat, brown, depressingly desolate landscape. I felt chilled, inside and out.

A few warmly wrapped villagers were setting up market stalls along the road by the petrol station. I asked them about the spring. They looked at me in bemusement. 'The miraculous spring,' I said. 'The old Kyrnychky spring.' A woman pointed without a word to the steppe beyond the petrol station. I walked off in that direction, sensing suspicious eyes on my back.

In thick undergrowth I found a rusty metal pipe. Water trickled into a muddy pit full of glass shards, bottle caps, and cigarette butts. The last miracle must have happened quite some time back.

A coincidence in Odessa

I got onto a minibus full of commuters who slept through the drive to Odessa with cricked necks and open mouths. The empty Budjak steppe rolled past the windows until factories, building supply stores, and filling stations indicated that we were nearing a city. Half an hour later, the minibus pulled up outside the main railway station, where the commuters massaged their tense necks and vanished yawning into town.

Winter was definitely upon us. In the city centre's grid of

streets, lined with splendid imperial facades, I saw three kinds of pedestrian. Some leaned into the icy gale-force gusts that swept off the sea and through the streets from east to west. Others advanced with a strangely erect gait to prevent the tail wind from sending them tumbling forwards. The third kind walked north or south, and only felt the full force of the wind when it ambushed them at a crossroads, blowing them sideways.

Odessa was the port metropolis with which Catherine the Great marked her conquest of the Black Sea coast. In the late eighteenth century, the tsarina gave orders that a city be conjured out of nothing in the middle of the steppe, with no Greek or other classical origins, even though its whimsically ancient name suggested otherwise. What was reminiscent of the multicultural societies of the Black Sea colonies of antiquity, however, was the ragtag population that soon made Odessa its home. With Russian patronage, French bureaucrats, Spanish officers, Italian architects, German industrialists, and merchants from Armenia, Greece, and Moldova congregated alongside communities of Bulgarians, Romanians, Tatars, Ukrainians, Poles, Turks, and Albanians.

Most importantly, however, Odessa became the centre of Russian Jewry. There were strict laws defining where Jews could settle in Catherine's empire. They were only allowed to take up residence in the western border regions, in a tract of shtetl land running from Lithuania in the north down through Poland to Ukraine. All of a sudden, Odessa formed a new gateway to the Black Sea on the southern edge of this area of Jewish settlements. The port's maritime traffic was controlled by other ethnic groups, in particular Greeks and Italians, but the Jews managed to find their niche in the export business as middlemen who made use of their connections in the shtetls to channel supplies of commodities from the northern hinterland to the coast. As the first Jewish traders rose to a prosperity and prominence in Odessa that remained a distant dream for their fellows in other parts of the tsarist empire, the port attracted a constant stream of would-be emulators. Yiddish became the second most common language after Russian. By the end of the nineteenth century, one in three Odessites was Jewish, and in the years leading up to the Second World War, there were more Jewish residents than Russians. Not even antisemitic aggression by their Odessan neighbours, which shook the city with dismal regularity in the nineteenth and early twentieth centuries, could deter new immigrants. These attacks became known by their Russian name, 'pogrom', meaning 'thunderclap', which radiated out from the Black Sea and entered languages around the world.

This Jewish age was brought to a temporary end by the Romanian occupation of Odessa during the Second World War. Tens of thousands were murdered by the Nazis' allies, while others fled and never came back. In the post-war years, Odessa's remaining Jews emigrated to Israel or became loyal Soviet citizens to blend in, concealing their roots so thoroughly that they could barely remember their past selves after a while.

On the upper floor of the synagogue on Vulytsya Osypova, the rabbi Avroom Wolf was poring over a file that his secretary had placed on the table.

'You remember the old lady in the fur coat, rabbi? We've gathered together all the papers. So far, everything's correct.'

The rabbi leafed through the file, the tip of his greying beard brushing the tabletop. I could see his eyes flicking from left to right and back again behind his spectacles. Eventually, Wolf picked up his ballpoint pen and inscribed a blue squiggle at the bottom of the last page. Odessa had a new Jewish inhabitant.

After the secretary had left the room, Wolf rolled his eyes theatrically at the ceiling.

'So many certificates! Mountains of certificates! Every day people turn up here, asking if they are Jewish, and I have to examine all their papers! These certificates are blurring into one before my eyes!'

Wolf had been born in Israel, but his Russian was rapid, snappy, and sparkling. Twenty-five years back, he had got himself posted as a rabbi to the Russian-speaking south of newly independent Ukraine, just three months after wedding his Israeli bride. In the 1990s, the couple had brought eight children into the world in Odessa at a time when the former Soviet planned economy had been abolished without there yet being a functioning market economy to replace it. Food supplies were patchy, and kosher food was practically unknown. For years, the Wolfs had eaten no meat or dairy products, the entire family living essentially on eggs, pasta, and trust in God.

The Jewish exodus from Odessa had continued in those difficult times. Each time Wolf put his signature to a sheaf of documents, he could be fairly certain that the freshly certified Jews would soon be emigrating to Israel or Germany. Nevertheless, a fairly stable congregation had formed in the reopened synagogue. People turned up having rediscovered not only their family origins but also their faith, eager to pray, live according to the laws, and read the scriptures. Early that morning, before I met with Wolf, I had seen them down in the central hall, dropping in at the synagogue on their way to work, wrapping the tefillin around their arms, and becoming absorbed in their recitations, their eyes closed. Two other synagogues in Odessa had reopened. There were a Jewish newspaper, a small museum, a few kosher restaurants – and Jews too, their number estimated at 10,000 by some, 30,000 by others. The community lived on.

'That's exactly what we wanted to achieve. We wanted to show that we cannot be destroyed. Hitler is gone, Stalin is gone, but we are still here.'

Wolf's ancestors hailed from Nuremberg. Some of them had been murdered; the survivors had fled to Israel.

'My wife's family story is much more interesting, though.'

His wife's great-grandfather had been a rabbi in Odessa. He had died in 1936, just in time to escape Stalin's terror and Hitler's horror. His three sons, all rabbis, had been less fortunate. Two of them had been shot as alleged counter-revolutionaries in 1938 at the height of the Stalinist purges, and the third had been killed in action during the war. Only the daughters had survived, and one of them had married another rabbi, Wolf's wife's grandfather. Shortly after the war, he had attempted to flee across the Polish border to the West and on to Israel. He was caught in the act and sentenced to twenty-five years in a labour camp.

'He toiled away in Siberia until Stalin's death. Seven years. In that whole time, he touched nothing that wasn't kosher – he subsisted on bread and water. When he came out, he was so thin you could see the water running through his body.'

It took until the sixties for the grandfather's family to be granted the right to leave the country at last. Fifty of them had set out, including Wolf's parents-in-law. His wife was born a few years later in Israel.

'Now, brace yourself!' Wolf leaned over the desk towards

me. I could see the punchline twinkling in his eye. 'When we arrived here in Odessa, we examined the synagogue's records. You'll never believe what we found. My wife's great-grandfather was a rabbi right here! There were eighty-three synagogues in Odessa back then. Eighty-three! And he was rabbi of the one whose rabbi I am now!'

I gave an appreciative smile. 'What a coincidence!'

His face fell. 'A coincidence?'

For a moment he stared at me in disbelief, then he burst out laughing. He slumped into his chair, shoulders trembling, looked up at the sky, and simply couldn't stop chuckling. 'A coincidence!'

Antelopes on the steppe

On the far side of Odessa, the main road bent away from the coastline in a wide arc to avoid the estuaries of two large rivers – first the Southern Bug, then the sprawling Dnieper delta. I took a bus to Kherson. Beyond this city, for the last 100 km before the Ukrainian border with Crimea, public transport thinned out. It was too cold for hitch-hiking. I rented a car, a small one built by an Uzbek manufacturer I'd never heard of, and crossed the Dnieper, which enters the Black Sea a few miles downstream from Kherson.

The Ukrainian radio station I listened to in the car devoted its airtime to a single subject. A few days earlier, the Russian coastguard had opened fire on three Ukrainian navy ships near the Crimean bridge to warn them off entering the Sea of Azov. The ships were impounded, their crews were taken prisoner, and now twenty-four Ukrainian sailors were languishing in Russian jails. Each side accused the other of having provoked the incident. Martial law had been declared in the

Ukrainian borderlands. As I drove, I rehearsed some Russian phrases to allow me to give a half-plausible explanation in case the authorities proved sceptical about what a foreigner might be up to in the area bordering Crimea during a state of emergency.

The road led through dull brown wintery steppe. The wind blew bits of dried-out bushes across the asphalt; these irregularly shaped objects came racing towards my car, half rolling, half bouncing, and then shattered with a snap beneath the wheels. Pheasants repeatedly fluttered across the carriageway, birds as brown as the steppe, the males with shimmering brightly coloured heads, the females virtually invisible as soon as they reached the other side of the road. Once, I saw a flock of cranes sailing along the verge, descending slowly and unfolding their legs just above the ground before diving into the hip-high grass.

In the nineteenth century, the largely untouched wild grasslands of the Crimean foreshore caught the eye of a German duke of the House of Ascania. Having run out of land to expand his sheep breeding operation in his native Anhalt, he purchased 600 square km from the tsar and called into being a German colony called Askania-Nova ('new Ascania') in the middle of the steppe. A good 2,000 sheep were driven out of Anhalt in 1828, and they chewed their first mouthfuls of steppe grass not long afterwards.

Russia was a let-down for the Anhaltians. Their sheep-breeding scheme wasn't profitable. Barely thirty years after the colony's establishment, they threw in the towel and sold the now 30,000-strong flock and the land to a man called Friedrich Fein.

Fein was an ethnic German, descended from the émigré colonists Catherine the Great had lured to Russia to settle the freshly conquered Black Sea coast. Most of them led quiet, inconspicuous lives as farmers in a scattering of villages south-east of Odessa. The Feins, however, were more ambitious. Fein and his progeny expanded Askania-Nova, made the operation profitable, exported wool, added all kinds of other animals to their sheep, and even established a zoo and later some botanical gardens on the steppe. As the nineteenth century came to an end, they had transformed Askania-Nova into one of the world's largest and most diverse wildlife parks. Russia's last tsar, Nicholas II, dignified the steppe colony with a visit in 1914 and marvelled at the antelopes, bison, zebras, Przewalski's horses, ostriches, and camels.

After this imperial visit, the German family, which by then had adopted the name of Falz-Fein, was ennobled with a barony. Not that it benefited them much. The October Revolution made it a dangerous time to be an aristocrat. Nicholas II was shot by the Bolsheviks in 1918, and the Falz-Feins fled to their ancestral homeland, Germany, where some of their descendants still live to this day.

Their wildlife park in the steppe remains, however. I drove along deserted country roads until the estate appeared before me – a huge biosphere reserve through fenced parts of which antelopes and Przewalski's horses gallop wild and free to this day. The park was public property during the Soviet era; now it is used as a research and nature conservation area by the Ukrainian Academy of Sciences. An elderly tour guide showed me around the botanical gardens and led me past endless stables and aviaries, listing dozens of species whose Russian names I had never heard before.

'However, those are only a fraction of the animals the Falz-Feins kept here.'

The guide had large melancholy eyes, which made her look

as if the emptiness of the steppe had permeated her soul. She told me that many Ukrainian holidaymakers used to stop in Askania-Nova on their way to Crimea, but the flow of tourists had more or less dried up since the annexation cut the peninsula off from the mainland.

'We've had almost no visitors in the past few years.'

The strip of land before Crimea had become a dead end. No one knew what would become of a visitorless Askania-Nova.

I continued south towards the Crimean border. The tour guide had told me about a village where the Falz-Feins had grazed some of their flocks of sheep before the Revolution.

Preobrazhenka lay directly on the border. Only 100 m from the edge of the village was the new fence the Russians had erected after the annexation.

I asked a few villagers about the Falz-Feins and wound up in the kitchen of Ludmila, a history teacher at the local school. Her old mother, Yekaterina, set down a plate of jellied pork and red horseradish on the table in front of me. Out in the yard, Ralf, a black Labrador, was barking: he didn't appreciate guests. There were white lace curtains on the windows. As we chatted, I watched the daylight dwindle and the curtains go grey.

Yekaterina talked about her father, who was born in 1894 and had tended the Falz-Feins' sheep as a young man. One time, when required to deliver something to his master, he had entered the family's castle, an enormous palatial manor where the Falz-Feins had lived in Preobrazhenka.

'He told us that an aquarium had been installed under the ceiling of one of the drawing rooms. It looked as if the fish were floating in the sky. My father talked about it for the rest of his life.'

After the Falz-Feins fled, the manor had fallen into disrepair and was later demolished. There were very few other traces of the family in Preobrazhenka. Their flocks had been nationalised after the Revolution, and their sheep-breeding business was turned into a sovkhoz, a state-owned farm. Simultaneously, the village had been renamed to match the sovkhoz, and both were henceforth known as Krasny Chaban ('red shepherd'). Only recently, once the annexation put Soviet memorials and Soviet place names on the hit list in Ukraine, had the village returned to its earlier name. Since 2016 it was called Preobrazhenka again, as it had been in the time of the Falz-Feins.

Ludmila and Yekaterina didn't think much of this re-renaming. God knows their village had more pressing problems. Virtually everyone who lived here had once worked in the sovkhoz. Yekaterina's late husband had been the farm manager, and she had administered the personnel records for forty years. Even the school where Ludmila taught had once been part of the sovkhoz. Since the collapse of the Soviet Union, however, the old state-owned farm was down to its bare bones. Half the village had been forced to look for new jobs. Most had found one in Armyansk, a small town nearby with a chemical plant – a large titanium factory. Soon, about 500 people from Preobrazhenka – roughly a third of the village population – had begun to commute to the factory in Armyansk.

The town wasn't far from Preobrazhenka. It was a few kilometres further south on the same road that traversed the village. Unfortunately, the Crimean border now ran exactly between the two places. The annexation meant that the titanium factory was now in Russia, whereas Preobrazhenka was still part of Ukraine.

For a few months, the villagers had continued to travel to work every day. They had seen the fence being gradually erected across the steppe, seen the Portakabins of the Russian border force appear at the side of the road and, a little later, the introduction of customs checks on the Ukrainian side too. They had seen the border gradually harden. It had become more and more difficult to drive to work in Armyansk each morning and back to Preobrazhenka each evening, but the villagers had carried on commuting to the titanium factory.

Until the day they were told that the factory would no longer employ any foreigners. Like the rest of Crimea, the works had been incorporated into the Russian tax, pensions, and social security system, and all the employees living on the Crimean peninsula had received Russian passports. Workers with Ukrainian passports were no longer needed in Armyansk. Too much red tape. At a stroke, all the commuters from Preobrazhenka lost their jobs. They hadn't moved anywhere, but now they were foreigners.

For a time, the villagers had protested against their dismissals. They blocked the railway line running through their village from the Ukrainian mainland to Crimea to cut off the titanium factory's supplies. This had brought the works to a temporary standstill, but their sabotage didn't get them their jobs back. Eventually, the factory had found alternative supply channels; the raw materials now came from Russia by ship.

I asked Ludmila and Yekaterina how the people of Preobrazhenka made a living now – and guessed the answer before I even heard it. Most of them, Ludmila said, went to work in the EU, especially Poland, to pick strawberries, change nappies, or clean offices. The village had become eerily empty since the annexation of Crimea. Most of the children in

Ludmila's classes were being brought up by their grandparents while their parents earned money abroad. Preobrazhenka's only permanent residents were the elderly, the young, and a few civil servants like Ludmila.

I ate my jellied pork. It was dark outside now, and the glass behind the curtains had turned black. Ralf the Labrador had stopped barking and didn't even bother raising his muzzle off the ground as Ludmila and Yekaterina accompanied me back across the yard to the village road. *Dogs*, I thought, *get used to everything, however angry it makes them at first. Like humans.*

Entry no. 5: *Mnemiopsis leidyi*

When the Falz-Feins fled Russia after the Revolution, only the ancient mother of the family's last patriarch stayed behind in the steppe – Sophie von Falz-Fein, an eighty-year-old woman who couldn't imagine that anyone would touch a hair on her head.

She was tragically mistaken. In June 1919, she was murdered in her home by two Bolsheviks who were obviously driven by a combination of greed and class hatred because, before robbing the old lady, they pointlessly stabbed her seventeen times. Their commander, a former bailiff for the Falz-Feins who had joined the Bolsheviks after the Revolution, had the two murderers shot without further ado.

I found Sophie von Falz-Feins' grave in an overgrown corner of the cemetery in Khorly, the village in which she spent the final years of her life. It stood on a small peninsula jutting out into the Black Sea a few miles north-west of the Crimean border. Khorly was a seaside resort, but now, in the middle of winter, it was practically dead. Only one of the many hotels was open – the Paradise, a cluster of small wooden bungalows in the style of hunting lodges.

The Paradise's concierge, Valeriy, was hoarding in his office hut a heavy bust of Lenin that had until recently stood in front of the village school. He had taken it in when people had started, one by one, to topple Lenin monuments in the surrounding villages.

'I was a pioneer once. I don't want Lenin to end up on the rubbish heap. Everyone here used to be a pioneer, even those who now want to knock down Lenin. Let them knock down other statues for all I care – I've given this one asylum.'

There was only one other guest at the Paradise apart from me. Mykhaylo was from the Donbass industrial region of eastern Ukraine. An engineer, he was supervising the construction of a field of solar panels way out in the steppe.

Mykhaylo was a second-generation Ukrainian Russian: like him, his parents were children of mixed-nationality marriages. In common with most Ukrainians, Mykhaylo spoke both languages fluently, with a slight preference for Russian, although this was more a question of habit than affinity. Even before the Russian invasions of recent years, the Ukrainian half of his heart had beaten harder in his breast than the Russian one.

Since we were the hotel's sole guests, on three consecutive evenings we both ended up in the only open restaurant in Khorly. During one of these meals, Mykhaylo told me about two school friends of his in the Donbass, a Georgian and a Ukrainian. After completing their schooling towards the end of the Soviet era, the three of them had been conscripted together as one of the last cohorts to serve in the Red Army. Mykhaylo's Ukrainian schoolmate had been dispatched to a military base in Russia and, after basic training, he had stayed on in the army. He was later promoted to a Russian special forces unit and sent to the Caucasus in the early 1990s. To Abkhazia, to be precise.

'Later on, he confided in me about the operations there. He told me how his unit whipped up the Abkhazians against the Georgians, how they armed them, whispered in their ears about having a state of their own, launched a referendum, and then got the populace to vote for secession from Georgia.'

Many years later, when soldiers started appearing in Crimea, Mykhaylo's phone rang. It was his Ukrainian schoolfriend.

'He was very agitated. He said, "They're stealing Crimea from us! What's happening is exactly like in Abkhazia. They're doing the same things we did all those years ago."'

Shortly afterwards, the old school friends from the Donbass had met up again – all three of them, the Georgian, Mykhaylo, and the Ukrainian. The Georgian said that some of his relatives had been driven out of Abkhazia during the civil war. He asked the Ukrainian why he had gone along with that.

'He had no answer.'

The Ukrainian schoolmate had left the army. He lived in Novorossiysk on the Russian Black Sea coast because he'd married a woman there. He regarded the annexation of Crimea as a crime and was ashamed of his mission in Abkhazia. He had the feeling that by getting involved in the one he had paved the way for the other.

The landlady of the restaurant in Khorly told me about a monk who was living as a hermit on a nearby island. The island was only a few miles off the coast, and I could make out its shoreline on the horizon as I set out westward from Khorly. I spent half the day enquiring in one village after another to see if there was a fisherman who would ferry me over to the island in his boat, but I was out of luck. Martial law had been declared a few days earlier, and that same morning the Ukrainian navy had banned fishermen from going to sea until further notice.

I eventually put the island and the monk out of my mind; instead, from the village of Lazurne I watched the sea freezing over. The icy wind was sweeping wave after wave up onto the shallow beach. I saw the flow gradually slow and the water become thicker and thicker, more and more pasty as it turned to slush that rolled sluggishly across the sand. Simultaneously, the sound of the breakers changed. The high-pitched swish of the water washing over the sand mutated into a more muffled, faltering, sliding noise, like the sound of a bartender scooping crushed ice.

As I stared at the water, a dead jellyfish washed up at my feet. It was fairly small, barely the size of my fist, and like a walnut in shape. Its body was tattered; it must have been floating around dead in the water for some time. I could still recognise the species, though. *Mnemiopsis leidyi*. It was hard to imagine, but the tiny creature in front of me had caused more lasting devastation to the Black Sea than any other.

The jellyfish had first appeared here in the early 1980s, a stowaway in the ballast tanks of a freighter that had come through the Bosporus, like so many invaders before it. In the absence of any natural foes, it spread within a few years to every corner of the sea and set about its labours of destruction. These jellyfish eat fish eggs and fish larvae as well as the plankton species that juvenile fish feed on. *Mnemiopsis leidyi* took a huge bite out of the Black Sea's food chain and brought the whole ecosystem to the brink of collapse.

By the late 1980s, the vast shoals of anchovies had dwindled to a tenth of their former biomass, and the other fish species that had provided a living to Black Sea fishermen for millennia were similarly decimated. All around the coast, boat crews found themselves out of work, with no clue as to how they were going to support their families. Dolphins too became a rare sight. Meanwhile, the phytoplankton at the bottom of the food chain whose natural enemies had been gobbled up by *Mnemiopsis leidyi* were able to multiply without restraint. Algal blooms became a frequent phenomenon, sucking oxygen out of the water and causing many scientists to fear that the sea's deeper anoxic layers might expand out of control.

For a few tense years, all the signs seemed to point to an impending unstoppable disaster. But then something unexpected happened. In the late 1990s, a new invader named *Beroe ovata* entered the Black Sea, a kind of jellyfish that feeds predominantly on other jellyfish. This proved to be the natural predator that could stop *Mnemiopsis leidyi* in its tracks. The two jellyfish still inhabit the Black Sea, but one checks the spread of the other, so that neither can cause major damage. The ecosystem has returned to its former equilibrium, though it has taken years for the fish stocks to recover.

I watched the jellyfish sink into the slush at my feet. Power, I thought, is not eternal.

Crimea

Qara deñiz

Like furnaces the mountains flare,
The sea puts on a blue collar.
People in need of swift repair
are forged anew in Crimea.

Vladimir Mayakovsky, 'Crimea', 1927

Tracks in the snow

I had been within a few hundred yards of the Crimean border in Preobrazhenka, but to cross it required a detour via Kiev. Throughout one whole day in January, I ran from one agency to the next in the snowbound Ukrainian capital to collect the necessary permits that would allow me to enter the 'Temporarily Occupied Territory of the Autonomous Republic of Crimea', as the annexed peninsula was known in Ukraine.

These papers were not the only obstacle. All travel links had been severed after the annexation; there were no flights, no trains, and no buses from Kiev any more. I took a night train back to Kherson, from where a minibus headed towards the border the next morning. It took the familiar road through the steppe, passed Preobrazhenka and soon afterwards reached the customs Portakabins on the Ukrainian side.

A thin blanket of snow had completely altered the landscape. Instead of brown emptiness, I was surrounded by an expanse of white. The other bus passengers and I joined the queue of pedestrians. In front of me, a woman hissed at her husband. He was holding the wrong passport, the Russian one. Shamefaced, he swapped it for his Ukrainian document.

The few Crimean residents who still visited the Ukrainian mainland on a regular basis didn't have an easy time of it at the border. They had been given Russian passports after the annexation, but since Ukrainian law didn't allow for dual nationality, everyone here, including the customs agents, turned a blind eye. The border crossers pretended to have only Ukrainian passports, and the customs officials pretended to believe them.

Beyond the Ukrainian border posts began no man's land. We hauled our luggage on foot for a few hundred metres through the steppe, until more Portakabins came into view on the Russian side. This time, it was the man I heard hissing at his wife.

'All right, I'm not stupid!'

He had the correct passport in his hand this time. The Russian one.

Cats were skulking around the barriers. One was dozing on the customs counter across which I pushed my passport.

'Is the cat Russian or Ukrainian?'

I tried to coax a smile out of the border guard, but her face didn't even twitch. Her superior, whom she summoned because my German passport bothered her, responded to my cat question.

'Everyone is welcome here. Russians, Ukrainians, Germans – everyone.' His lips were twisted into a spokesperson's rictus. 'The cats have been living here since the day we set up the border crossing. Would they really do that if we were the evil occupiers Western newspapers say we are?'

The cat on the counter stretched its legs in its sleep. It didn't look as if it particularly cared whose hand fed it.

Minibuses were waiting on the other side of the Portakabins. A two-hour drive brought us to Simferopol, the capital, which lies in the Crimean interior. I took a taxi from the bus station into the snowy city centre. The driver was a Crimean Tatar. He told me that the name for the Black Sea in his language was *Qara deñiz* and that he liked Soviet war films.

'Because the Germans always say the same words in them.' He repeated the words the way he'd heard them in films: *Russisch Schwein! Russisch Schwein!* ('Russian pig! Russian pig!') Then he laughed until he was red in the face.

I met Yelena, whose name was not really Yelena but something else, in a pub in the city centre that evening. A mutual acquaintance in Kiev had put us in touch. The pub was virtually empty, but when Yelena stepped up to the table where I was waiting, she asked if I minded moving to a quieter corner. She pointed to a couple at a nearby table.

'They're talking too loudly.'

It was only when we got chatting that I grasped the real reason: she was scared of someone listening in on us. Yelena was Russian, like most people in Crimea but, unlike most people here, she was far from overjoyed that Crimea was now part of Russia.

Until the annexation, Yelena had been a lecturer at the same city university where her mother had taught before her. All her life, she had loved the cosmopolitan university environment: the mixture of foreign languages, the conferences abroad, the constant turnover of visiting scholars and exchange students. All of that had come to an abrupt end five years ago. The sanctions that had been imposed after the Russian annexation had forced Western academic institutions to halt their cooperation with Crimean universities.

Yelena felt cut off from the outside world. The worst thing, however, was that no one else appeared to share this feeling. Her colleagues and students were delighted by Crimea's alignment with Russia and didn't miss a thing. 'Now we're part of a huge country,' they said, 'and we can travel from here to the Pacific without leaving our homeland, so why do we need the West?' The numbers studying in the philological faculties had collapsed; no one wanted to learn a European foreign language any more. The only rise was in Chinese, the language of the supposed ally, which Russian TV presented as a substitute for the lost West. Crimea was shifting its sights.

After a while, Yelena had quit her job as an academic.

'I couldn't lecture to those people any longer. They didn't want to learn anything about the world. I have nothing to teach them.'

Now she was working for an agency that arranged weddings abroad. She travelled all over Europe inspecting hotels, restaurants, banquet rooms, and castles for customers from Russia and Ukraine. For each of these trips, she would cross the Crimean border and then spend days on buses until she reached Western Europe. Back in Simferopol, the sanctions made her life tough. Crimea was cut off from the international payments system, and many software companies also blocked their programs on the peninsula. Despite not having the easiest working conditions, Yelena enjoyed her job. She loved weddings, even though she herself had never married.

Her sister had been living in Germany for a long time and kept asking Yelena how much longer she was going to hold out in Crimea. She didn't know. It was difficult for her to discuss things with friends, as few people here shared her views, and she was even more wary of expressing her opinions with strangers. Her life in Crimea had become lonely. All the same, there were many things holding her back. She didn't want to give up her mother's house. Her salary at the agency wouldn't cover the cost of living in the West. She knew it wasn't easy to find skilled work in Europe, and she didn't fancy ending up working in a call centre. She wasn't sure if she could face starting all over again in her early forties.

'If I were seventeen, I'd leave tomorrow,' Yelena sighed. 'But I'm not seventeen any more.'

As we chatted, we watched fresh snow start to fall outside the pub windows, thicker and thicker, until the flakes were swirling in the beams of the street lights like bubbles in champagne flutes. By the time we left the pub, the snow lay ankle-deep on the pavement. I watched Yelena walk away, leaving a trail of footsteps behind her, and for a moment, as if in a weird dream, I felt as if I should erase her tracks so no one could follow her.

Today we, tomorrow you

In the centre of Simferopol, there was a brand-new monument to Catherine the Great. A fine layer of snow covered her forehead, her shoulders, her majestic bosom, and her outstretched arm. It was a copy of an older monument erected to mark Russia's first annexation of Crimea, a memorial to the tsarina who had seized the peninsula from the Tatar khans in 1783. The Bolsheviks had pulled it down after the Revolution. An inscription on the base confirmed that this copy had been raised after the second annexation:

'Newly erected in honour of the reunification of Crimea with Russia in the year 2014, forever.'

This 'forever' oath is a constant in the history of Russian conquests of Crimea. Catherine had sworn it when she incorporated the peninsula into the Russian Empire in 1783 'from now on and for all time'. When the Russian Empire had folded into its Soviet successor, Nikita Khrushchev had shunted Crimea from one republic of the Soviet Union into another, from the Russian SFSR into its Ukrainian counterpart, an administrative manoeuvre with ramifications that the general secretary did not predict, because he assumed that Russia and Ukraine would be united forever. When a mere four decades later they no longer were, Crimea was suddenly part of an independent Ukraine. Twenty-three more years had passed when Russia took back what was supposed to have been Russian forever. My mind went back to the poster I had seen all over the peninsula shortly after the annexation: Putin's likeness accompanied by three Russian words – 'Crimea. Russia. Forever.'

A small relief had been sculpted on the base of the monument to Catherine. It featured eight men bowing their heads (capped with fezzes, turbans, and other exotic headgear) to the tsarina – stylised representatives of the Crimean peoples, subjugating themselves gladly to their new empress. Here, in a footnote, so to speak, the time before the dawn of the forever-time was hiding in plain sight – Crimea's earlier, non-Russian history.

When, two days later, the snow suddenly began to melt as quickly as it had fallen, I set out to look for the old Crimean peoples who had inhabited these parts before the Russians came. There were no longer eight, but I found three at least: the Tatars, the Karaites, and the Krymchaks. Some of them even still wore headgear.

South of Simferopol in the foothills of the Crimean mountains lay an area strewn with tiny villages above whose houses I saw increasing numbers of towering minarets the further I got from the capital.

In Sokolinoye's mosque, small plastic dishes were dotted around the carpet in the precise places where meltwater was trickling through from the snow on the roof. The murmur of the imam during midday prayers was punctuated by the sounds of dripping.

I struck up a conversation with a man called Ruzhdi outside the mosque. He was wearing a *taqiyah*, a Muslim skullcap. Ruzhdi was a Crimean Tatar, like one in five of the 2,500 villagers.

The mosque was an old fieldstone building with a pencil-shaped minaret not much wider than Ruzhdi's shoulders. The minaret was new, and Ruzhdi had helped with its construction. The Bolsheviks had torn down the original minaret after the Revolution while converting the mosque into the cultural centre of a kolkhoz.

Ruzhdi was in his mid-fifties, a man with a charismatically greying beard and barely suppressed rage in his eyes. He had been born in Uzbekistan in a camp settlement near Samarkand. His parents had lived through the 1944 deportations when Stalin had carted the entire population of Crimean Tatars – just under 200,000 people – to Central Asia after accusing them of collectively collaborating with the Germans. Many hadn't survived the journey; others had been separated from their families on the way.

His father had ten brothers and sisters, Ruzhdi said. 'I know five of them: four uncles and an aunt. I never met the other five. They could walk past me here in this village, and I wouldn't recognise them. Many people who were exiled are still searching for their relatives today.'

There once lived in Sokolinoye, Ruzhdi told me, an old man, a Tatar, now dead, who had escaped deportation because he had fought on the front line in 1944 – not for the Germans but against them. Returning to Sokolinoye, which had once been almost exclusively inhabited by Tatars, he had found the village empty. He asked questions to which he got no answers. When he went to Moscow to ask the same questions, the response was to put him in a labour camp by the Arctic Ocean. The old man had shown Ruzhdi the rehabilitation decree he kept in the glove compartment of his car. He had served twenty-five years before being released.

'All of this is temporary,' Ruzhdi's father used to say in

Uzbekistan. 'They have turned against the Almighty, and their system will not endure.' Ruzhdi had heard these words over and over again throughout his childhood and adolescence until, in 1989, his father said, 'The ice is breaking. We're going home.'

The return had not been easy. Many Tatars had been prevented from settling in their ancestral villages because these had long since been occupied by other people. Instead, they had been allocated areas in the hinterland where the soils were dry and hard to till. The authorities had refused to register the Tatars until they found work, and firms wouldn't employ them until they were registered. Nor had the local Russians reacted with particular joy to the new old neighbours. Ruzhdi remembered the distribution of bread rations in the settlements in the 1990s, when food was scarce following the collapse of the Soviet Union. Sometimes, when Tatars queued up to wait for their rations, the Russians would hiss, 'We haven't been waiting for you to come back all this time. Go and get your bread somewhere else.'

The Tatars had stayed, though. Ruzhdi and his parents had been fortunate enough to come across a pragmatic village headman in Sokolinoye who didn't put any obstacles in their path. They and the other returnees had built houses for themselves, found work, irrigated the land, and reopened the mosque. Much the same had taken place in many villages in the Crimean interior. Nowadays, almost one in ten inhabitants of Crimea was a Tatar. Before the deportations it had been one in five.

That angry glint in Ruzhdi's eyes flared up when I asked him about the new political circumstances. Many Crimean Tatars had opposed the annexation from the start because they were terrified of living under Russian rule again. Their leaders were arrested, sentenced, and intimidated by the new regime, and the Mejlis, the minority's representative body, was labelled an extremist organisation and disbanded.

Instead of answering my question, Ruzhdi led me into the small cemetery next to the mosque. This burial ground had also had to be re-established, he said. There was no longer a Muslim cemetery in Sokolinoye when the Tatars returned. It was only when they dug up the soil around the mosque that they struck bones, which they then gathered up and buried in a mass grave in the middle of the new cemetery. On top of it they laid a fragment of an old gravestone found along with the bones under the turf. The fragment was small, and the remaining section of the Tatar Arabic inscription contained only two verses, but to the Tatars it seemed a fitting tribute.

Ruzhdi translated the verses into Russian for me. As he recited them, he looked me fixedly in the eye, as if to make sure that I got the message.

TODAY WE, TOMORROW YOU
TODAY US, TOMORROW YOU

Some 100 km north of Sokolinoye, in the coastal city of Yev-patoria, I met Viktor Tiriyaki. He was wearing a black hat made of wavy Karakul sheepskin, which made his weary face look pale. His grey beard must once have been red, since a few hairs had not yet lost their old colour.

Tiriyaki was the spiritual leader of the local Karaite com-munity, a Turkic-speaking minority that, as far as I knew, followed the Jewish faith. I knew I didn't know much and, after a few minutes chatting to Tiriyaki, I knew I wouldn't learn much more from this conversation. He was a morose and mistrustful man who played his cards extremely close to his chest. I didn't hold this against him. History had taught the Karaites that it was better if the world didn't find out too much about them.

Tiriyaki took my pen and drew a tree in my notebook, its trunk forking into three branches.

'Those,' he said, pointing to the roots, 'are the commandments.'

'These' – the three branches – 'are the New Testament, the Talmud, and the Qur'an.'

'This' – the trunk – 'is the Torah. Our only scripture. Karaites believe in the Jewish faith as it was when Jesus Christ was born and before other things were subsequently added.'

The Karaites had never accepted the Talmud. This had isolated them from all other Jews, who had never really known what to make of the Karaites. This had worked to their advantage in the Russian Empire – unlike other Jews, the Karaites had not been subject to restrictions on the professions they could pursue. A few of them had made large fortunes, especially in the tobacco trade. This wealth was visible in the old *kenesa* – the Karaite synagogue in whose hall I was sitting with Tiriyaki, a sumptuous religious complex with vine-draped colonnades, marble tombs, carved wooden interiors, and warm stained-glass windows.

When the Nazis invaded Crimea in the war, they didn't know what to think of the Karaites either. Were they Jews? The Nazis commissioned an assessment by a Polish Jewish historian who, against his better judgement, declared the Karaites to be non-Jews, clearly to spare them the fate he would later suffer himself: he perished in the Warsaw Ghetto. His scheming paid off, however. The Nazis murdered the Crimean Jews but they spared the Karaites, whom they classified as a Turkic people.

Not long afterwards, the Karaites had a second stroke of luck. Their lenient treatment by the Germans could well have been a good reason for Stalin to have them deported alongside the Tatars, especially as the two minorities spoke very similar languages. Yet this cup too passed over them. For Stalin, the Karaites appeared to be Jews.

The *kenesa* in Yevpatoria had been closed down after the war, just like Crimea's churches, mosques, and Jewish synagogues. The historic religious complex had been converted into a 'museum of atheism', and the outbuildings were used as grain silos. The community hall had become a nursery, which Tiriyaki had gone to as a boy, knowing full well that his grandmother had still been praying in the *kenesa* only a few years earlier.

There were now only a few hundred Karaites living in Crimea. Many had emigrated to Israel in the 1990s. The devout core of his community, Tiriyaki said, consisted of forty people.

We had been talking for less than half an hour when the old community leader began to give me signals that he'd said everything he was prepared to say.

'If you have no further questions …'

But I do, I longed to cry, *hundreds of them*. Yet Tiriyaki's expression was so forbidding that I confined myself to the central question whose insolubility had saved the Karaites' lives twice. Where were they from? Were they a Turkic people that had converted to Judaism in the distant past? Or were they Semitic immigrants who had only become Turkic-speaking in Crimea? I knew that this matter was controversial among the Karaites too.

Tiriyaki stared at me impassively. His face was hard to read – not so much as the twitch of a muscle.

'Origins are a card that politicians love to play. They are of no consequence to the faithful.'

He stood up and offered me his hand. I was already halfway to the door when he uttered a few final words as a send-off.

'The Karaites lived here under the Tatar khans, under the tsars, the Soviets, the German occupiers, the Ukrainians, and now the Russians again. No one could drive us out. We are still here. That is all that counts.'

From Yevpatoria I travelled back to Simferopol, the Crimean capital, where I met Dora Pirkova, a petite elderly lady who was wearing a brown felt hat with a narrow brim – not for religious reasons but against the cold.

'I've no time for religion,' she said. 'I grew up in the Soviet Union.'

Meltwater was dripping from the roofs of Simferopol. A leaking, gurgling gutter hung over the entrance to the Krymchak cultural centre. We ducked through the falling droplets. Once inside, Dora removed her felt hat and knocked the water from the brim.

'Welcome.'

She was the centre's chairwoman.

The Krymchaks were a Jewish Turkic-speaking people like the Karaites, but with the slight difference that they abided by the Talmud. This slight difference had spelled their downfall.

The cultural centre comprised three small rooms in a residential building. Two of these were packed with exhibits. Dora led me into the room at the back. On the facing wall hung a picture, a sort of triptych, whose panels were painted with scenes from Krymchak history: religious festivals, folk dances, village weddings, traditional crafts. Moving from left to right, these depictions traced developments from the distant to the more recent past. At the far right-hand edge, three men with machine guns were mowing down a crowd.

On 11 December 1941, armed Nazi troops rolled into Karasubazar, the old Krymchak capital east of Simferopol. They drove together the entire population, some 6,000 people, and marched them out of town, until they came to the side of a country road where graves had already been dug.

The only survivor of the ensuing massacre was a fifteen-year-old Krymchak girl called Gurdzhi Riva, who fell into the graves with the executed and played dead. When night came, she clambered out and fled. It was she who brought news of what had happened to the small clusters of Krymchaks living in other parts of Crimea.

Dora's mother, who had been little older than Gurdzhi Riva at the time, escaped in 1942 on one of the last ships to set sail from occupied Crimea for Georgia. She lived in Tbilisi until shortly after the end of the war. When she returned to Crimea, she found very few Krymchaks alive. The only people who had survived were a few families who had fled early enough and the young men, such as Dora's father, who had been fighting on the front line when the massacre took place. Her parents met in 1947 in Simferopol. Their daughter was born a year later.

Dora's parents had spoken the Krymchak language together, but they didn't dare pass it on to their children. It was the Stalinist period; Krymchak sounded like Tatar and, if you lived in Crimea, it was not advisable to sound like a Tatar. Very occasionally, Dora would hear her father humming Krymchak songs as he worked. He had set up in business as a cobbler. His work tools – old-fashioned pliers and hammers – were exhibited in a display case at the cultural centre.

After Stalin's death, the Krymchaks tentatively asked the

Soviet authorities whether it might be possible to introduce Krymchak lessons at one of the schools in Simferopol, but their request was rejected. They were informed that the Krymchak people had unfortunately been wiped out by the fascists. Since they no longer existed, they needed no schooling.

By the end of the Soviet era, there were very few people left in Crimea who spoke Krymchak. Dora's parents had been overjoyed to see the Tatars return from exile in the 1990s. Their languages were so closely related that they could converse with one another. Her father had often gone to market in Simferopol to chat with Tatar traders.

In the last seconds before her father shut his eyes for the final time in 2007, he had sung an old Krymchak song:

Mummy is gone, Daddy is gone
Only I am still here
A lonely orphaned child.

With these verses on his lips, one of Crimea's last Krymchak voices had fallen silent. Another one, Dora's mother's, had faded away a few years later. Now, Dora said, there were only three people living on the peninsula who mastered the language of their ancestors, and all three of them were well over eighty.

As with the Karaites, the Krymchaks espoused a variety of opinions about their origins. Some thought they were a Turkic people who had turned to Judaism; others saw themselves as Turkicised Jews. Dora said that both theories had their supporters in Crimea. To be more precise, the two theories ultimately had one supporter each, two aged amateur ethnographers who had engaged in fierce arguments until an electric shock had suddenly extinguished one of them a few years back. The other man was ninety-seven years old. It was likely that the question of the Krymchaks' origins would remain unresolved.

In total, there were only just over 200 Krymchaks left alive in Crimea. The rest had emigrated in the 1990s to Israel and Germany, the two countries where immigration was comparatively easy for Jews at the time. Dora's children lived in Israel. She herself had never entertained the thought of leaving Crimea, but she respected her children's decision.

'I could understand young people's desire to go to Israel.'

She looked into my eyes pensively.

'But to Germany?'

The love story of Alla and Vladimir

The Institute of Biology of the Southern Seas is located on Sevastopol's harbour promenade in a magnificent white building whose classical facade had adorned almost every postcard of the city since the late nineteenth century.

Inside, I met Vladimir. He was a plankton specialist, and he introduced me to his laboratory colleagues, a group of Russian oceanographers hunched over their microscopes with one eye squinted, like Cyclopes straining in pursuit of science. They all welcomed Crimea's change of nationality – and that of their institute – from the bottom of their hearts. Only one colleague had been of a different opinion, they said, and he had left the institute. They had no idea what he was up to now. When he left, his plan had been to write a play – a political parable about the invasive organisms in the Black Sea.

Vladimir and his colleagues were still investigating the chaos that the killer *Mnemiopsis leidyi* jellyfish had unleashed in the sea. They told me of copepods whose stocks had been reduced to such sensitive levels that similar crustacean-like plankton had occupied the vacated biological niches. As I listened to them, I could see their departed colleague's play taking shape in my mind.

Vladimir invited me to dinner after he finished work. We drove out of the city centre in his car, passed through the darker outskirts, bought a chicken and two bottles of wine somewhere along the way, and eventually entered the prefabricated tower block where he lived with his wife, Alla, and Max, Alla's eleven-year-old son from her first marriage. The table was laid. Max was already in his pyjamas, but he was allowed to stay up. Alla filled my plate and Vladimir my glass. A winking Christmas tree bathed the living room in changing traffic-light colours.

It was just under six years since Alla and Vladimir had got to know each other at a sanatorium in southern Crimea, where they had both been taking advantage of the spa facilities. Between therapeutic baths and contrast showers there had developed between them what Vladimir smilingly called a 'spa romance'.

Alla shot her husband a slightly reproachful glance. 'A spa romance that led to a family.'

Alla was Ukrainian. She came from Uman, a city in the centre of the country. She had been sent to the Crimean spa by her employer, a Ukrainian TV channel. Alla reported on social affairs.

She'd had no trouble finding a job after deciding to move to Sevastopol to be with Vladimir. There weren't many journalists in Crimea who spoke good Ukrainian; her TV station was happy to have a correspondent. Max was about to start school when he and Alla moved in with Vladimir in 2013.

She soon realised why it had been so hard to fill the correspondent post. When she interviewed passers-by on camera in the street, not one person would speak to her in Ukrainian. Sometimes Russian Crimeans would hiss at her because they felt constantly insulted that their peninsula had been lumped in with Ukraine after the collapse of the Soviet Union, and so they would tell Alla where to stick her Ukrainian questions. On a visit to an orphanage, children younger than her own son explained that they hated the Ukrainians. They then took a shine to the reporter during her visit, and when Alla left they begged her to stay here and not go back to her 'stinking Ukraine'.

'Oh, Allochka.' Vladimir gazed tenderly at his wife. 'You take it too much to heart. There are idiots everywhere.'

Barely a year after Alla and Max had moved to Sevastopol, Ukraine began to simmer with unrest. While Alla continued to film entertaining reports on Crimea for the Ukrainian-language broadcaster, Russian TV stations in Crimea propagated horror stories about the demonstrations in Kiev. They said that Ukrainian fascists were attempting to seize power, that speaking Russian would soon be banned in Ukraine, and that there was a threat of ethnic cleansing in Crimea and the Russian-dominated east of the country.

Like most Russians, Vladimir couldn't figure out what he should make of the TV images he was seeing. He was particularly frightened by reports about Tatars supposedly planning revenge campaigns against Russians in Crimea. Vladimir remembered his military service in the Red Army, when brawls among recruits regularly divided the barracks into Soviet ethnic groups – Tajiks, Chechens, Uzbeks, Armenians, and Tatars – who would gang up and vent their hatred toward the Russians. Vladimir sensed that things were getting hairy when Tatars came out onto the streets of Simferopol in a display of solidarity with the Ukrainian protestors in Kiev. He was therefore glad when soldiers in unmarked uniforms appeared in Crimea soon afterwards. Everyone could guess who had sent them.

Max had just started school, and he remembered how his classmates had started painting their uniforms then. He attended a primary school offering extra Spanish. The old red sleeveless jumper he showed me had a slightly darker patch on the chest, where the school badge had once been sewn on. The badge featured Don Quixote and Sancho Panza next to a flag illustrating Spanish–Ukrainian friendship, half yellow and red, half yellow and blue. When the soldiers popped up in Crimea, many children had painted over the flag with the colours of the Russian tricolour – white, blue and red.

'And then—' Max's voice cut out here for a second, as he'd forgotten to take a breath while he was telling his story at full tilt. 'Then Vladimir woke me up one morning and said, "Max, we're part of Russia now."'

Not long afterward, the compulsory Ukrainian language lessons at Max's school were dropped. The badge with the Ukrainian flag was abolished too. Max had grown out of his old jumper before the badge could be replaced by a new one.

Alla lost her job, because it had become impossible for her broadcaster to employ correspondents in Crimea after the annexation, and because no one in Ukraine wanted to watch entertaining reports about the peninsula any more. Her Ukrainian mother, whom she phoned every day, had gone half mad with worry for her daughter; it was hard to convey to her that the events were confusing but not imminently life-threatening.

Vladimir felt as if his research institute were on the way

up since the annexation. He had started there in the dying days of the Soviet Union and could clearly remember the years of decline, when the scientists' budgets had been cut further and further, and he and his colleagues were forced to use their research ships to offer courier services to other Black Sea countries so that they could plough at least this revenue into maintaining essential infrastructure and equipment. The absolute nadir was the day when a strip club called Rasputin had moved into one wing of the institute. As Vladimir told me this, shaking his head, I realised that he and his colleagues largely blamed Ukraine for the ruin of Soviet science. Research facilities suffered in Russia too after the collapse of the USSR, but nowhere had they sunk as low as in Crimea.

The situation improved, Vladimir said, once the institute belonged to Russia. There was more money – for research projects, for equipment, for staff. The hated strip club had moved out. The flipside was the sanctions, which made it hard to work with research centres in the West, but Vladimir hoped that this would be sorted out one day.

Max had begun high school a year ago. There were no Ukrainian lessons there either, but he spoke to his grandmother in Ukrainian on the phone every evening. It was more complicated to visit their relatives in Uman than before but, every once in a while, Max and his mother would set out on the long slog across the Crimean border.

Alla had found a new job. She now worked for the same institute as Vladimir, in the public relations department, where she explained the results of the marine scientists' work to a wider audience. She liked her job, even though many of her Ukrainian friends had repudiated her. They saw her refusal to leave Russian-occupied Crimea – as tens of thousands of Ukrainians had done since the annexation – as a betrayal.

But Alla had stayed. Max had stayed. And Vladimir had stayed with them. I listened to the three of them putting their memories into words with a sense of relief. I knew that many Russian-Ukrainian families had splintered over the Crimea conflict, because their relatives and friends and broadcasters had fed them contradictory versions of the story for so long that they no longer shared a language in which to discuss it. Here, though, in this small Soviet flat, under the pulsing lights of a plastic Christmas tree, three people had been stronger than so many others.

The end of a bridge

Winter was moving into a milder phase as I set off from Sevastopol on the last leg of my journey. All the snow was gone from the plains; I could see it only in the distance, on the higher levels of the Crimean mountains, which reared up in front of me as I headed south. The road looped up the slopes in sharp bends before overcoming the western foothills and plunging down on the other side into an altered landscape, a Mediterranean world of cypresses, palms, and olive trees. The southern margins of Crimea were a distant outpost of the same subtropical vegetation zone whose imported plants were familiar to me from Sochi and Abkhazia.

In Yalta there was a huge Lenin memorial on the waterside promenade, which was ringed with palm trees and over-shadowed by snow-capped peaks. It was Lenin who in 1920 had signed the Decree about the Use of the Crimea for the Treatment of Workers, which led to the peninsula's annexation in the name of the proletariat: 'The sanatoria and spa resorts of the Crimea, which used to be the privilege of the upper classes, the wonderful dachas and villas used by large landowners and capitalists, and the palaces of former tsars and grand dukes, are to be used as sanatoria and healing places for workers and farmers.'

A young painter called Oxana, whose phone number Alla and Vladimir had given me in Sevastopol, drove me to the Livadia Palace on the southern edge of Yalta. It was a Monday, and the old tsarist residence was closed, so we were only able to peer in through the windows of the stately apartments in whose four-poster beds Soviet farmers had been allowed to sleep after the Revolution.

'Farmers in palaces! It's barbaric!'

Oxana didn't think much of Lenin. She was a monarchist at heart. She painted seascapes in oil on large canvases, works in the style of the Romantic landscape artist Ivan Aivazovsky with which Yalta's business class decorated their living room walls. Once, Oxana told me, a public prosecutor had ordered a portrait of the last Russian tsar from her. The picture was to show Nicholas II inside the Livadia Palace, his summer residence. While painting the picture, Oxana had set up her easel in the palace for a few days to be able to capture the original backdrop.

'I don't know how to describe it, but as I painted, I suddenly felt a bond with the palace. It was as if I had lived there once, in a former life.'

She had fine long hands, which she ran through her hair as she spoke with affected aristocratic elegance.

On our way back into town, Oxana complained about the impact of the sanctions on Crimea.

'All the Western brands have vanished from the shops. It's impossible to buy anything decent any more. If it goes on like this, I won't have a clue what to wear. That doesn't matter to most people here, but I'm accustomed to quite a different lifestyle.'

In general, however, Oxana didn't have many objections to the annexation that, to her mind, had finally returned Crimea to its rightful place in the old world of the Russian tsars. The Soviet error of cleaving the peninsula from its traditions and making it an appendage to impoverished Ukraine had been corrected. Not for the first time, I was stunned by how differently people interpreted events here to bend them to their own narrative.

After parking the car in Yalta, Oxana and I strolled along the promenade until we suddenly came to a fountain whose basin was shaped like the Black Sea – my whole journey reduced to a diameter of 5 m. I walked up to the edge of the basin in fascination. In three strides, I had covered the Russian Black Sea coast, then one each for Abkhazia and Georgia. It took me a few seconds to travel the length of the Turkish coast; the Balkans and Ukraine were negotiated equally swiftly, and finally I was standing by the small concrete peninsula in the form of Crimea that stretched out into the middle of the bowl.

In the spot where the eastern end of Crimea almost touched the Russian coast, someone had wedged a stick between the concrete shores to represent the new bridge that had been built over the Kerch Strait the previous year. My journey's final destination was within touching distance.

To the right of the country road lay the sea; to the left, the mountains soared steeply up into the sky. The bus laboured on the winding road along the southern edge of Crimea, past wind-ruffled pine trees and cypresses. Only between Sudak and Feodosia, where the mountains smoothed out, did the road shake off its coils. The southern vegetation disappeared, the landscape became flat and featureless, and from here until the end of the journey I saw nothing but the brown expanse of the steppe.

The road terminated in Kerch, at Crimea's eastern tip. A bitter wintry wind sliced through the city. It was at its fiercest on the bare hill that reared up out of the steppe to the south of the centre and was scattered with the ruins of an acropolis. In the seventh century BC, on the site of present-day Kerch, Greek seafarers had built one of the first trading colonies on the northern Black Sea coast – ancient Pantikapaion.

Examining the traces of this distant past in the city's archaeological museum, I suddenly found myself staring at an empty plinth. It looked a bit like the remains of one of the Ukrainian monuments to Lenin, but the missing item here was something very different – a statue of Mixoparthenos, a mythological figure who was half woman, half snake. A small slip of paper explained its absence.

THIS PIECE IS CURRENTLY PART OF THE EXHIBITION
'CRIMEA – GOLD AND SECRETS OF THE BLACK SEA'
IN THE ALLARD PIERSON MUSEUM
(AMSTERDAM, THE NETHERLANDS)

A research assistant working at the museum told me what had happened from his perspective.

'The Dutch have stolen our statue.'

I was familiar with this story. It was one of the odd consequences of the annexation. The piece had been sent from Kerch to the Netherlands on loan in 2013 and exhibited there, alongside many other archaeological treasures from Crimea. Soon afterwards, Russia incorporated the peninsula into its territory. When the exhibition in Amsterdam came to an end, the loans were due to be returned to their owner – but all

TROUBLED WATER

of a sudden it wasn't clear to whom they actually belonged. The Crimean museums from whose collections they were taken had been Ukrainian institutions until the annexation, but they were now de facto in Russia. The Allard Pierson museum in Amsterdam soon found itself being pressured by both sides to return the items. The Crimean museums wanted their exhibits back. The culture ministry in Kiev, on the other hand, argued that the loans remained Ukrainian property and belonged in Kiev.

The people in Amsterdam began to get nervous. They couldn't afford to return the art treasures to one party and be sued for compensation by the other; the value of the exhibits ran to €1.5 million. At a loss, the directors of the Allard Pierson addressed a request to a Dutch court to examine the legal standing of the conflicting demands. The results of this process were pending, and the Mixoparthenos statue was still in storage in an Amsterdam warehouse.

'We'll never get it back.' The staff member of the Kerch Museum, a man whose deeply furrowed brow conveyed his pessimism, didn't have much confidence in the Dutch judicial system. 'It's all an excuse to punish Crimea. They cannot accept that we want to be part of Russia. It's the Americans pulling the strings.'

He showed me a photo of the lost statue. It was carved from white stone and was about 50 cm tall. Mixoparthenos, the snake woman, had a human torso that divided below the navel into two long diverging and spiralling tails that curled up by her sides. The mythical creature was holding the ends of these two snake legs in her hands.

The Mixoparthenos myth originated on the shores of the Black Sea. Herodotus related that the snake woman was already living in the land of the Scythians before the Scythians arrived there. There she is said to have come across the sleeping Heracles and stolen his horses. When the hero awoke, the snake woman told him that he would only get his horses back if he slept with her. Heracles agreed. Following their night of passion, Mixoparthenos bore three sons. (Herodotus doesn't go into the anatomical details of how a woman with no lower body can make love or give birth.) The three sons turned out to be fully human and, as they grew up, Heracles prophesied that only one of them would develop into a man able to draw his father's bow. The successful son's name was Scythes, and he became the founding father of the Scythians. It was the shape of the bow in his hand that the Greeks later associated with the form of the Black Sea.

Disconnected from its myth, the snake-tailed Mixoparthenos figure lingered on as a decorative motif long after ancient times. An American designer discovered it in 1971 while scanning a collection of illustrations in search of a logo for a new coffee house in the West Coast metropolis of Seattle. In white on a green background, he drew a long-haired female figure holding splayed snake tails in each hand on either side of her body. This coffee house grew over the years into a global chain and later modified its logo, because the splayed tails were considered too erotic for a family business. The brand design now consists of only the snake woman's face, long hair, hands, and the tips of her forked tail – but look closely and Mixoparthenos is still recognisable in the green-and-white Starbucks logo.

There was no longer a Starbucks branch in Kerch. It and other Western chains had been forced to cease business in Crimea due to the economic sanctions. I had been struck in cities all over the peninsula by how many former fast food restaurants had been taken over by local proprietors after the annexation. Most of them had simply kept the logos of their Western predecessors and made minor adjustments to the brand names to suggest to their customers that nothing had changed. I saw an old Burger King that now called itself Big Burger, a McDonalds that now traded as RusBurger, and a Kentucky Fried Chicken that had turned into Crimean Fried Chicken. One Starbucks branch was now called Starducks, replacing the Mixoparthenos figure with a duck, and another one was known as Coffee Croc and emblazoned with a grinning crocodile.

Since the annexation, the former Starbucks branch in Kerch was called Cappuccino Coffee-Bar, its green-and-white logo featuring a steaming cup of coffee. I stood in front of the café for a long time, staring at the distorted sign. I wondered how many people in Kerch were aware that Mixoparthenos, the snake-tailed mother of the Scythians, had vanished from their city not once but twice – the first time from the archaeological museum, the second from the Starbucks logo.

On the day of my departure from Kerch, before I set off on the long journey back to the Crimean border and on to Berlin, I climbed one last time up the acropolis mound above the city, where the Mixoparthenos statue had been found among the temple ruins in the late nineteenth century.

In the hazy winter light, I saw the Crimea bridge sticking out into the sea from the eastern side of town. Its carriageway melted away into the mist and the far shore was invisible, but I knew that over there was the Taman peninsula and the old fishing cooperative where my trip had begun.

The bridge was finished, and from this vantage I could see cars travelling in both directions. It was 19 km long, and a taxi driver had told me the day before that it was just under half an hour's drive from one end to the other.

I had taken almost a year to get to this point.

The Ark

Epilogue

You have not changed at all, wicked sea,
But I have changed; I'm not who I was!

Mikhail Lermontov, 'I salute you, wicked sea', ca. 1840

They poured aboard from all directions. Some came from Russia, some from Turkey, others from Ukraine, and a few from Moldova and Georgia. From every coast of the Black Sea they rolled up in their heavily laden vehicles, and one after another they disappeared into the ship's giant belly.

The heat was oppressive, even though the September sun hung low over the water. Eight months after the end of my journey around the coast, I had returned to the Black Sea, this time to cross it. I wanted to get closer to the centre I had circled for almost a year. In Chornomorsk, a small Ukrainian port south of Odessa, I watched from the upper deck of a freight ferry called *Sea Partner* as the vehicle decks filled up with lorries.

An hour earlier, when I was passing through the customs checks on foot, a brief and violent summer thunderstorm had swept over the harbour, and a whiff of rain still hung in the air. A front of leaden clouds was moving slowly away inland. Silent flashes of lightning were twitching above the loading cranes, but they did not herald thunder. The lorries trundled on board in an endless procession as the sun sank over the west of the harbour basin and the stormy light gradually gave way to darkness. High above the ramps I saw a flock of gulls flapping through the beams of the harbour floodlights. For a few seconds, the bottoms of their wings stood out bright orange against the night sky before their silhouettes plunged abruptly into the dark.

I was the only passenger who had not embarked at the wheel of a lorry. One by one, the hauliers gathered out on deck, an international bunch, their rough faces leathery from the sun, amid a cloud of body odour and cigarette smoke. The men – there was not a single woman on this ship – nodded in passing, exchanged silent handshakes, or patted each other on the shoulder. Many seemed to know one another from previous crossings. I heard Turkish greetings and Russian curses amid scraps of other languages. The *Sea Partner*, with a Panamanian flag at its stern, was an ark for the peoples of the Black Sea.

Not long after the total darkness of night had engulfed the harbour, the bow doors rose up and closed the ship's maw. The engine droned as its torque increased and, with a dull throbbing, the *Sea Partner* detached itself from the quayside. The ground beneath my feet immediately seemed to lose all its solidity, and through the ship's metal hull I felt the sea's viscous embrace. Peering down from the upper deck, I saw a small red boat steering a course parallel to ours far below us. By the end of the breakwater, it had closed to within a couple of feet of us, and a man leaped from the ferry onto the smaller boat. The pilot was leaving us. Our escort vessel made a sharp turn and headed back to the harbour, leaving the *Sea Partner* to head out into the open sea.

Chornomorsk slipped slowly away behind us. The small port had been given its name less than three years ago. In the Soviet era, it had been called Ilyichovsk in honour of Lenin's patronymic, Ilyich, before the Ukrainians renamed it during their reforms. Chornomorsk was now named after the Black Sea, and it struck me shortly after we had cast off that our port of destination to the east of the mouth of the Bosporus was called more or less the same in Turkish: Karasu. The voyage of the *Sea Partner*, scheduled to last a little more than twenty-four hours, would take it from 'black sea' to 'black water'.

As the ship glided across the Gulf of Odessa, the last visible sign of the receding land was a semicircle of distant lights. The almost-full moon waned behind the clouds to a yellow slit glaring down at the waves like an evil eye. The lorry drivers stood on deck, smoking and staring into the distance, their faces relaxed, grateful for a break and a view of something other than asphalt.

I struck up a conversation with a Russian from Samara, who was transporting wooden beams from the Volga to Turkey.

'Be happy you're taking this ferry in summer. You wouldn't like being tossed about in the winter storms. Everyone just hangs over the railings then.'

Sanya was short but stocky, and were it not for his beer belly, he might still have passed for the water sportsman he'd been before becoming a long-distance trucker; he had represented Russia in kayaking competitions. He showed me some bikini photos of his wife, a buxom blonde whose number he'd saved in his phone under Zayats ('bunny').

'Not bad, eh?'

I nodded appreciatively.

'Show me yours.'

When the gong sounded for dinner, we went down the metal stairs to the cafeteria together. Above the serving counter hung a printed A4 sheet with a crossed-out smiling pig's head on it, accompanied by the Turkish words *Domuz yok* ('no pork'). I heard a driver in the queue ahead of me swear under his breath in Russian.

'Bloody hell, no pork, what the fuck …'

The culture clash seemed to be restricted to this, though. Sanya and the four other Russians with whom we shared our table regularly travelled up and down the Black Sea coast, and all of them knew the few dozen terms in three or four languages that every haulier needed to survive. The same was true of the other drivers, whether Turks, Ukrainians, Moldovans, or Georgians. Even though the men ate in separate groups according to their mother tongue, they would loudly wish everyone a tasty meal from one table to the next in a variety of languages, their messages gratefully received despite much dodgy pronunciation. Even the two Ukrainians who sat down at our table after their meal with tankards full of beer got on fine with the Russians. There was no mention of the war between their countries until I raised the issue, and it was quickly dealt with.

'Are we supposed to kick lumps out of each other in here, all because a few millionaires are arguing out there?'

Two of the men had loads of timber – Sanya Russian birch, Oleg Ukrainian pine. Sasha, Vova, Yura, and Andrey were carrying Siberian coal to Turkey. They all mocked Dima, who was on his way from Kharkiv to Istanbul: his lorry was full of menstrual pads.

Later that evening, the passengers separated into two groups. The Turks stayed sitting around the tables of the cafeteria, while most of the others, including us, gradually moved on to the bar next door. This wasn't alcohol-related; I saw tankards of beer on the Turkish tables too. What divided the drivers were the different on-board television channels. The ones in the cafeteria showed Turkish crime movies, those in the bar Russian ones. In the spirit of old Soviet linguistic fraternity, the Ukrainians, Moldovans, and Georgians watched with the Russians.

Our table was the loudest. Soon the table was heaving with bottles of vodka that the drivers had picked up in the duty-free shops at the harbour. Vova cut slices of cured pork fat. The evening took its typical Russian course.

At some stage – I was no longer entirely sober – I all of a

sudden felt transported far back in time. To me, this ship with its polyglot hauliers resembled the Black Sea communities of ancient times, one of those patchwork colonial settlements where Greeks had got drunk with Scythians in defiance of all boundaries between civilisation and barbarism. Along the coast I had encountered only remnants of those old multi-ethnic societies, which had been torn apart over millennia by order-loving imperialists and nationalists, but here, in the middle of the sea …

My reveries were shattered by an argument – an argument, I later realised, that had broken out not along national lines, but between two Russians. I've no idea how it started. I was chatting to Sanya when, out of the corner of my eye, I saw Sasha jump up and confront Andrey, looming over him and yelling.

'Out! We're taking this outside! One of us is going to take a dip!'

He turned on his heel, stomped off towards the exit, and disappeared through the steel door leading to the deck.

Andrey remained seated.

Vova pushed his chair back with a screech.

'I'll go and see what's up with him.'

A few seconds later, we heard the sound of bodies slamming into metal walls outside. I was about to leap to my feet, but Sanya grinned and laid his hand on my arm.

'They're only fooling around.'

After a few minutes, Vova came back in, panting.

'The guy's completely out of control. I try to calm him down and he starts laying into me.'

Now it was Andrey's chair that screeched.

'If he's looking for trouble, he's going to find it.'

We heard more thuds against the outside wall. Then Sasha

came back through the door, followed by Andrey, both of them with bloodied hands.

Sasha slumped into his chair next to mine. A long string of blood was trailing from his right ear. He stared at the tabletop, breathing hard. He looked as if he'd had enough.

Andrey, however, was just getting into his stride. He grabbed a full tankard from the table and held it right in front of Sasha's face.

'You want trouble, eh? Real trouble?'

He drew back the tankard. Sasha shut his eyes in total resignation, waiting for the blow to land. Andrey banged the tankard down on the table and seized one of the empty vodka bottles.

'Trouble?'

He drew back his arm. Sasha screwed up his eyes.

Andrey dropped the vodka bottle and picked up a table knife. Uneasy now, I tried to catch Sanya's eye. He laughed.

'Russian tradition.'

Andrey yanked Sasha's head backwards and held the knife to his throat.

'Trouble?'

Sasha put up no resistance. He let it wash over him like a whipped dog.

Then everything happened at amazing speed. Andrey mashed his left hand into Sasha's face, reached back with his right hand and stabbed Sasha with all his might. It was only when he pulled back the knife that I saw that he'd been clasping it the wrong way around – it was the blunt end, not the blade, that he had rammed into Sasha's ribs. But the pain was obviously serious enough to bring a howl of anguish from Sasha. He doubled over forwards, gasping for breath, and rested his forehead on the table. He stayed in this position, motionless and whimpering, his arms clutching his aching chest.

Two of the other Russians tried to twist the knife out of Andrey's fist.

'Get your shit together, man!'

I made the most of the distraction of the escalating brawl to slip out to my cabin.

The next morning, I saw Sasha at breakfast. His right ear was encrusted with blood, but he was otherwise in good spirits.

'It happens.'

A few pieces of fitness equipment were mounted on the upper deck, but even in the morning, the late-summer sun was blazing down so mercilessly that no one fancied doing any exercise. I was alone on deck. Most of the drivers were lounging in front of the televisions in the cafeteria or sleeping off their hangovers in their cabins.

There was nothing but water in every direction. We had half of the journey behind us and were equidistant from the north coast and the southern shore. The sea had a metallic blue glimmer, the sunlight glancing and bouncing off the surface. Behind the ship, where the propeller had churned up the water, a brighter trail stretched out to the horizon, flanked on either side by parallel skeins of foam stretching out into the distance like train tracks.

Two small green songbirds were darting around the ship's superstructure after insects. Finches? Buntings? I wasn't sure. I'd been watching them swoop and dive for some time when I began to wonder how these birds had ended up on this ship.

And if they planned to travel back with it.

Or if they were going to start a new life on the other shore. Like so many others.

Acknowledgements

My thanks go out to everyone who shared their stories with me.

Many friends and supporters played their part in this book's development. Thomas Hölzl and Diana Stübs were a particularly great help. There could have been no better translator for this text than Simon Pare.

I am grateful to the Foundation for Polish-German Cooperation, which partially funded my research trips and was not put off by the fact that barely any Germans or Poles live by the Black Sea nowadays.

I cannot adequately express my thanks to fate and its accessory, Andrey Zatsepin, for guiding me at the right moment to the right shore.

I would also like to thank all the authors whose works were sources of reference and inspiration to me. I have listed them on the following pages in alphabetical order, but it is worth highlighting Neal Ascherson and Charles King, whose books about the history of the Black Sea region leave precious few unresolved questions – hopefully the very ones that guided my steps on this journey.

Bibliography

Anderson, Tony, *Bread and Ashes: A Walk through the Mountains of Georgia* (London, 2003).

Apollonius of Rhodes, *The Argonautica*, trans. Robert C. Seaton (London, 1912).

Ascherson, Neal, *Black Sea: The Birthplace of Civilisation and Barbarism* (London, 1995).

Achkinazi, Igor, *Krymchaki: Istoriko-etnograficheskiy ocherk* (Simferopol, 2000).

Babel, Isaac, 'The King' in *The Collected Stories of Isaac Babel*, trans. Peter Constantine (New York, 2002).

Blok, Alexander, 'Scythians', trans. Andrew Wachtel, Ilya Kutik, & Michael Denner, *From the Ends to the Beginning: A Bilingual Anthology of Russian Poetry*, accessed online.

Brown, Kate, *A Biography of No Place: From Ethnic Borderland to Soviet Heartland* (London, 2003).

Çelebi, Evliya, *An Ottoman Traveller: Selections from the Book of Travels of Evliya Çelebi*, trans. Robert Dankoff & Sooyong Kim (London, 2010).

Dimitrov, Petko & Dimitar Dimitrov, *The Black Sea, the Flood and the Ancient Myths* (Varna, 2004).

Doksanaltı, Ertekin & İlker Mimiroğlu, 'Giresun/Aretias-Khalkeritis Island', *Anodos: Studies of the Ancient World*, 10 (2010).

Dzyatkevich, Viktor, *Plemzavodu Krasny Chaban 75 let. Stranitsy istorii v sobytiakh i sudbakh* (Kalanchak, 2005).

Ellison, Grace, *Turkey To-Day* (London, 1928).

Florensky, Pavel, *Detyam moim. Vospominania proshlykh dney* (Moscow, 2004).

Freely, John, *The Black Sea Coast of Turkey* (Istanbul, 1996).

Fridman, Eman & Douglas Bowden, 'The Russian Primate Research Center – A Survivor', *Laboratory Primate Newsletter*, 48/1 (2009).

George, Andrew R., ed. & trans., *The Epic of Gilgamesh* (London, 2003).

Gronau, Dietrich, *Mustafa Kemal Atatürk oder die Geburt der Republik* (Frankfurt am Main, 1994).

Hall, Edith, *Inventing the Barbarian: Greek Self-Definition through Tragedy* (Oxford, 1989).

Herodotus, *The Histories*, trans. George Rawlinson (London, 1992).

Ivanov, Vitaly & Vladimir Belokopytov, *Oceanography of the Black Sea* (Sevastopol, 2013).

Kappeler, Andreas, *Kleine Geschichte der Ukraine* (Munich, 1994)

—— *Die Kosaken. Geschichte und Legenden* (Munich, 2013).

Karakina, Elena, et al., *Putevoditel po evreyskoy Odesse* (Odessa, 2008).

Kassabova, Kapka, *Border: A Journey to the Edge of Europe* (London, 2017).

King, Charles, *The Black Sea: A History* (New York, 2004).

—— *The Ghost of Freedom: A History of the Caucasus* (New York, 2008).

—— *Odessa:. Genius and Death in a City of Dreams* (New York, 2011).

——— *Midnight at the Pera Palace: The Birth of Modern Istanbul* (New York, 2014).

Leigh Fermor, Patrick, *The Broken Road: From the Iron Gates to Mount Athos* (London, 2013).

Lermontov, Mikhail, *A Hero of Our Time*, trans. Natasha Randall (New York, 2009).

——— 'Privetstvuyu tebya ya, zloye more' in *Sobranie sochineniy* (Leningrad, 1979).

Magris, Claudio, *Danube*, trans. Patrick Creagh (London, 1989).

Mayakovsky, Vladimir, 'Krym', in *Polnoye sobranie sochineniy*, vol. 8 (Moscow, 1958).

Mandelstam, Osip, 'Tristia', trans. Burton Raffel & Alla Burago, in *The Complete Poetry of Osip Emilevich Mandelstam* (Albany, 1973).

Marsden, Philip, *The Spirit-Wrestlers: A Russian Journey* (London, 1998).

Mikvabia, Surab, et al., *Sukhumskiy obezyaniy pitomnik. K 90-letiu so dnya osnovania* (Sukhum, 2017).

Mucha, Stanisław, *Tristia. Eine Schwarzmeer-Odyssee* [documentary film], 2015.

Ovid, *The Poems of Exile: Tristia and the Black Sea Letters*, trans. Peter Green (Berkeley, 2005).

Öztürk, Bayram & Ayaka Amaha Öztürk, 'Biodiversity in the Black Sea: Threats and the Future', in Zafar Adeel et al., *Mankind and the Oceans* (Tokyo, 2005).

Pamuk, Orhan, *Istanbul: Memories and the City*, trans. Maureen Freely (New York, 2005).

Paustovsky, Konstantin, 'The Colchis', trans. Helen Altshuler, in *Selected Stories* (Moscow, 1970)

——— *Southern Adventure*, trans. Kyril Fritz-Lyon (London, 1969).

Raabe, Katharina & Monika Sznajderman, eds., *Odessa Transfer. Nachrichten vom Schwarzen Meer* (Frankfurt am Main, 2009).

Ransmayr, Christoph, *The Last World*, trans. John E. Woods (New York, 1990).

Reid, Anna, *Borderland: A Journey through the History of Ukraine* (London, 2015).

Rolle, Renate, *The World of the Scythians*, trans. F. G. Walls (London, 1989).

Rossianov, Kirill, 'Opasnye svyazi. Ilya Ivanovich Ivanov i opyty skreshchivania cheloveka s chelovekoobraznymi obezyanami', *Voprosy istorii estestvoznania i tekhniki*, 1 (2006).

Rostovtzeff, Michael, *Iranians and Greeks in South Russia* (Oxford, 1922).

Ryan, William & Walter Pitman, *Noah's Flood: The New Scientific Discoveries about the Event that Changed History* (New York, 1998).

Sakalli, Abdulla & Nuri Başusta, 'Sea Surface Temperature Change in the Black Sea under Climate Change: A Simulation of the Sea Surface Temperature up to 2100', *International Journal of Climatology*, 38 (2018).

Steavenson, Wendell, *Stories I Stole* (London, 2002).

Stoker, Bram, *Dracula* (London, 1897).

Strabo, *Geography*, trans. Horace Leonard Jones (London, 1917–32).

Webster Wilde, Lyn, *On the Trail of the Woman Warriors: The Amazons in Myth and History* (London, 1999).

Westerman, Frank, *Ararat: In Search of the Mythical Mountain*, trans. Sam Garrett (London, 2008).

Voloshin, Maximilian, 'Kultura, iskusstvo, pamyatniki Kryma', in *Krym. Putevoditel* (Moscow, 1925).

Xenophon, *Anabasis*, trans. C. L. Brownson (London, 1922).

Yanko-Hombach, Valentina, et al., eds., *The Black Sea Flood Question: Changes in Coastline, Climate and Human Settlement* (New York, 2007).

Zaitsev, Yuvenaliy & Vladimir Mamaev, *Marine Biological Diversity in the Black Sea: A Study of Change and Decline* (New York, 1997).